BLOOD IN THE FORUM

Blood in the Forum
The Struggle for the Roman Republic

Pamela Marin

continuum

Continuum UK, The Tower Building, 11 York Road, London SE1 7NX
Continuum US, 80 Maiden Lane, Suite 704, New York, NY 10038

www.continuumbooks.com

First published 2009.

British Library Cataloguing-in-Publication Data
A catalogue record for this book is available from the British Library.

ISBN 978 1 84725 167 1

Map of the Forum used with permission from the University of Michigan Press from
Millar, F., *The Crowd in Republican Rome* (1998) based on a map from *Roman Voting
Assemblies* (1996), drawn by Jenny Graham.

Typeset by Pindar NZ, Auckland, New Zealand
Printed and bound by MPG Books Ltd, Cornwall, Great Britain

Contents

Maps and Illustrations

Dedicated to Peter Derow
in memoriam

Chronologies

GENERAL CHRONOLOGY OF THE ROMAN REPUBLIC

753 BCE	Traditional foundation of the city of Rome
753–509	The Regal period, characterized by the rule of kings, ending with the death of Tarquinius Superbus (the Proud) by L. Brutus
509–264	early Republic
264–133	middle Republic
218–201	Second Punic War with Carthage. Hannibal crosses the Alps
149–146	Third Punic War, resulting in destruction of Carthage
146	Fall of Corinth
133–31 (or 27)	late Republic

CHRONOLOGY OF THE SECOND CENTURY BCE

146	Defeat of Carthage and Corinth
133	Tribunate of Tiberius Gracchus
122	First tribunate of Gaius Gracchus
121	Death of Gaius Gracchus
116	Senatorial committee sent to Jugurtha in Numidia
112–106	War against Jugurtha
107	Marius elected consul
106	Cicero born (3 January); Pompey born (29 September)
105	Cimbri and Teutones begin attacks in Northern Italy
104–100	Marius has five successive consulships
103	Saturninus' first tribunate; land for Marius' veterans
100	Saturninus' second tribunate, unrest and riots in Rome; Caesar born

CHRONOLOGY OF THE FIRST CENTURY BCE

53	Death of Crassus at Carrhae; continued riots in Rome, no consuls until July
52	Death of Clodius on the Via Appia; Cato supports Pompey as sole consul
51	Cato is defeated in only attempt for consulship; Cicero bids for triumph, after being sent to Cilicia
50	Attempts by senate to reconcile Caesar and Pompey unsuccessful
49	Civil War begins; Cato and eldest son flee with Pompey Cato assigned to Sicily but leaves the island to Caesar's legate; Bibulus offered command of Pompey's fleet after Cato's refusal
48	Battle at Dyrrhachium; defeat at Pharsalus; Pompey's death; Cato in charge of anti-Caesarian forces; Cicero returns to Italy
47	Cato travels to North Africa (Utica)
46	Battle at Thapsus; Cato's death; Caesar returns to Rome in July and travels to Spain to deal with anti-Caesarian forces
45	Caesar returns to Rome in October; various *Catos/Anticatos* published
44	Caesar assassinated; Brutus and Cassius leave for Macedonia
43	Cato's daughter Porcia dies
42	Defeat at Philippi; deaths of Brutus, Cassius and Cato's eldest son
40?	Sallust's *Bellum Catilinae* published
29–19	Composition of the *Aeneid* by Virgil
27	Augustus proclaimed first emperor of the Roman Empire
14 CE	Death of Augustus

Acknowledgements

There have been so many films, documentaries, books and biographies about the late Roman Republic that the general reader and scholar may feel overwhelmed, and, therefore, I am indeed grateful to Michael Greenwood at Hambledon Continuum for persuading me that a new perspective on the late Republic would be of great interest. My fascination regarding this period of history is spread over many years, including graduate work in the US, UK and Ireland. Many parts of this work result from my Ph.D thesis: *Cato the Younger: Myth and Reality*, begun at Oxford under the auspices of Christopher Pelling and Andrew Lintott, while its completion at University College, Dublin was overseen by Andrew Erskine and Philip de Souza. I am, of course, indebted to each of them for their support while writing this project.

At Hambledon, everyone has been very helpful during this process. I wish to thank Penelope Whitson and Alice Eddowes as production editors for keeping me aware of developments, but, more specifically, Ruth Stimson as my copy editor for her painstaking and informative queries and corrections, which have greatly added to the accuracy of this text. I must also thank Andrew Erskine again for reading through the first chapters of this book and to many other colleagues who have clarified small, but necessary points. Of course, any errors within are entirely of my own making, but hopefully, these are few. I am particularly grateful to the libraries at UCD and Trinity, as well as the Sackler library at Oxford, who allowed me access to clarify more general issues. Finally, I must thank my husband Barry Gleeson for his support during the rather lengthy process that this work has entailed.

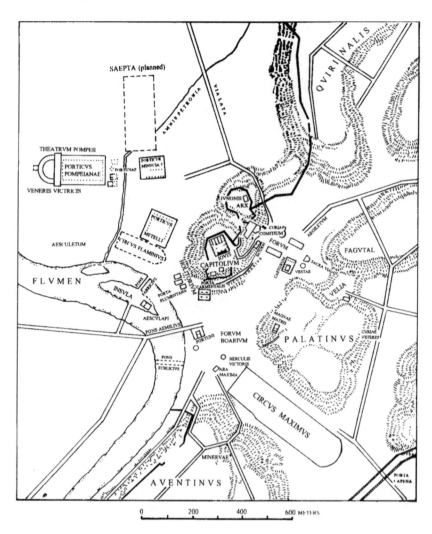

The Roman Forum c.53 BCE

Roman Italy

(Spain) Hispania

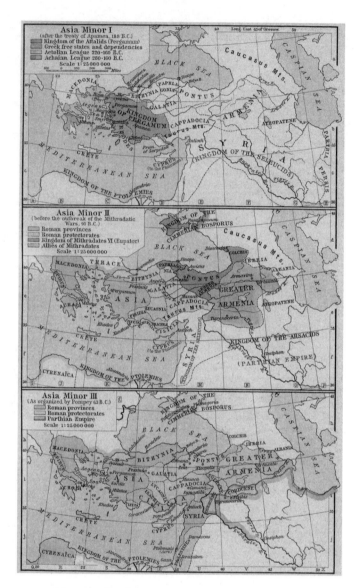

The growth of the Roman Empire in Asia Minor

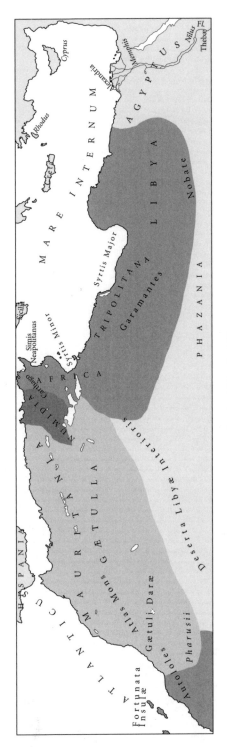

Ancient North Africa

Introduction

The screen darkens and slowly the image of the Forum comes into focus. Temples, monuments and elaborate houses surround government buildings such as the senate house, where laws are made, treaties debated and politicians argue the issues of the day. Men in togas stroll across the marbled squares while the voices heard on the streets reveal the cosmopolitan nature of the city. Market traders, artisans and ordinary citizens walk through their city, a city of empire but still a republic. The names of forgotten generals and heroes are etched on statues, triumphal arches are abundant and the tombs of the dead line the roads leading to the city. It is a city of commerce, trade and law. It is a lively and busy city. It is Rome.

Ambitious young men are beginning their election campaigning while others are practising their oratory in the law courts. Traders from around the known world are hawking their wares and a small group of onlookers is listening to a politician explain a new land policy or the benefits of a new tax. Children are rushing to school while women and servants are buying food at the numerous stalls, the bakeries and wine bars are doing a roaring business. A slave is cleaning the latest graffiti from the front of a house and a washerwoman is collecting the urine from the reeking city sewers. A labourer slowly climbs the six floors to his small room while an aristocrat listens to the newest poetry. Actors are practising for the night's performance and small gangs of youths are debating the latest sporting results.

Elsewhere, a beggar holds out his hand to a passing soldier. A former consul stands and surveys the scene, but sighs as he walks towards his house. The twilight is coming and soon the city will be dark, forbidding and alien. Trade will continue, women will emerge from the shadows of temples and bodyguards will protect those afraid of what the city will become. The voices in the Forum become distant as the man enters his elaborate house in the night with its ornate decorations, his spoils from overseas commands, amidst the gentle whispers of music. Outside his window, he can see the countless poor, the masses of humanity that may have elected him once upon a time, but this is not the Rome he grew up to admire and fight for. The myths of the past have no place in this Rome.

Every month thousands are coming in to the city. There is no food, little employment and everywhere the cries of abandonment echo in the slums. Men die in faraway lands while politicians proclaim the glory of Rome. Those ambitious young men are now arguing that changes must be made as they campaign in the streets. There must be land, there must be food – Rome must now provide. Ordinary men have lost their farms as they fought for Rome and now their families continue to crowd into the city. The tribunes – voices of the people – are clamouring for reward now that their enemies are destroyed. Centuries ago, the small farmer left his plough to protect the city, but now Rome is a world power and has been for the last few generations. The ideals and dreams of Rome have not changed, but perhaps the people have. There are now only the armies of the politicians, the small farmer has disappeared and while the life of the city continues, Rome itself has been transformed. There are slaves, immense riches and the political arena closed to only a few. As he closes the window and the screen grows dark, the ex-consul wonders what direction will his city now take?

This is the story of the last century of the Roman Republic (133–44 BCE), with particular emphasis on the period from the dictator Sulla to the death of Julius Caesar (82–44 BCE). Many of the issues that concerned this last generation had their foundations prior to Sulla, but reached fruition in these last decades. The musings of the ex-consul above could have been from any time during that last century, but the imagery of Rome itself and what it stood for resonates across the centuries to the present day.

It is the Rome of *Spartacus*. Associated with Cicero, Caesar and Augustus, Rome was a world centre. There are generals, heroes, poets, villains and loose women. It is a world familiar yet somewhat alien. We can understand their laws, their customs and their words as well as their sports, their bloodthirsty nature and their inhumane desire for glory, dignity and honour. Caesar argued that his dignity and personal honour had been insulted as he crossed the Rubicon, but it was power that he sought, which perhaps resonates more to a modern reader. Republican Rome and the struggle for dominance was a fact of life, of politics and, even, of survival.

Ancient Rome consists of not just the individuals that come to mind, but also those masses who voted every summer for the following year's magistrates. The names of Sulla, Caesar, Pompey and Cicero are perhaps some of the best known figures in late Republican politics, but the governmental structure allowed others to succeed, such as Cato the Younger, Bibulus and Brutus. It was the poets, the generals and the politicians, along with the ordinary man on the street, that made Rome great. The religious practices, the Vestal Virgins and the senate itself are components of one of the greatest civilizations that ever existed. Rome continues to fascinate because we see ourselves in its citizens and its struggles.

This book tells the story of the last decades of Rome – what succeeded, and why the Republic ultimately failed. Was this failure inevitable? Was its destruction attributable to one man – Julius Caesar – or was he perhaps the most visionary of his colleagues in realizing that Rome had indeed changed and that single control was necessary? Had Caesar been stopped earlier, would Republican Rome have continued or were there too many problems within the small city-state and its vast empire? Was the Republic doomed to failure? Are the actions of men like Brutus and Cassius in assassinating Caesar worthy of admiration, or was it the final gasp of a fallen world?

There are no clear answers, but the best that can be said is that the individuals who struggled to survive in Rome were led by its past and its promise. The myths that surrounded its formation led to the idealism of the century under consideration. It is convenient to look at the events of this period of Rome's history as a gradual progression to sole leadership, but those who lived in the late Republic did not know its future, and every day brought new challenges and rewards. It is the 'everyday' sense that this book tries to convey and in the end, one will hopefully better appreciate the men and women who lived in the greatest city that has ever existed.

1

What it Was to be Roman

'... It is true that Lucius Quinctius Cincinnatus was ploughing his field when he was told that he had been appointed dictator ...'

CICERO, ON OLD AGE 16

'He paused for a moment and shed tears, only saying: "So my field will be unsown this year, and we shall be in danger of not having enough food to support us." Then he kissed his wife and instructing her to look after things at home, went off to the city.

I am led to narrate these details for no other reason than to make clear to everyone what type of men the leaders of Rome were at that time, that they worked with their own hands, led self-disciplined lives, did not complain about honourable poverty, and, far from pursuing positions of royal power, actually refused them when offered.'

DIONYSIUS OF HALICARNASSUS, ROMAN ANTIQUITIES 10:17

In the year 458 BCE, and again in 439, Cincinnatus was approached to assume the dictatorship in order to deal with an ongoing military struggle against the Aequi, a tribe in central Italy. This legendary story of the small farmer leaving his crops to attend to the political and military crisis of the early Republic found resonance as the centuries passed. Indeed, the late Republican orator and politician Cicero could use this analogy without any explication for his audience. However, some four centuries later, Rome was very different – its wars were fought far from the Italian peninsula, immense wealth had been acquired and its political system was open to many from outside of the city of Rome itself. Yet, this traditional view remained a key component of Rome's literature, myths and aspirations.

When referring to their past, the Romans idealized their history. Cincinnatus was regarded as one of the Republic's heroes, somebody who embodied virtue and simplicity in his lifestyle and approach to life. After resolving the threat from the Aequi, he stepped down from dictatorship after 15 days. This almost immediate resignation was viewed as the ultimate example of civic duty, modesty, good leadership and, above all, service to the *res publica*. A second dictatorship to deal with threats from the plebian class further strengthened the view of Cincinnatus as the ideal Roman, who returned to his farm and his modest life.

There was an obsession with *virtus* – the embodiment of moral integrity as it pertains to the Roman perspective:

> The Roman aristocrat was expected to show courage and wisdom, the two qualities most important for a general and a magistrate. In this context wisdom did not denote a rarefied philosophic detachment or an intellectual enquiry into first causes and the nature of things. It meant practical political judgement, which was of little use unless expressed in words at meetings of the Roman people and of the senate, in such a way as to influence the course of events.[1]

A fragment of the second century BCE satirist, Lucilius, helps to further define this concept:

> Virtue is knowing what is right and useful and honourable for a man and what things are good, and again what are bad, what is shameful, useless and dishonourable ... and besides all this, thinking our country's interests to be foremost of all, our parents' next, and then thirdly and lastly our own.[2]

Therefore, it appears that Roman aristocratic *virtus* centred on courage, justice, wisdom and temperance, with particular focus on achievement in the political, military and religious duties that each individual undertook for the *res publica*. Figures such as the great Cato the Censor (234–149 BCE) were considered role models. Cato came from an agricultural background, returning to his farms when not involved in political and military business. He abhorred luxury and ostentatious displays of wealth, encouraging the passage of legislation aimed at strict restrictions on dress and entertainment; regardless of his persuasive rhetoric, these did not pass. Cato instituted numerous economies within the city and on his farm, the latter of which were written down in a number of texts. The first Latin author of note, Cato the Censor typified the ideal Roman, but few were able to emulate him in practice. He was also obstinate, rigid in his approach and full of self-importance, but the historian Livy, while mentioning this briefly, is admiring:

> This man possessed such ability and force of character that in whatever station he had been born he must have been a fortunate and successful man. In no department of business, whether public or private, was the requisite knowledge lacking to him, he was equally versed in the affairs of town and country life. Some men have reached the highest posts through their knowledge of law, others through eloquence, others again through their military reputation. This man's versatile genius made him at home in all alike, so much so indeed that whatever he took up you would say that he was born for that one

thing alone. In war he was a most doughty fighter and distinguished himself in many famous battles, and when he reached the highest posts he proved himself a consummate general. In peace, if you consulted him you found him a most able lawyer, and if he had to plead in a case, a most eloquent one.

Personal quarrels – far too many of them – kept him busy, and he himself took care to keep them alive, so that it would be difficult to say who displayed the greater energy, the nobility in trying to suppress him, or he in worrying the nobility. He was undoubtedly a man of a rough temper and a bitter and unbridled tongue, absolute master of his passions, of inflexible integrity, and indifferent alike to wealth and popularity. He lived a life of frugality capable of enduring toil and danger, with a mind and body tempered almost like steel, which not even old age that weakens everything could break.[3]

Cato the Censor would serve as the symbol of Roman's greatness, and what Romans believed they too were capable of. In the last decades of the Republic, his great-grandson, Cato the Younger, would take on that mantle of stubbornness and integrity; his contemporary, Cicero, believed that this Cato 'with the best of intentions and highest regard for the Republic, he acts as though he lives in Plato's Republic than in the sewers of Rome.' Cato the Younger was nevertheless, a formidable force – one whom Caesar would grow to hate.[4]

The first century BCE politician and historian Sallust would later argue that these early struggles showed Rome at its best, and its downfall was due to Rome's successes during the third and second centuries BCE – by conquering their enemies, such as Corinth and Carthage, the Romans began to fight among themselves, rather than being united against a common foe. Sallust comments that desire for wealth and power had superseded the past 'but in these degenerate days ... who is there that does not vie with his ancestors in riches and extravagance rather than in uprightness and diligence?'[5] Yet, there had been attempts in previous centuries to limit luxury, so the argument, while convenient for Sallust's own literary purposes, can only be used to show one aspect.

The last century of the Republic was filled with individuals who grew up with the ideals of the past surrounding them, but competition, desire and greed would colour their lives. The Roman vision of its past and, even more, *virtus*, interwove itself into everyday life. Individuals, such as Cincinnatus and Cato the Censor served as a moral compass, but the reality was somewhat different.

LIFE IN ROME

It is estimated that up to 320,000 people lived either in the city of Rome or its environs in 70 BCE. This figure included citizens, slaves and other freeborn non-citizens, both men and women. It is clear that 'in spite of vast expansion, before and especially after the Social War, a huge population and a very substantial proportion of citizens, always lived within a shortish distance from the political centre.'[6] This is of particular importance as involvement within the political structure was an essential element of citizenship. With so many people in and around Rome itself, the people who voted in elections and on legislation, were able to participate on an almost daily basis.

The city of Rome, which traditionally was founded in 753 BCE, spread over seven hills. The original government had been based in a swampy valley next to the Palatine Hill, where, during the Republic, many senators and other wealthy and influential individuals lived. They could walk down the Via Sacra, one of the oldest streets in Rome itself, and attend to the business of running the city and, later, the foreign territories acquired through numerous treaties, wars and simple expansion. As the capital, Rome was not just for government functions, but a real, living city.

Everything was mixed in together – temples, political institutions, law courts, shops and houses. In the centre of the Forum, there were shops and merchants intermingling with senators. There was no rational planning to the city, with few major thoroughfares, excepting the Via Sacra (running from the Forum to the Palatine Hill) and the parallel Via Nova. The Forum was perhaps the most important area in the city (and one which was duplicated throughout the cities of the Roman world). Not just reserved for political business, there were temples, shops, the courts and other elements of Roman civilization. The Capitoline Hill loomed over the Forum, with its grand temples of Jupiter, the temple of Concord and other symbolic reminders of the gods.

The Palatine Hill, next to the Forum, was where the wealthy lived. Its inhabitants included Clodius and Cicero, the latter moving there in 62 and ironically, given their fractious relationship, the two were next-door neighbours. The Aventine Hill was the region of the plebs, while others lived within the ancient *pomerium*, which was the religious boundary of the city – not in a physical sense, but the land within was Rome, while the land outside was referred to as belonging to Rome. Elections and successful generals awaiting triumphs could not enter this sacred area, and thus had to remain outside the city, usually at the fields of Mars to the north. An attempt to limit traffic in the city was a temporary response to the overwhelming volume of people, but due to the numerous festivals and holidays, thousands could crowd into the city itself.

There was no equivalent of the modern police force in Rome. The wealthy hired bodyguards, or, in the last decades, used their own personal armies to secure order. One example was during the trial of Milo for the murder of Clodius, where Pompey's army was nearby to insure order. The aediles were nominally responsible for the safety of the city, but communities banded together at times, for their own protection and that of their neighbours. It was not usually considered safe to go out alone at night, yet it was not completely dissolute and dangerous either. Most wide-scale violence appears to have occurred around political events, such as elections, or groups either protesting against an individual or supporting one, such as the violence between Clodius and Milo's gangs throughout the 50s BCE.

City planning may not immediately come to mind when one thinks of ancient Rome. Built on an ad hoc basis over several centuries, Rome still had numerous merits. It was a very clean city with sewers, running water into some wealthy homes, fountains for the lower classes and an extensive bathhouse system. There were no permanent theatres in the city until Pompey's Theatre in the last years of the Republic – theatres were constructed from wood on a yearly basis and then dismantled, often with the ornamentation providing decoration for the senatorial sponsor's home afterwards. The aedile of 58, M. Aemilius Scaurus, moved the marble columns that had been installed in his own temporary theatre into the atrium of his own house – a constant reminder of the splendour of his own magnificent building.

It was, nevertheless, an extremely crowded city, and numerous plans for its extension were thought of, but did not reach fruition until Augustus. A useful term, as coined by the scholar Florence Dupont in her *Daily Life in Ancient Rome*, is 'labyrinth' and she continues:

> Unless you were born and brought up in a particular Roman neighbourhood, it would seem like a labyrinth where it was impossible to find anyone you might be looking for. Even those who were familiar with a particular locality might easily lose their way. As soon as you strayed from the main thoroughfare, road names and house numbers vanished. The essential landmarks were public monuments, temples, colonnades and city gates.[7]

By the first century BCE, it appears that many notable figures had moved out of Rome itself – to villas with vast gardens overlooking the city. Perhaps it was also a way to distance themselves from the increasingly violent mobs that paraded through Rome at various times, in particular during the election contests. It was also an opportunity for more space and even to show one's great wealth – the historian Sallust, who was accused of massive embezzlement and even thrown out of the senate, had a huge property with trees surrounding his elaborate dwelling. Sallust and Cicero, both plebeians, illustrated how much Rome had changed – there were few real differences between the patrician and plebeian classes, at least in terms of monetary equality.

PATRICIAN VERSUS PLEBEIAN, AND THE EQUITES

There were few real distinctions in the late Republic between the patrician and plebeian classes. In reality, it was wealth (or access to wealth) that allowed an individual to pursue a political career, regardless of patrician or plebeian status, as well as ambition, ability and experience. Bribery, extravagant games and public displays of largesse were also intrinsic to the Roman system, with men such as Caesar borrowing large sums to cover expenses. The political offices were unpaid, but many could expect a posting as a provinical governor following their praetorship or consulship, although some, like Verres in the 70s BCE, let their greed overtake their administration and they would return to Rome dripping with gold, jewels and other prizes. In Verres' case, unfortunately, the ambitious young orator Cicero had also been in Sicily and having a reputation for honesty and integrity, he was approached by the islanders to prosecute Verres, in which he was successful.

New men, those without consular ancestors, had a somewhat more difficult time. After the conflict of the orders in 287 BCE – when the plebeians finally secured equal political rights with the patrician class (members of Rome's first families), many were able to enter into politics, but by the first century BCE, still very few men ran for political office from outside a small group of aristocratic families. In fact, there were only four who achieved the top post – the two most notable were Marius (first consulship in 107), who had showed great military abilities, and Cicero (in 63), who again was considered an excellent orator and may have been elected in an attempt to stop the renegade L. Sergius Catilina (Catiline).

One position that was restricted to plebeians only was the tribunate, established in 494 BCE, which allowed the office holders to not only propose legislation, but also to veto any they felt contrary to the public good. The reality was, however, far from the ideal. It has been convenient to look at Tiberius Gracchus in 133 BCE as the starting point for the tribune as a revolutionary figure, due to his *lex agraria*, but substantial research has shown that there were a few tribunes throughout the second and third centuries BCE that tried to present popular-type legislation. Throughout the first century BCE, for which we have more documentation, there were a number of individuals who utilized the tribunate as a stepping-stone to a political career, either as tool of powerful senators or for their own desires. Sulla's attempt to restrict the powers of the tribunate in 81 was the focus of much agitation and unrest over the subsequent decade, notably in 75 and 73, before Pompey and Crassus restored the full range of powers, including the important right of veto, in their first consulship in 70.

Another important point was that patricians could assume political office at an earlier age than their plebeian counterparts. One example, in particular, which has caused problems with determining Julius Caesar's year of birth (was it in 102 or 100?) is that Caesar was elected consul for 59 – as a patrician Caesar could run prior to the (at the time of election) minimum age of 42; therefore, scholars tend to favour the year 100 for his birth date. Pompey, of course, was only 35 when he was elected, but his outstanding military abilities meant that he not only bypassed the *cursus honorem* (sequential order of holding office), but for his first political office was able to assume the consulship, again contrary to the guidelines that Sulla had established during his dictatorship.

Equites were another rank of the Roman political system (literally 'knights', in practice the equivalent of the merchant class – there was a property qualification to the rank). It was considered inappropriate for a senator to engage in business himself, but he could employ individuals to do so on his behalf. By the middle of the second century BCE, the equites, traditionally excluded from the senatorial offices, began to agitate for some sort of involvement within the *res publica*. The tribune Gaius Gracchus made a move towards recognizing their merit – he proposed that the knights should constitute the jury in extortion trials. This meant that any provincial mismanagement and judgement accordingly was now in the hands of equites and not the senatorial class. Throughout the first century, this honour would be removed and reinstated several times, but while Gaius Gracchus may have wanted to divide the wealthy classes, there are numerous instances where the knights worked with the senatorial classes. There was fluidity within the system as well – a son of a senator who preferred a business career and remained out of politics would be an eques, while the son of an eques who desired a senatorial career would be elevated to the senatorial class with his first election.

The equites remained a powerful force in Roman Republican politics. It was they who dealt with the tax collection in the provinces and were directly affected by the piracy threat, and who provided money and loans to all in Rome. There were some very negative comments about Brutus and his money-lending practices – not just because of his exorbitant interest rates, but largely because he was from the senatorial classes. Nevertheless, there was competition between the two groups, but in the race for senatorial dominance, those seeking political office employed numerous ways to achieve their goals.

ARISTOCRATIC COMPETITION IN ROME

There is no doubt that the aristocratic male was born and reared to take his rightful place in Roman politics. From childhood, he was assured of his birthright, but more than that, everywhere he looked, examples of his family and other illustrious individuals were scattered around Rome. In the second century BCE, it was common for successful generals to build elaborate temples and other buildings in thanksgiving to the gods for their victories. Furthermore, the very houses they lived in were a dedication to their families, their ancestors and the glorious deeds and political offices that their fathers, grandfathers, and so on had held. In funerals, the masks of the deceased and their ancestors were paraded in lengthy processionals through the city before the dead were entombed. Even the triumphs paraded through the streets to the delight of the ordinary person, with their displays of wealth, slaves and the general in war paint akin to Jupiter himself, would turn the heads of children.

There were not enough political offices to go around. The supreme prize of the consulship could only be held by two men per year. The praetorship had eight posts, while the more numerous lesser offices could provide a starting point, but to get a triumph, to succeed, to be a consul – it was out of the reach of most, and those families who had held the consulship in the past were loath to allow anyone outside of their circle to hold a major political office.

Family connections and supporters could perhaps assure election to the lower offices, but elaborate games, massive feasts and large-scale bribery characterized almost all rises to the top. It was necessary to spend money, make connections and promise much to get the praetorship, let alone the consulship; this meant that only the rich, or those who borrowed heavily, could progress. Even Cato the Younger, renowned for his integrity and refusal to use bribery, and greatly respected by the people, failed to be elected to consulship for 51 BCE, because of his adamant repudiation of ordinary electoral practices.

Competition for political office was ruthless, with mud-slinging, attacks on one's opponents and open bribery to one and all. It was considered public duty, it was what those involved had been raised to achieve, and it was the Roman system of political dominance. Men believed that they deserved the riches and glory that military and political success offered. Thus, Caesar declared that it was his personal dignity that had been insulted when he was refused the consulship *in absentia* in both 59 and 49. In the former case, he stepped down from his *imperium*, forsaking his triumph; in the latter, Caesar had an army and he would not listen to the senate or its compromises. His personal *dignitas* was under threat.

It was a combination of these factors that characterize the Roman system. From running for election to religious involvement, all were done as a sense of duty, of fulfilment of destiny and, above all, what was expected, praised and admired by the families, their colleagues and their city. Aside from politics, another area in which men had to achieve was religion – whether they personally believed or not, it was part of what was expected.

RELIGION

Polytheism – or the belief in many deities – was central to the Roman religious system. There were two main forms of religion, personal and state, both of which are important for an understanding how religion was essential in the late Republic. While some of the intelligentsia may have disdained religious practice in favour of philosophy, it was still a fundamental part of the *res publica* and it flavoured all transactions from public holidays to military battles to running the assemblies themselves. Essentially, nothing could be achieved without performing the religious rituals, as it was believed that prosperity was dependent on the gods. Religion permeated all aspects of life – at home, at war and in politics.

THE HOUSEHOLD AND FESTIVALS

The *lars familiaris* was considered the protecting spirit of the household, with its shrines usually located in the atrium or at the hearth. Usually, the women of the house were responsible for the proper maintenance and observance of the shrine, giving a portion of the families' main meal every day. A movable festival in late December/January – the Compitalia – saw feasts and games (until the latter was outlawed by the senate in 68 BCE), which was an opportunity for neighbourhoods to join together in celebration of household deities.

Numerous festivals dotted the Roman calendar, in fact, every few days saw another religious holiday. One of the most important (and popular) was the Saturnalia, which celebrated the Temple of Saturn – originally a day (December 17), by the late Republic, it had extended into a week of role reversal between masters and slaves, with gambling, pranks and massive banquets. No stranger to fun, the late Republican poet Catullus remarked that 'it was the best of days'[8]. With such distractions, it is believed that Catiline was planning his insurrection during this festival time in 63 BCE, but was thwarted.

There were extensive games and theatre performances every September for about two weeks at the *Ludi Romani*; the population would have only just recovered from celebrations in honour of Rome at the Septimontium (early September) and many festivals throughout the summer months as well. Another popular festival – in honour of the she-wolf who had suckled the infants Romulus and Remus – was the Lupercalia, which took place over several days in February. Following a sacrifice of two goats and a dog, young women lined up to receive whip-lashings which were thought to promote fertility and ease pain in childbirth. Another festival aimed solely at women were the rites of the Bona Dea festival. The goddess of fertility, virginity, healing and women, the good goddess appealed to women of all social classes, but the rites performed on December 4th were held in the household of the wife of a prominent magistrate, usually the

Pontifex Maximus. Men were forbidden to attend and one of the most famous scandals in the late Republic occurred when the young aristocrat P. Clodius gatecrashed the event at the home of Julius Caesar in 62 BCE by dressing as a woman. Unfortunately for Cicero, he was able to destroy Clodius' alibi at the ensuing trial, earning him Clodius' lasting enmity.

It is not clear how involved the ordinary person was in religious practices as opposed to participation in the various feasts, festivals and games that accompanied religious occasions. Priesthoods were not full-time jobs, but leading individuals filled those positions as it was considered part of their duties to the state. One example would be the heavily contested election for the Pontifex Maximus – or high priest – in 63, Caesar went up against Catulus, the latter considered an example of Roman virtue and integrity. After vicious mud-slinging attacks, where Caesar even accused his rival of embezzling funds in the rebuilding of the temple of Jupiter, Caesar secured the post.

RELIGION AND POLITICS

The senate, along with most of the assemblies, could only meet when certain religious restrictions had been fulfilled. First, it could only meet in a consecrated building, usually the Curia Hostilia, but certain other buildings could be used for specific and special purposes, for instance, on 1 March, which was the Roman New Year (when they would meet in the Temple of Jupiter) and for councils of war, which took place in the temple of Bellona. This temple was located outside the city walls and represented the ancient war goddess Bellona, who usually accompanied Mars into battle. After a prayer and a sacrificial offering were made, and auspices taken (observing birds in the sky), the senate could begin its business. It is quite probable that these practices were often abused – in 59 BCE, the consul L. Calpurnius Bibulus, annoyed with Caesar, first announced that the auspices were not favourable and then retired to his house to 'watch the skies' as a delaying tactic to prevent Caesar's legislation from being passed; Caesar, however, pushed through his laws illegally. The following year, the tribune Clodius passed his *lex Clodia de obnuntiatione*, which forbade the use of such tactics, but it was not retrospective.

Taking the auspices was important in a military sense as well. Crassus went ahead with battle at Carrhae having ignored the unfavourable omens, and complete annihilation of the Roman troops along with Crassus' own death was the result. In 249 BCE, the consul Claudius Pulcher, annoyed that the sacred chickens wouldn't eat, threw them overboard, saying that if they wouldn't eat, they could drink. The Romans attributed his catastrophic defeat on having ignored the auspices. Lightening and thunder were considered positive if happening during the taking of the auspices, but not if they occurred before or after. It appears that a Vestal Virgin may have been struck by lightning in 114 BCE, which was seen as an ominous sign – the Vestals were viewed as the gods' representatives on earth and such a death would have prompted great fear and unrest among the people.

The senate would also consult the Sybilline books, which were sacred texts written by prophetic priestesses, the Sybils, who had been prominent in the Etruscan and early Republican period. They were partly burned in 83 BCE, but Rome sent out envoys to all Roman cities to get as many copies as possible sent to them. In times of crisis and calamity, the senate would use the books for advice and suggestions. In fact, Publius Cornelius Lentulus, believing the oracle that 'three Cornelii would dominate Rome,' joined the conspiracy of Catiline in 63 BCE. According to Suetonius, another oracle which proclaimed that only a king could control Parthia may have led to claims that Caesar was aiming for the kingship when he began to organize an attack against Asia Minor in 45–4 BCE.

As noted above, most educated Romans appeared to pay only lip-service to religion, preferring philosophy and philosophical debate. It was part of every well-to-do young man's training to study in Greece, and among the prominent individuals of the late Republic, a large proportion spent some time there, such as Cicero, his friend and correspondent Atticus, Caesar, Cato and later, Brutus. Even the young poet Horace was drawn into the struggle between the assassins of Caesar – Brutus and Cassius – and Octavian while studying in Athens in the late part of the 40s. The major influential schools were Epicureanism and Stoicism, neither of which accepted the pantheon of gods as espoused by Roman religion. The Epicureans emphasized the neutrality of the gods and their lack of involvement in human affairs, which argued that the composition of atoms was a random affair. Lucretius' *De Rerum Natura*, a first century BCE poem that uses the logic of Epicurus to dispel anxiety about death, was considered a fundamental text or handbook to the role of Epicureanism in Rome. The idea that all Epicureans were hedonist or simply pleasure seeking is mainly based on the consul Lucullus' extravagant displays of wealth, but the philosophy focused more on reaching tranquillity (and pleasure) by knowledge, friendship and living a simple lifestyle.

Stoicism, based on the third century philosopher Zeno, also advocated free will, virtue and control over one's emotions. Only then, it was believed, could man control himself and his world. Furthermore, knowledge could be obtained by reason – the ancients were not necessarily Stoic in the modern concept, rather they were taught freedom from passion by way of reason and truth. Using logic, concentration and intelligence, the Stoic could therefore free himself from irrational anger or hasty decisions, to the detriment of his own wellbeing. Although Zeno had counselled that a retreat from public life was necessary to achieve one's goals, the Romans again modified this philosophy to suit their political nature. One of the great examples of Stoicism in the late Republic was the politician Marcus Porcius Cato the Younger, but even though Cicero pokes fun at the young man during his *Pro Murena* in 63 BCE (Murena being on trial for excessive bribery for the consulship of 62) he treats him with respect and even admiration. Cicero also notes Cato's illustrious ancestors, in particular, his great-grandfather, Cato the Censor, who was a role model for this new generation.

DEATH AND FUNERALS – ADMIRATION OF ONE'S ANCESTORS

Romans had a deep respect for death and funerary practices. The idea of an afterlife was perhaps an anathema to the philosophical mind, where both Epicureanism and Stoicism argued nothingness after life, but the traditional Roman view was similar to that of the Greeks. The idea of an underworld, controlled by the Roman god Pluto, with the ferryman Charon demanding payment to cross the river Styx, was an important part of Roman mythology and belief. After crossing, one would have to pass the three-headed dog Cerberus before going to be judged; after that, they would be sent to the fields of Asphodel if they were neither virtuous or evil, sent to Tarturus if they were evil (where they were punished for their deeds), or the ultimate, sent on to the Elysium fields (paradise) for the heroic or blessed. In Virgil's *Aeneid*, the hero Aeneas went to Hades, but with a golden branch, he was able to enter and leave the underworld. The depiction of the fields of Asphodel in Book VI illustrate a ghostly, misty world where the shades of the dead wandered aimlessly, as the ferryman warns that 'this is land of shadows, of sleep and drowsy night.'[9]

A typical upper-class funeral incorporated mourning women, musicians and, sometimes, mimes and dancers. Wearing the masks of the deceased and his ancestors, a procession would lead through the city, stopping at the Forum and reading a eulogy. Thus, Mark Antony's famous funerary oration of Julius Caesar in March 44 BCE was not particularly unusual. This procession would then continue outside the city to the site of the burial or cremation, since no Roman could be buried within the city walls. Many were buried along the major roads leading out of Rome; one of the best documented was that of the Via Appia, where monuments to the dead, including many illustrious families, lined the streets.

The lower classes, lacking the necessary funds for elaborate funerals, belonged to burial clubs that accumulated a common fund with members' small financial contributions. These clubs would then provide the necessary services after death, the most important of which was an acknowledged place of burial. Although some organizations, such as guilds or *collegia*, were banned at times throughout the last century BCE, burial clubs were allowed to continue as they provided a most necessary function – the proper burial of their members.

Via Appia (Depiction of 1891)

The masks carried by the aristocracy during the funeral procession were not death masks, but, in fact, had been made during life. They had no connections with magic, nor were they used to conjure up the dead. Used as representatives of the deceased's family background, they politicized the importance of the individual and their family in an overtly public manner. They defined status and represented a link between the generations. In an age of veneration for one's ancestors, the masks used in the funerary procession were not just symbols of the past, but also put 'pressure on family members from expectations' that the images signified.[10] If they failed, there was another way to save their wealth, their families and, quite possibly, their reputations.

VOLUNTARY DEATH IN ROME

The concept of voluntary death was widely accepted throughout the ancient world. *Voluntaria mors* carried with it no real stigma, unlike the modern concept of suicide from a Christian perspective, and was, in some cases, desired rather than feared. One of the most influential texts of the time was Plato's *Phaedo*, which deals with the concept of the soul, but it is obscure about the specific detail regarding when it was acceptable to kill oneself. Socrates argues that it was against the gods' will to commit suicide, except if a sign was received by the individual. The Stoics later established three specific criteria, which included: state-imposed death, incurable physical pain, or if one was under intolerable shame, but 'what Plato (was) trying to forbid is suicide from mere indolence or from fear of facing the ordinary hardships of life.'[11] Suicide was not acceptable as a result of mental instability, but was honourable in cases of extreme physical pain and terminal illness.

Therefore, in the face of defeat, whether personal, political or military, it was perfectly acceptable to seek death. The usual method was with a dagger, either self-inflicted or with the assistance of a friend, slave or otherwise. Other ways, particularly for women, included hanging or jumping, while starvation and poison were rarer.[12]

If one was to be executed by the state, it was preferable for the condemned to kill themselves so that their families would retain their property and social status, while those involved in military disasters might commit suicide rather than be taken prisoner, as some of Crassus' legions did following the spectacular defeat at Carrhae in 53 BCE. During the civil war between Pompey and Caesar, one of the generals – Vulteius – believing escape was impossible, encouraged his soldiers to kill themselves rather than be taken prisoner. Perhaps one of the most famous deaths was that of Cato the Younger in April 46 BCE, following Caesar's victory at Thapsus. Although it has taken on mythical proportions, thanks to Seneca's later obsession, his death represented the simple fact that Cato firmly believed that liberty and freedom, indeed the very things that Rome itself represented, had been irrevocably destroyed by Caesar.

POLITICS IN ROME

It was the combination of senate, popular assemblies and magistrates that the Greek historian Polybius particularly admired. Whilst his second century BCE account showed a familiarity with Roman institutions, there has been considerable debate on what type of government Rome really had. Was it a democracy (since citizens could vote) or an oligarchy (since it was only the wealthy or those with wealthy connections who could afford a political career)? The term Republic need not influence such a debate. Although the immediate connection with democracy might be made with Athens, Athens was not itself a typical Greek system (and you had to be a citizen to vote). As Nicolet notes 'the great majority of Greek constitutions ... were timocratic: as a rule only the rich and noble could belong to the civic body or at any rate hold high office.'[13] Therefore, on the surface, Rome appears to be more democratic than its Greek counterparts, and it is in that context that the debate belongs, rather than comparison with modern ideals of democracy. That is a point, however, which will be addressed below in greater length.

THE POLITICAL OFFICES

There were five main political offices: consul (chief magistrate of the state), of which there were two; praetors (jurisdiction and overseeing provinces) of which there were eight; aediles (two curule, two plebeian) who were responsible for the day-to-day running of Rome; quaestors (financial matters) which were increased by Sulla to 20; and 10 tribunes of the plebs. Censors were normally elected every 10 years and were awarded to ex-consuls of hopefully exceptional merit, who were responsible for assessing property and, increasingly, in enrolling new citizens.

There were also extraordinary commands that an individual might be appointed to, for instance, to deal with a specific need or threat, such as Pompey during the 60s BCE, when he was selected to try and resolve the problem of piracy threatening the grain supply to Rome in 67. During this time, two men also appointed themselves as dictators. The first was Sulla, the other, and with more disastrous results, was Julius Caesar. During the first part of 52 BCE, as elections had not been held the previous summer due to extensive violence, Pompey also held the sole consulship, which was in essence a dictatorship, only with a time limit. Pompey did appoint a co-consul (his father-in-law in September 52) and unlike Caesar, did step down for the incoming consuls of 51 BCE.

If there weren't delays or violent riots, some 44 individuals were elected every year for the main political offices. While the assemblies that elected these individuals are mentioned at length below, it might be interesting to compare modern and ancient representation. In many English-speaking countries, such as the UK, Ireland and the USA, elections take place every four to five years. In a country such as Ireland, there are 166 members of its parliament (or *Oireachtas*) for a population of four million (2006 census) with voting rights for a little over three million citizens. This means that the ordinary elected official represents some 18,000 people. Rome had a voting pool of around 400,000 citizens; therefore, on a yearly basis, 11,000 people were represented, which is a smaller number than in many other modern societies. Although these numbers are perhaps somewhat arbitrary, it does make one pause to consider how representative modern governments are in comparison to the ancient world.

THE ASSEMBLIES

Magistrates were elected by voters in the popular assemblies. There were four assemblies, although only three were used for practical political purposes in the last decades of the Republic. The fourth – the *comitia curiata* – is mentioned for one particular situation that had a major impact on politics during the 50s BCE. The division between the classes was most notable in the more senior elections, rather than for lesser ones.

The main three assemblies were *the comitia centuriata* (election of senior magistrates such as censors, consuls and praetors), *the comitia tributa* (election of quaestors, curule aediles and other junior magistrates) and the *concilium plebis* (election of plebeian aediles and tribunes). The last (and the oldest) the *comitia curiata*, had ceased to have any practical importance in the late Republic, although in cases of a patrician seeking adoption by a plebeian, it would go through this assembly (this became important in 59 BCE when the patrician P. Clodius Pulcher sought to relinquish his patrician status in order to run for the plebeian tribunate). However, our focus should be on the first three assemblies during this time period.

Both the *comitia centuriata* and the *comitia tributa* had voters of both patrician and plebeian background, whilst the *concilium plebis* was restricted to those of plebeian descent. Both the *comitia tributa* and *concilium plebis* had voting units arranged on a regional basis, with 35 tribes (or units) with only four reserved for the urban voters. What would appear to be out-dated by the end of the Republic, with an estimated one million inhabitants in Rome itself, was in fact a reflection of Rome's early agricultural and rural bias.

The *comitia centuriata*, however, was divided into 193 classes on purely financial (and military) considerations, so that the first 18 centuries were restricted to those on a high income and gradually decreased to those with little or no wealth. It was in this assembly, which elected the most senior magistrates, that there was no distinction between rural or urban inhabitants, but money talked. One of the centuries from the first class (nos 19–70) would be selected by lot to announce their vote first and then each century would reveal their decision until consensus had been reached. When a majority was reached, voting stopped regardless of whether those in later centuries (nos 98 to 193, 97 being the number for a clear majority) had registered their results. It would therefore appear in most circumstances that the poor of Rome did not influence the election of the senior magistracies to any great extent, but the psychological aspect of having a vote, regardless of property status, is of utmost importance.

OLIGARCHY, REPUBLIC OR DEMOCRACY?

Democracy is a difficult term. Its modern equivalent is open to much interpretation, but overall, ancient authors were particularly opposed to democracy in real terms. Plato, not the most objective of philosophers in this regard, had seen first hand the danger that unchecked democracy could inflict. The state-ordered death of Socrates after a trial and conviction for corruption of the young, resonated throughout the ancient world. The experience of Athens, which would ultimately lead to its destruction, was hardly a positive result. The distinction between democracy and *politeia* (rule of the many) was an important development. Aristotle's view is particularly astute:

> Two elements ... are especially important. One is the far juster and more careful assessment of the merits of government by the multitude, where this is based on the acceptance of a common good, and on some willingness to pursue it together, and where

it is also organized in a way that uses the capacities of its citizens and restrains their more malevolent and dangerous characteristics in an effective way. The second, in the endless decisively, but for a long time every bit as consequentially, was Aristotle's decision not merely to contrast a healthy with a pathological version of rule by the multitude, but also to reserve the term *demokratia* for the pathological version.[14]

The idea of democracy in the ancient world, even its very usage, was considered an extremely hostile term. In fact, the Romans never used the term democracy, nor was it a Roman concept. The political author John Dunn has noted that 'the unit of political authority in Roman public inscriptions … was the senate and people of Rome (*Senatus Populusque Romanus:* SPQR). In that formula (and by no means only in that formula), the senate came first.'[15]

It has often been argued that Rome was principally an oligarchic system of government, but more recent scholarship has tried to present a more democratic element. Part of the problem has perhaps been a concentration on specific leading individuals, such as Caesar, Pompey and Crassus. Furthermore, the mid-second century BCE Greek author Polybius, used as evidence in many modern introductions to the Roman system of government, notes a three-sided approach to an unwritten constitution: oligarchy, the people and courts. This has actually resulted in even greater confusion in understanding the fundamentals of the Roman system, which has much more in common with modern types of representational government than is perhaps realized.

The idea of the Roman Republic itself as a term should not be dismissed, but perhaps the term oligarchic democracy would be a better compromise to encompass both the wealth of its participants as well as the reliance on the masses for their votes. Without wealth, many men could not afford to run for political office, but without the voting structure that all Roman citizens were entitled to participate in, these men would not have been elected in the first place. Perhaps the best definition is that popular participation was a key element in Rome, but that does not necessarily mean a full-scale democracy as seems to be the ideal in the twenty-first century, at least in the West.

There has been much debate about the structure of Roman Republican politics, with some interesting results. John North, in a 1990 article, 'Democratic Politics in Republican Rome', raises an intriguing idea, which cuts straight through many misconceptions – we may talk about the political motives in presenting legislation, but why did the voters support them? He contends, however, that 'if there was such a thing as Roman democracy, it was non-participatory to an extreme degree.' Professor Fergus Millar, in his *The Crowd in Rome in the Late Republic* (1998), disputes this, arguing that popular participation and the crowd were a fundamental aspect of the Roman governmental structure. A later work by Henrik Mouritsen, *Plebs and Politics in the Late Roman Republic* (2001), uses the geographical restraints of the city itself to demonstrate how limited some functions were. A puzzling question has always been how many people could have listened to, or even have heard, the speaker at the rostra in the Forum? Within the dimensions of this space, the vast numbers that Millar suggests cannot be sustained. While Rome may have had a participatory electorate, there were no newspapers, no radio and no television – thus, elections were won on foot and by reputation.

Furthermore, no ordinary citizen could propose legislation – it was up to the presiding magistrates or tribunes – they could only vote or veto it. While anybody could run for political office, it was usually the wealthy or those who could secure loans, such as the young Caesar, who were successful. Military success was also an important component. While the aristocracy may have been more fluid in relation to admittance to the top classes, whether by marriage or money, Rome was not a democracy in the sense that ancient Greece, especially Athens, professed to be. The *capite censi* (those counted by head) were restricted to the lower property classes, which meant that the rich had the first votes. While the concept of democracy is impossible to assign to the late Roman Republic, perhaps due to our modern inconsistencies with the term, there was nevertheless, an element of popular participation that must be recognized.

ROME AT WAR

Politics and war were inextricably linked. The military prowess displayed on the battlefield was a prerequisite for success in the political arena. Many a young man showing such skill and success could parlay this into a long-term political career. The first man over the wall of an enemy fortress was awarded a gold wreath – the *corona muralis*, whilst a simple laurel wreath – known as the *corona civica* – was the ultimate achievement for saving the life of a fellow Roman. These honours were brought out at major festivals, the winners continually reminding others of their successes. For a more senior figure, a triumph through the streets of Rome was the ultimate achievement. Yet, it was part of the very fabric of society that military victories could be exploited by these men; thus, those that were successful could never rest on their laurels, but in fact, had to seek more and more advantageous commands or provincial governorships to increase their prestige and their wealth. The ordinary citizen was perhaps not affected by the extensive plundering and pillaging that occurred, seeing only the benefits bestowed on the city of Rome, but in the struggle for pre-eminence, rules were broken. Therefore, while many officials may have been corrupt, the entire system lent itself to such behaviour. The Romans at war were again different from other ancient societies, in particular, the Greeks.

The Romans diverged from the traditional Hellenistic model by controlling and supervising the troops in front of them from the rear; it was a risky tactic to lead from the front because, in the thick of a battle, it was extremely difficult to determine the weaknesses of the enemy, gaps in the opposite formation and when to call the reserves in the back into the action. Furthermore, the Romans had a unique advantage over their enemies: they relied on their citizens and allies to make up their armies. Most other city-states used mercenaries, who were paid out of the public purse – their loyalty laid with the commanding general, but not necessarily to the ideals of the state they were fighting for. The Roman army, on the other hand, were fighting to not only protect Rome, but also their own interests, property and families.

Another element, unique to the Romans, was the sheer numbers that could be mobilized for battle. This is important, particularly during the early centuries of the Republic, but the traditional army ideal of the small farmer was to cause numerous problems as, over time, more and more lengthy stays abroad by this soldier-class meant that their farms fell into disarray or were sold due to increasing debts. There were attempts by several tribunes to remedy the matter, but the rapidity of Roman expansion resulted in only temporary measures. The rise to professional armies was perhaps unavoidable, but more than that, as the senate did not adequately recognize that without a state-sponsored army, it would fall to individual generals to provide for their troops, and ultimately, reward them with booty and the possibility of land upon retirement.

Also unique was the Roman determination to win at all costs. Interlinked with the notion of protecting Roman interests was the fear that this was an enemy that could ultimately destroy Rome itself. Under the Hellenistic concept of war, suing for peace at the point of surrender was recommended; the Romans, however, considered that complete annihilation of their enemy was the better course. It was not particularly the deaths of the enemy that they sought, but rather, destruction of the enemies' resources and ability to rehabilitate themselves so that they could not pose a threat to Rome in the future. The infamous Third Punic War (149–6 BCE) could be construed as directly related to this concept. The Romans had been able to subdue their enemy following the First and Second Punic wars (264–41 and 218–1 BCE respectively), but even the suggestion of Carthage rearming and therefore, potentially threatening Rome again was anathema. This was echoed by the esteemed Roman Cato the Censor's sentiment 'Carthage must be destroyed,' and coloured the first half of the second century, offering a plausible reason to the determination to engage against Carthage again. While it was indeed an obsession, much like the modern world, the perceived threat of an enemy is nevertheless understandable.

Yet, the Romans were not particularly a warmongering nation. In the first few centuries of its existence, Rome had been one of several tribes in the area. However, as they began to consolidate their position by absorbing these other individuals, the practice of defending itself and, in the process, acquiring more territory was an inevitable consequence. Excepting its complete destruction of the city of Carthage, the Romans usually left the ruling classes alone, incorporating them into a patronage system that was effectively hands-off. Thus, war was not necessarily the main goal, but securing its borders against others was a major objective.

The charge of imperialism against Rome is a valid one. Rome tried not to subjugate its conquered foes, although the collection of taxes and enslaving its prisoners of war, particularly the leaders, could be construed as a harsh measure. Once there was surrender, the Romans would move in and establish a quasi-governmental structure, usually, as noted above, with the locally recognized rulers if that was possible. There was also the possibility of the locals acquiring Roman citizenship over time, particularly in the Italian peninsula, although this was a contentious issue.

The repercussions to a city or region that betrayed Rome were swift. The southern Italian cities who willingly went over to Hannibal during the second Carthaginian war had their rights stripped, higher taxes imposed and lands confiscated – many of these cities would not have their rights fully restored until the aftermath of the Social War in the early 90s BCE. If there was further insurgency against Rome, Rome might then establish its own heavy presence in that region, such as creating its own ruling class who, in turn, were answerable to Rome.

In its first few centuries, Rome relied on the propertied class for its army. There were two reasons for this. The first was that the army, cavalry and so on provided their own arms and equipment; therefore, only those with money could pay their way. The second was that if the men involved had property and money, they would have more of a stake in the battle, fighting not just for the *res publica*, but also to protect themselves. This type of psychological propaganda was a major element towards the motivation of the Roman army and its impact and implications cannot be overestimated. The mercenary armies of the Hellenistic countries, hired for a battle, were not defending their own lands, while the Romans were themselves fighting for everything they had, and also for what Rome represented.

The idea that the armies of the later Republic were different to those that came earlier is a misconception. The general and consul Marius did reduce the property qualification in the late part of the second century BCE, by the year 107, when he desperately needed troops to fight against Jugurtha in Numidia, but this had been gradually building over the previous few centuries. As Rome increased its frontiers, a more professional army emerged. The idea of soldiers leaving their fields for a short campaign was a viable option up until the fourth and third centuries, but as wars increasingly took place away from the

Italian peninsula, longer and longer terms away from the home were required. Unfortunately, a catch-22 began to develop – one needed a property qualification to be conscripted, but after lengthy campaigns, for instance, in Greece or Spain, veterans returned to face large debts. Many lost their farms and, therefore, could not be considered as viable conscripts in the future. There was also an even graver economic and psychological consequence. Those landless veterans would crowd into the nearest urban centre, usually Rome, but without the prospect of continuous work, could fall into poverty, calling upon the state to provide for their food and very existence.

The greatest change to the army is credited mainly to Marius, which will be discussed in more detail in Chapter 2; however, it is sufficient to note that this new, more professional army became increasingly reliant on the general and his success – their loyalty, particularly with the promise of booty, reward and honours, in turn could be used as a standing threat by ambitious individuals. Perhaps Marius, in his eagerness to resolve immediate border problems did not foresee the repercussions of his hasty decision to open the army to all, but over the next century, the implications would be clear.

TERMINOLOGY

Throughout the twentieth century, many major historians used terms such as *optimates* and *populares* to define the political 'parties' that major figures belonged to, such as Caesar the *popularis* or Sulla the *optimate*. *Optimates* stood for the group of individuals who supported senatorial dominance, while *populares* were those who pandered to the public, often in opposition to senatorial practice or sentiment. It has been implied that these were political parties similar to their modern counterparts, which has been extremely misleading. Instead of couching Roman politics and political life in modern terms, it is perhaps better to re-evaluate the terminology itself for a clear understanding.

In the first instance, the terms *optimates* and *populares*, while convenient for the historian, is rather confusing for the reader. Cicero uses *boni* or the best men to categorize those individuals who predominated in senatorial matters, but many times, those politicians also passed popular measures, such as corn doles or agrarian legislation. The fluidity between personal ambition, senatorial acquiescence and voter awareness meant that the concept of political parties, such as was in vogue in historiography during the mid-twentieth century, has been replaced by an awareness of the temporary nature of alliances and motives. This shift has been most helpful in a better understanding of the flexible nature of Roman politics.

The terms used within this book are senatorial/*boni* and popular, but not in relation to the individuals themselves, rather their legislation and proposals at a specific time, which may eliminate some confusion. After all, many modern politicians present legislation that is pro- or anti-governmental policy, but at the same time, or later in their career, change their positions. The same is true of Rome. While Cato the Younger has been long assumed to be overtly pro-senatorial, his *lex frumentaria* during his tribunate in 62 illustrates another side. The very fact that Cato ran for and was successfully elected to the tribunate – a position that had taken on very negative press in the late Republic – demonstrates that political figures were flexible in their approach. Clodius is characterized as a *popularis* – with its very malevolent connotations, but the view of him also needs an overhaul. We are dependent mainly on Cicero, his bitter enemy, for a characterization of Clodius, but recent scholarship has provided new ways to view this most contentious of politicians. The same is true with others, and it is the intention of this work to separate the terminology and look at the individual themselves and, in particular, their actions.

Other concepts, such as the role of clients and patronage, have also fallen out of favour. It is important to recognize that many prominent individuals had supporters and even the basic layout of the Roman house, with its open atrium to welcome visitors, illustrates this. Support, both from those seeking assistance as well as offering it, particularly concerning potential voters, was an integral element of both personal and public life. Exhaustive studies have been done elsewhere with varying degrees of acknowledgement, ranging from placing *clientae* reliant on someone as a fundamental factor in that individual's success, to others downplaying its (and their) seemingly rigid structure. The more preferable term would perhaps be supporters, but with an understanding that such groups were flexible and fluid, changing frequently as need arose.

SOURCE MATERIAL: ANCIENT AND MODERN

Using primary source material can raise contentious issues: the authors may be influenced by contemporary events, their own personal feelings or even incorporate popular myths within their writings. Some individuals have earned animosity through vindictive contemporary accounts, while others have been glorified beyond recognition. It is important to look at the actions that can be agreed on and then work outwards from that; personality by necessity comes afterwards. Such individuals as Catiline and Publius Clodius Pulcher have been demonized, but in the last 20 years reappraisals of both have been extremely effective in opening up the debate about Roman politics and adding colour to the tapestry of its history. It is important that the definition of importance be readdressed. Just because Julius Caesar was ultimately successful, this cannot negate the role that others, perhaps maligned as minor characters, played. The ancient authors are used throughout, but when there is a conflict, this is noted in the endnotes. For the most part, these accounts are used to add the flavour and excitement of elections, battles and ordinary daily life.

2

A Blueprint for Civil War? Sulla and the 80s BCE

In the half century prior to the dictatorship of Sulla in the early 80s, a number of issues had come under political scrutiny. These included the growth of large estates, conscription to the army and extensive economic difficulties in Rome itself. While numerous politicians attempted to deal with these, particularly from the middle part of the second century BCE, the fact that they were not resolved would have serious repercussions in the late Republic. In fact, it might be argued that the *ad hoc* solutions led directly to problems that ultimately doomed the *res publica*.

THE LAND PROBLEM

One of the consequences of the more lengthy campaigns outside of the Italian peninsula meant that smaller farmers, who traditionally made up the citizens' militia, could not farm their lands and accumulated debts while away. These soldier-farmers, therefore, lost their smallholdings either by dispossession or, simply, being bought out. Resulting from this was less of a demand for free labour as the larger farms were mainly worked on by slaves. The population migration to Rome became more pronounced following Roman successes over Greece (149 BCE), Carthage (146), and Rome gaining control of Spain the following decade, particularly as great wealth and an influx of slaves flooded into the city and countryside.

In 133 BCE, Tiberius Gracchus, grandson of the famous Scipio Africanus (who had defeated Hannibal) through his mother Cornelia and related by marriage to some of Rome's most illustrious families, was elected tribune of the plebs. He was determined to tackle the dispossession issue head-on, and he presented legislation that was quite far-reaching in its scope and treatment. It was intended to resolve the problem of the landless citizenry.

Tiberius proposed that a land commission of three men be appointed to allocate small holdings to landless citizens by reclaiming all public lands that were now illegally held in private hands. He allowed for some lands to remain in private hands – 500 *iugera* for the land-holder with an additional 250 *iugera* for each of the first two sons, not an inconsiderable amount (a *iugera* is

Bust of Sulla

comparable to the modern measurement of 3,000 square yards, 5/8ths of an acre or 2,530 square metres). This bill would therefore provide relief for Rome's poor and, with this mass settlement, it would solve conscription problems as citizens would have enough land to meet the property qualification and be eligible for any future military involvement. This would also reduce the number of slaves needed for farming and, consequently, possibly decrease any slave unrest and uprisings. However, there were already some rumblings of discontent from the senate.

This limit of 500 *iugera* was not new, but Tiberius was determined to enforce the previous legislation; furthermore, it would appear that the new holders of the land had to pay a small rent, so while the wealthy would lose the excessive land, the poor would not receive it for free. One other aspect was the new holders could not sell it back for money, so that the previous user could not bribe or intimidate them into selling or abandoning the 30 *iugera* that each landless citizen had been allotted.

Yet the senate and the increasingly wealthy *equites* were not pleased. Aware that there would be some opposition, Tiberius instead took his measure to the people first, rather than consulting the senate, which was an outrageous breach of traditional protocol. At the plebian assembly, his fellow tribune Octavius, encouraged and supported by the senate, interposed his veto, but Tiberius paid no attention.

In the ensuing riots, Tiberius encouraged the people to depose Octavius for not acting in the best wishes of the electorate, which was swiftly passed. Tiberius may have got his legislation, but at a grave cost – the manipulation of the political system to serve one person's wishes would increasingly be considered as a viable option by many following, with disastrous results.

In the end, however, the laws were passed. The three land commissioners appointed were Tiberius, his brother Gaius and Appius Claudius Pulcher (Tiberius' father-in-law). While they would rotate the chair of the commission every year, there were no deadlines imposed on the work of the commission itself. The most immediate problem was money. The senate had initially allocated a mere pittance, but Tiberius found another way to get funds. When King Attalus III of Pergamum died, leaving his kingdom and estate to Rome, Tiberius proposed to the people that the personal fortune should be given to the land commission, which was approved. It should be noted that Tiberius' father had been the patron of Pergamum, so Tiberius' move, while against senatorial practice, was not necessarily the complete insult and insubordination as might be perceived, but nevertheless, it was a snub to the superiority of the senate.

While Tiberius may have had good motives behind his agrarian legislation, the fact remains that Tiberius ignored the senate, deposed a fellow tribune and had taken over the financial and administrative responsibilities of the senate in seizing the Pergamum monies. His opponents argued that he was setting himself up as a king (*rex*), particularly when Tiberius announced that he would be seeking a second tribunate, which implies two things: first, Tiberius feared prosecution for his actions during 133 (holding office again would make him immune from prosecution); second, he may have felt that without his presence as tribune, his agrarian legislation might ultimately fail. However, Tiberius faced several problems as he sought re-election.

In the first instance, many of his supporters had left Rome and returned to their rural homes; therefore, it was perhaps more difficult for him to secure an easy election. There were also problems at the initial election meeting, where there had been senatorial resistance to Tiberius' re-election amid abuse by Tiberius' friends towards the voters, and thus, this first attempt was adjourned. When the assembly resumed on the Capitoline hill, the senate itself was meeting down in the Forum. A violent riot broke out, with some later blaming Tiberius himself for raising his hand to his head as a gesture to disrupt the proceedings. Whether this was deliberate or not is not clear, but the senate itself was not amused. The *Pontifex Maximus*, Scipio Nasica, who was first-cousin to Tiberius, urged the presiding consul, P. Mucius Scaevola, to declare a state of emergency and do whatever was necessary to stop Tiberius. Scaevola, himself a lawyer, suggested legal measures, but Nasica, not pleased, turned to the senate and announced that he would go up the Capitoline hill to deal with Tiberius and they were welcome to join him. He then led a group of senatorial colleagues into the melee:

> The attendants of the senators carried clubs and staves which they had brought from home; but the senators themselves seized the fragments and legs of the benches that were shattered by the crowd in its flight, and went up against Tiberius, at the same time hitting those who were drawn up to protect him. Of these, there was a rout and a slaughter, and as Tiberius himself turned to fly, someone laid hold of his garments. So he let his toga go and fled in in his tunic. But he stumbled and fell to the ground among some bodies that lay in front of him. As he tried to rise to his feet, he received his first blow, as everybody admits, from . . . one of his colleagues, who hit him on the head with the leg of a bench; to the second blow claim was made by Lucius Rufus, who plumed himself upon it as having done some noble deed. And of the rest, more than three hundred were slain by blows from sticks and stones, but not one by the sword.[1]

In the ensuing violence, Tiberius was clubbed to death and some 200–300 other supporters were routed and killed on the Capitoline hill. The victorious senators then dumped the dead into the Tiber as if they were common criminals. The very thing that Scaevola had wanted to avoid – a constitutional and legal crisis – had occurred under the leadership of Rome's most senior priest – Scipio Nasica. A tribune, whose body and actions were sacrosanct, had been murdered in cold blood. Nasica was blamed by the Gracchan supporters for his role and the senate, for his protection, sent him on a mission to Pergamum, where he was poisoned, apparently by other supporters of Tiberius Gracchus.

While the senate may have good cause to fear Tiberius Gracchus in his attempt to secure a second tribunate, which was completely against tradition, the resolution of the problem, with such violence, appalled ordinary people. A tribune, clearly acting in their interests, had been violently ambushed and murdered. The fact, however, remains that while Tiberius' death could have avoided, his methods *were* unconstitutional, or at the very least, against tradition (or *mos maiorum*). He had bypassed the senate in proposing his legislation and had himself deposed a fellow tribune in his efforts to pass his agrarian laws; furthermore, he had also appropriated monies from Pergamum without approval. His agrarian reforms addressed a serious problem in Rome, but the methods by which he achieved his goal were contradictory to traditional Roman practice. The following year, 132, saw the anti-Gracchan base begin a systematic campaign to drive his allies into exile, in another constitutionally unprecedented measure, giving the consuls a right to order a one year period of exile of any Roman citizen. The next ten years saw an uneasy truce between the two sides.

GAIUS GRACCHUS

Tiberius' younger brother, Gaius Gracchus, began his political career with his election as quaestor in 126 BCE, which he served in 125. His next political office was that of the tribunate, which he secured for 123. While Tiberius' tribunate had been characterized mainly by his agrarian legislation and disregard for senatorial procedures, Gaius proposed an entire programme of legislative and socio-economic reforms that would have far-reaching consequences.

Gaius first proposed a law that any official who had been deposed by vote of the people should be barred from holding any further political office. This was clearly aimed at Octavius, the tribune that Tiberius had removed from office, but in the end, and with the influence of his mother, Cornelia, Gaius abandoned this measure:

> Having first stirred up the people ... he introduced two laws, one providing that if the people had deprived any magistrate of his office, such magistrate should not be allowed to hold office a second time; and another providing that if any magistrate had banished a citizen without trial, such magistrate should be liable to public prosecution. Of these laws, one had the direct effect of branding with infamy Marcus Octavius, who had been deposed from the tribunate by Tiberius; and by the other Popillius was affected, for as praetor, he had banished friends of Tiberius. Popillius, indeed, without standing his trial, fled out of Italy; but the other law was withdrawn by Gaius himself, who said that he spared Octavius at the request of his mother Cornelia. The people were pleased at this and gave their consent, honouring Cornelia no less on account of her sons than because of her father; indeed, in after times, they erected a bronze statute of her, bearing the inscription: 'Cornelia, Mother of the Gracchi.'[2]

His other proposals, however, would reach fruition.

His next move was to propose a law making it illegal to exile any Roman citizens without a trial. By making it retroactive, Gaius was fundamentally overturning the 132 BCE exile of the pro-Gracchan supporters. It had a further implication that the courts could not put to death any Roman citizen without a trial. This would remain in force throughout the next century, envoked particularly in the 60s BCE and the infamous Catilinarian conspiracy (see Chapter 5), but disregarded during the various civil wars of the 80s and 40s BCE. With this move, many of his political opponents fled Rome, and Gaius set about his overall reform programme.

He ordered the construction of new roads in order to facilitate communication and transport of goods, as well as a monthly subsided corn ration – a *lex frumentaria* – for citizens as there had been a recent plague of locusts in Africa, which meant a shortage of cheap grain, and argued that the extortion courts should be manned by the *equites*, not senators, in order to reduce corruption, particularly in the provinces.

The continuing conscription crisis was reflected in his next measure. Boys under the age of 17 were not to be conscripted, while soldiers would now be given free uniforms, thereby reducing some of the financial constraints on army enlistment. He also proposed legislation that Italian allies with Latin rights should be given full Roman citizenship and that allies with no rights should be given Latin rights. Although aided by his fellow tribune, Fulvius Flaccus, this particular measure failed, perhaps due to fear that Gaius would win additional popular support on the Italian peninsula, but also perhaps to an overall reluctance in Rome to hand out such privileges to their allies. This particular issue would become a major issue in the 90s BCE and lead to war. Gaius ran for a second tribunate in 122 BCE, which he easily won. On this occasion, the senatorial elite did not oppose his candidature. It was during this second tribunate that he proposed the above Italian citizenship reforms, but this time, his opponents struck back, arguing vehemently against this measure. They began to gather their ammunition against him.

In relation to land, Gaius went much further than his older brother. He made major adjustments to Tiberius' laws. The land commission was given power to deal with public land outside of Italy, was empowered to plant colonies and to grant land to deserving individuals. Gaius proposed that the cities of Scolacium and Tarentum, both in southern Italy, be colonized. Perhaps the most contentious resettlement was, however, Gaius' proposal for Carthage – to be renamed Junonia. The tribune M. Livius Drusus proposed an alternative to Gaius' land programme which illustrated the senatorial opposition to Gaius. Drusus proposed creating 12 colonies with 3,000 settlers each compiled from the poorer classes and also a relief from rents due from those who had been resettled under Tiberius' earlier 133 BCE *lex agraria*. In relation to the Italian question, Drusus offered a way of redress against provincial mismanagement. Although known as the *leges liviae*, they were never enacted, but nevertheless, undermined popular support for Gaius' own proposals.

In fact, Drusus was so successful that Gaius lost his bid for a third tribunate, while a vocal opponent to the Italian citizenship was elected consul for 121 – L. Opimius. Unfortunately for Gaius, the new consul was also adamantly opposed to him. When Gaius organized a mass protest on the Aventine hill, the senate passed a new measure – the *senatus consultum ultimum* or martial law. This new mechanism of proclaiming a danger to the *res publica* was constitutionally insecure; the methods taken by the senate had no legal precedent, but for the moment, it was enough to enable the marshalling of troops from a general waiting on the Campus Martius for his triumph. On the night before the fight, Plutarch notes that:

Gaius, as he left the Forum, stopped in front of his father's statue, gazed at it for a long time without uttering a word, then burst into tears, and with a groan departed. Many of those who saw this were moved to pity (him); they reproached themselves for abandoning and betraying him, and went to his house, and spent the night at his door.[3]

Opimius quickly gathered a further armed force of senators and supporters and confronted Gaius and his followers. Much like the violent scenes of a decade earlier, which resulted in Tiberius Gracchus' death, a pitched battle took place within the city itself. Hundreds were killed, but Gaius appears to have escaped. He committed suicide the next day. Opimius hastily established a tribunal that condemned some 3,000 people accused of being Gaius' supporters. Although he was later prosecuted for these actions in 120, the consul Carbo was able to secure his acquittal. Opimius went on to build the Temple of Concord in the Forum.

The land question, which both Tiberius and Gaius had tried unsuccessfully to deal with, remained unsolved and continued to be a major issue throughout the next century.

THE ARMY

As discussed in the previous chapter, the army in Rome had traditionally come from the farming class, but from the mid-second century BCE, the available pool had diminished considerably. Gaius Gracchus' measure excluding boys under the age of 17 is a good example of how dire the situation really was; furthermore, he also provided for free uniforms for those enlisting. Whether that also included all weaponry is not clear, but at least changes were occurring gradually.

It is generally accepted that the consul Marius (cos 107) overhauled the entire composition of the army and eventually removed the property qualification entirely, taking soldiers from the urban poor and landless farmer class. It is more likely, however, that in Marius, the final hurdle in a series of changes was cleared. In essence, over the past century, and particularly from the 140s with the lengthy campaigns in Greece, Carthage and Spain, there had been a paucity of available men. With more campaigns, additional men were needed in North Africa and the Italian borders. A few measures had already been proposed, such as the gradual decrease in the property qualification and providing free uniforms, but Marius made the dramatic leap to abolishing the property qualification as well as providing equipment.

With the fear of the barbarians to the north, in 107 Marius removed the necessity of owning land and was able to enlist many of the disenfranchised, the urban poor and the unemployed side-by-side with the traditional property owners. There were several benefits for these individuals from the lower classes, such as the possibility of land as a reward when they finished their lengthy service, taking part in the 'romanization' of newly conquered territories or troublesome border areas by mass resettlement by veteran soldiers and, finally, a large trained reserve remained to be called into duty if there were any problems, both externally and, unfortunately, internally during the subsequent civil wars of the 80s and 40s BCE.

Marius himself is a fascinating figure. Born in Arpinum, he appears to have been part of the local equestrian class and was elected to a local office. He was, however, a *novus homo* or 'new man,' meaning that no ancestor of his had been elected to political office in Rome, but he was ambitious and hopeful. There is a story that as a child, he had found an eagle's nest with seven eggs in it – a prophecy that foretold his eventual election as consul for a record seven times. Marius, in fact, would establish the eagle – one of sacred animals of the god Jupiter – as a symbol of the senate and people of Rome (SPQR). He showed superb potential as a young man when he served with the army in Numantia and his talents caught the eye of his commander, P. Cornelius Scipio Aemilianus Africanus (who had overseen the destruction of Carthage in 146 BCE). Around the same time, Marius ran for one of the 24 special military tribunates, handsomely winning one. Later, he ran for the quaestorship (123), which he possibly served in Asia, and was elected tribune for 119 BCE with the support of the Metelli clan.

The relationship with one of Rome's most powerful and wealthiest families – the Metelli – was particularly advantageous to the young Marius. Although they were of plebian origin they had served with great distinction from the mid-third century BCE, both politically and militarily. It was Q. Caecilius Metellus (later) Numidicus, who first supported and then turned against his lieutenant, Marius, creating one of Rome's great personality conflicts.

As tribune, Marius proposed a law narrowing the passages down which voters passed to cast their vote, thereby preventing outsiders from harassing voters. It had only been 20 years before this (139 BCE) that voting by secret ballot had been introduced, however, this first attempt was rejected by the senate; later, Marius brought his law before the people, who enthusiastically supported him, much to the dismay of the Metelli.[4] Before then, oral voting meant that senatorial figures could assure themselves of the voting outcome, particularly by those that had pledged their support or received financial assistance to make up their minds, e.g. the infamous bribery that seemingly characterized every election.

Marius had some problems in securing his next political office. He ran unsuccessfully for the aedileship, and in 116 BCE barely won election as praetor. He was promptly charged with *ambitus* or electoral bribery, but managed to secure an acquittal. From 114–13, his *imperium* (political power) was continued and he was sent for two years to Lusitania (modern southern Portugal and

Spain), where he was involved in a minor military operation. The break with the Metelli, following his legislation during his tribunate, does not seem to have been permanent. In 109, Q. Caecilius Metellus took Marius with him as his legate in his campaign against Jugurtha.

Numidia, now comprised of modern day Tunisia and eastern Algeria, had originally sided with Carthage during the second Punic war between Carthage and Rome (218–04 BCE), but in 206, the new king of the eastern portion had switched his allegiance to Rome, while the western part remained true to Carthage. With a successful victory against Carthage, the king of eastern Numidia – Massinissa – was given the entire area of Numidia as a reward for his support. It was not until his own son and heir to the throne, Micipsa, died in 118 BCE, that problems began to surface within the province, which would soon involve Rome.

Micipsa was succeeded to the throne by his two sons, Hiempsal and Adherbal; however, Massinissa's illegitimate grandson, Jugurtha, put forth his own claim. Hiempsal and Jugurtha, who enjoyed support among the Numidians, had quarrelled almost immediately following Micipsa's death and Jugurtha ended their rivalry by having him killed. This action led to war being declared between Adherbal and Jugurtha, with the former running to Rome for its assistance. The senate ordered that the territory be divided into two parts, Adherbal receiving the eastern half, while Jugurtha received the less populated and less developed western area.

Jugurtha had been sent to Spain when his uncle, Micipsa had ascended the throne in 148 and it is believed that while he was there, he had made several important Roman contacts. It is probable that extensive bribery assisted the senate in making their decision to validate Jugurtha's claim, but another reason may have been to try and stop the fighting due to Numidia's situation as a profitable client kingdom. Regardless of this outcome, Jugurtha resumed hostilities against Adherbal when the latter returned from Rome.

By 112, war had resumed and this time, Rome could not turn a blind eye when several Italian businessmen were killed. In 109, the consul Q. Caecilius Metellus took command of the Roman troops against Jugurtha, with Marius as his legate (or subordinate commander in the field). Through successful strategic military planning, Jugurtha was easily overwhelmed. Marius argued that Metellus was prolonging the war in Numidia and should be replaced as commander by himself. Although there was some precedent during the second Punic war and later in 131, where tribunes proposed legislation for a special election to select a replacement commander, it was a somewhat unusual tactic. However, in 108 another tribune passed similar legislation, and taking the unusual step of approaching the people directly, it was decided that Marius would replace Metellus – against the wishes of the senate.

Quickly replacing Metellus as commander in the Numidian war, Marius was able to secure a treaty with Jugurtha on quite favourable terms to the Romans. The battle of Muthul in 108 was the pinnacle of victory, with Marius reorganizing a few groups and leading some 2,000 soldiers to relieve Metellus. Another general, P. Rutilius Rufus, had successfully held the Numidian forces near the river Muthul. By the time evening fell, all of the Roman troops were able to reunite. Jugurtha, however, swiftly retreated and never again met the Romans in battle – he returned to guerrilla warfare with somewhat better results:

> The whole conflict was more like an encounter with robbers than a battle; the horse and foot of the enemy, mingled together without standards or order, wounded some of our men, and cut down others, and surprised many in the rear while fighting stoutly with those in front; neither valour nor arms were a sufficient defence, the enemy being superior in numbers, and covering the field on all sides. At last the Roman veterans, who were necessarily well experienced in war, formed themselves, wherever the nature of the ground or chance allowed them to unite, in circular bodies, and thus secured on every side, and regularly drawn up, withstood the attacks of the enemy.[5]

In the meantime, however, Marius began to plan for the consulship. Metellus was not pleased, his comment that Marius should wait until Metellus' own son was eligible has been widely circulated. The irony was that Metellus' son was 20 and would not become eligible for some 20 years. Marius paid no attention to Metellus and successfully ran for the consulship for 107 BCE. His first concern was to secure more men for the military and he set about reforming the criteria in relation to enlistment.

His first move was to abolish the property qualification, which would have significant repercussions, but the main goal at this time as perceived by Marius was simply to increase the numbers available. The property qualification originally had been about 11,000 sesterces, but this had been lowered by the Gracchan legislation to 3,000 sesterces of property value.[6] Marius, however, decided to eliminate this and recruited without any inquiry as to the property of prospective soldiers. Although it might appear that thousands may have rushed into military service, the next few decades would see a balance between the poor and propertied within the ranks. One disadvantage that may have been overlooked by Marius in his eagerness to recruit more men, was the shift from the personal responsibility of the farmer-soldier to that of the successful general, rewarding his troops with booty and the promise of land when a campaign finished. This would become a major problem in the first century BCE when soldiers began to look to their generals, and not the state, to reward them for their services. It also meant that the army became increasingly loyal to their general, who, in turn, could rely on those soldiers, not just in war but also in times of peace as viable support, and indeed threaten the stability of Rome itself, as the generals could call out their soldiers to pass legislation, or worse, be used to secure power over rivals within the political system itself.

Metellus, disappointed by Marius' election and displeased by Marius' appointment as commander in Numidia, had returned to Rome, but was overwhelmed and surprised by the enthusiasm and praise he received from both the senate and the people, the former perhaps already regretting the transfer of the command to Marius, particularly when Metellus had effectively curtailed Jugurtha's actions before Marius had even been elected consul. Giving the title Numidicus to Metellus, the senate illustrated how they felt about the conflict. When the war ended in 106, the senate furthermore recognized Lucius Cornelius Sulla as the conqueror of Numidia – not Marius.

Lucius Cornelius Sulla – hereafter Sulla – was an extremely competent military leader. Marius had sent the youth to talk with the king of Mauretania, Bocchus, who was convinced by Sulla to betray Jugurtha. Although the honour of capturing Jugurtha should have belonged to Marius since he was the overall commander, Sulla had other ideas. Taking the credit, Sulla was even rumoured to have created a signet ring celebrating his accomplishment. Thus, both Metellus and Sulla were recognized for their contribution – the glory was not Marius', which was to cause problems later between Sulla and Marius with disastrous results.

Unusually, however, Marius was to receive an even greater honour, being elected *in absentia* for a second consulship for 105. Marius then turned his attention to a northern threat – the advancing Cimbri and Teutones tribes into southern Gaul. Both tribes were closely aligned, probably originating from modern Jutland, but had moved from northern Europe through to the Danube region, ultimately coming into conflict with the Romans near the Italian borders. In 109, the consul M. Junius Silanus had been set to deal with them, but he was completely defeated and destroyed. A few years later, in 107, Marius' co-consul L. Cassius Longinus, was also defeated. His second-in-command was only able to save what was left by having his army 'march under the yoke,' a complete and utter humiliation in the field.[7] The following year, another consul – Q. Servilius Caepio – marched to Gaul and subdued the disloyal town of Tolosa (modern Toulouse), but when a new consul, Gn. Mallius Maximus – also a *novus homo* like Marius – was appointed to assist Caepio, the two quarrelled and could not be reconciled. Without their cooperation, the two tribes, now on Rhone, were able to destroy both Caepio and Mallius' separate armies, with a loss of possibly some 80,000 soldiers. Italy itself now was faced with a barbarian invasion.

Marius had been elected twice for consul already in 107 and 105, and he returned to Rome with the captured Jugurtha in tow. Marius celebrated a magnificent triumph with Jugurtha in the front. Jugurtha was later strangled in 104 and the province of Numidia was split into two – western Numidia was added to the lands of Bocchus, the king of Mauretania, who had assisted Sulla, while the eastern half continued to be governed by local leaders. It would again become important in the civil war between Pompey and Caesar in the 40s BCE, and serve as the final resting place (at Utica) of one of Caesar's greatest foes, Cato the Younger.

A previous law, which had tried to regulate election to political offices and the time ideally that one had to wait, appears to have been repealed, and Marius would find himself elected consul for five successive consulships (104–100 BCE). As the two barbarian tribes moved into Spain and northern Gaul, Marius had some time to prepare his army for his new command against the Cimbri and Teutones. He chose as one of his legates the capturer of Jugurtha, the young Sulla, illustrating that regardless of any personal difficulties between the two, he was able to recognize the outstanding military skills that his subordinate held.

It was not until 102 that the two tribes, perhaps strengthened by Marius' apparent lack of resistance, decided to invade Italy, but from two fronts. The Cimbri decided to invade Italy through the Alps, while the Teutones would go along the Mediterranean coast. This division, however, worked in Rome's favour as they could deal with each in a much more managed approach. Marius refused to engage with the Teutones, and in fact, was able to block their path. Without waiting for their reinforcements, the Teutones attacked the geographically better placed Romans and thousands were killed. Having hidden some of his troops, Marius was then able to decisively destroy the Teutones as his soldiers came from behind and routed the enemy without mercy:

> Under this double attack (the barbarians), could not hold out long, but broke ranks and fled. The Romans pursued them and either killed or took alive over a hundred thousand of them, besides making themselves masters of the tents, wagons, and property, all of which, with the exception of what was pilfered, was given to Marius by vote of the soldiers.[8]

Marius' co-consul of 102 BCE, Q. Lutatius Catulus, had less luck against the Cimbri. He was unable to hold the Brenner Pass (a mountain pass between Italy and modern Austria) and the Cimbri were able to advance into Italy itself. Marius curtailed his triumph over the Teutones and hurried to assist Catulus. At the battle of Vercellae in Cisalpine Gaul (territory on the Italian side of the Alps) in the summer of 101 BCE, Marius, along with Sulla and Catulus, was able to finish off the Cimbri with a complete victory, killing a huge portion of the enemy (estimated between 60,000 to 120,000) with thousands captured. The threat to Rome was over.

THE ITALIAN QUESTION

The Italian allies paid taxes and provided soldiers to the Roman army, yet they had few rights. They had two categories of representation at Rome: the higher level had Latin rights; the second were without any rights at all. Latin rights referred to those cities who remained unincorporated into the Roman state, and could be construed as intermediaries between Rome and other allies. They had the right to enter into contracts and business with recourse to the courts in Rome; furthermore, they could intermarry with Roman citizens. But they could not vote or run for political office in Rome itself, and resentment was growing. Gaius Gracchus had tried to resolve the problem, but failed.

As reward to his soldiers and without recourse to the senate, Marius immediately bestowed Roman citizenship on all of his troops, including those who were from the Italian allies. Although the senate may have questioned this, Marius' argument that he could not distinguish between the voices of Romans and Italians in battle was all that was necessary. But how to deal with the remainder of the Italian allies would consume the senate and Rome itself within a decade, leading to war.

The year 100 BCE was Marius' final year of his seven successive consulships, and it would not be a particularly pleasant one for him. It had not been an easy election for him and Marius had had to rely on a difficult alliance with the tribune Saturninus and his ally G. Servius Glaucia. In his previous tribunate in 103, Saturninus had proposed that each of Marius' veterans should receive an allotment of 100 *iugera* in north Africa, but, unfortunately, he was later to be tried for his insulting behaviour to ambassadors acting on behalf of Mithridates VI of Pontus. He was acquitted by an appeal to the people, but Saturninus had gone too far. The censor, Q. Metellus Numidicus, tried to have him thrown out of the senate for his immorality, but his colleague refused. Saturninus began to go around Rome proclaiming that he was heir to the Gracchan tradition, particularly in terms of agrarian reform or, as his opponents would argue, agrarian rewards.

When elected for his second tribunate in 100, Saturninus went much further in his agrarian pursuits. He now proposed that lands recently reclaimed from the Cimbri in northern Italy were to be used for Marius' veterans. He suggested that further colonies be established in Sicilia, Achaea and Macedonia, with Italians also admitted to these settlements. Unfortunately, this part of his plan created great resentment at Rome – the decision to give Roman citizenship was never an easy one, and Saturninus came up against a great deal of opposition from both the senate and the people.

A clause in his *lex agraria* in relation to the resettlement of Marius' veterans imposed an obligatory oath on every senator to uphold the law on penalty of expulsion and exile. Metellus Numidicus, Marius' old enemy (and the censor who had tried to expel Saturninus) refused, but only went into exile to Rhodes for a year until the efforts of his son allowed him to return. Subsequently, it appears that he involved himself little in public affairs, dying in 91 BCE.

With echoes of Gaius Gracchus, Saturninus also proposed a *lex frumentaria*, which would supply corn to the plebs at a nominal price. This, however, met with greater resistance, as the quaestor Q. Servilius Caepio announced that the treasury could not finance this and other tribunes interposed their vetoes. Refusing to compromise, Saturninus ordered that the voting continue, but Caepio contrived to end the meeting with violence. Although the senate proclaimed the proceedings null – due to thunder being heard – Saturninus' measure was ultimately successful due to the threat of Marius' veterans massed around Rome.

However, all was not well between Saturninus and Marius. The former, along with his friend Glaucia, decided to run for political office for 99 BCE. Saturninus was elected to the tribunate for an unprecedented third time, while Glaucia, who was praetor at the time, ran for the consulship. One consulship was filled without a problem, but another individual, Gaius Memmius, had a good chance of being elected second, thereby eliminating any possibility for Glaucia. Hired agents of Saturninus and Glaucia proceeded to beat Memmius to death while the actual election was taking place.

The next day, the senate declared both men public enemies and called upon Marius to defend the *res publica* against his former allies. Marius had no choice and, following a ruthless battle in the Forum itself on the 10th December 100 BCE, he captured Saturninus and his followers in the capitol. Assured that their lives would be spared, Marius took them to the *curia hostilia* (part of the senate house), but in the end, Saturninus was stoned to death.[9] Glaucia was found in a nearby house, dragged out and also killed. Marius, perhaps disgruntled and frustrated, left Rome for the east and went into retirement.

The episode had a strange postscript. Some 40 years later, in 63 BCE, a certain Titus Labienus accused a former senator, Gaius Rabirius, of the murder of his uncle, one of Saturninus' followers. The actual charge was the archaic *perduellio*, roughly equivalent to high treason in a military sense, which had recently been replaced by the law of *maiestas* in the late Republic. Julius Caesar and his uncle Lucius were appointed as special commissioners to try the case, which was considered 'a particularly ancient procedure'.[10] Parts of Cicero's elegant defence speech on behalf of Rabirius give a clear indication of the chaos and uncertainty of the time: 'Marius and L. Valerius (consuls in 100) . . . order whoever wishes the Republic to be safe to take up weapons and follow them. All obey . . .'[11] Cicero further argued that to hide was 'tantamount to an utterly shameful death, to be with Saturninus to madness and crime', that the situation called for immediate action, and to condemn this now elderly man for involvement in the battle and later deaths of Saturninus and his followers was folly. The *res publica* had been in serious danger and the outcome was a result of Saturninus' own treasonable activities, but sadly for Rabirius, Cicero's speech had little effect – he was condemned and sentenced to death by crucifixion. However, as the people were about to ratify the decision, Metellus Celer pulled down the military flag from the Janiculum hill, which automatically dissolved the assembly. It has been suggested that this trial was a mere mechanism by Julius Caesar to demonstrate that the *senatus consultum ultimum* could not just be used to 'eliminate legislators who had forced through important measures that the senate opposed.'[12] In end, however, the trial never resumed and Rabirius was never formally convicted; his end is not known.

Following the deaths of Saturninus and Glaucia along with their followers, Rome was relatively calm. The Italian question remained a sore, slowly festering until it erupted in 91 BCE. The situation was perhaps exacerbated by passage of the *lex Licinia Mucia* in 95, which removed Latins and Italians from the citizen rolls, and provided for the prosecution of those who falsely claimed to be Roman citizens, while a subsequent *lex Minucia* tried to regulate the status of children when only one parent was a Roman citizen. These measures illustrate an effort by the senate to limit the citizenship, but when M. Livius Drusus was elected tribune in 91 BCE, with a platform of reform including the citizenship question, things swiftly changed.

Marcus Livius Drusus was the son of the Livius Drusus who had been elected as tribune back in 121 as an opponent to Gaius Gracchus. His proposed agrarian legislation had been effective in undermining Gaius' own reforms, but these collective measures had never been passed. He was later elected consul in 112, where he had a successful campaign in Macedonia before securing the censorship in 109. Dying in 108, he left a legacy of senatorial support for his son, who himself was elected tribune in 91 BCE.

A rivalry between the younger Drusus and his former brother-in-law Q. Servilius Caepio, praetor for the year, characterized the beginning of 91. The two had been great friends, with Caepio married to Drusus' sister Livia, but following an alleged argument about a golden ring between the two men in the late 90s, Livia divorced Caepio and married Marcus Porcius Cato. A grandson from the first marriage would be the later assassin of Caesar, Brutus, while Livia's only son from the second, also Marcus Porcius Cato, would be Caesar's greatest political enemy. It was a most illustrious line, with marriages and alliances made with some of Rome's great figures of the first century BCE, with even the adopted son of Livius Drusus producing the wife (Livia) of the future emperor of Rome, Caesar's heir Octavian.

Drusus had numerous ideas that appear to have been initially supported by the senate. He wanted to return the jury courts back to joint senatorial and equestrian composition, undoing Gaius Gracchus' previous legislation that had given the *equites* complete control. He also set up an agrarian commission to grant more land to the urban plebs, both around Rome and in its colonies. His final non-contentious legislation was a *lex frumentaria*, which saw a reduction in the price of grain. Drusus' downfall, unfortunately, was his next move.

Drusus proposed that the Roman citizenship be extended to the Italian allies. The second century CE Roman historian Appian writes that the *lex agraria* was proposed so that Drusus could count on the urban plebs to continue supporting his Italian bill, while Livy states that it was with Italian support that he forced through both his grain and land distribution programmes.[13] Drusus unfortunately made a major miscalculation when he decided to meet with the heads of the various Italian states and formed an association with them, including a particular friendship with the Marsic leader Q. Poppaedius Silo. It was also alleged that Drusus had accepted an oath of allegiance from their aristocracy, which would have gained him a large support base, however, there is no clear evidence on this point.[14] Even the hint of scandal would be enough for his enemies to claim that Drusus was a traitor.

It may be that Drusus saw a genuine need to resolve the Italian question, but his move was vehemently and violently opposed by the majority of Romans. He lost support from the senate, the *equites* and even from the Italian landowners who did not want to lose their land in Drusus' agrarian reforms. These landowners would have benefited from Roman citizenship, but perhaps it was a question of profit over privilege. Through the agitations of the consul L. Marcius Philippus and of Drusus' sworn enemy, Q. Servilius Caepio, much of Drusus' proposed legislation was annulled. Perhaps the scholar Arthur Keaveney is correct when he says that Drusus 'lacked the true killer instinct,' by not vetoing the actions of the senate.[15]

In the autumn of 91 BCE, as Drusus was returning to his house surrounded by his usual entourage of supporters, he was stabbed and died a few hours later with the weapon still in his side.[16] The repercussions of his assassination were immediate and swift. Upon hearing of his death, along with the expulsion of some of his Italian supporters from Rome, the Italians began to marshal their forces together – as Appian states, 'they decided that they could not longer tolerate that those men who were working for their political advancement should suffer such outrages, and since they saw no other avenue for obtaining the Roman citizenship, they decided on open rebellion.'[17]

THE SOCIAL WAR

The revolt that triggered the Social War (*socii* – allies) is generally believed to have begun at Asculum in Picenum and then spread through central Italy. A new state was set up with its capital in Corfinium, which was renamed Italica, and a replicate Roman governmental structure was created, with consuls, praetors and other political offices established. The allies also created their own coinage with an Italian bull raping the Roman world. Ironically, many of the soldiers who were to fight for the Italians were, in fact, seasoned veterans from Rome's many campaigns, but there was no generals of comparable quality on the Italian side, which would ultimately lead to great difficulties. In the short-term, however, the Italians were able to win on the battlefield, much to the chagrin of the Romans.

The Romans faced a two-front revolt, in both the north and south. In the north, the consul Publius Rutilius Lupus was advised by Marius, who had recently returned from retirement, and Pompeius Strabo; while in the south, the other consul, L. Julius Caesar, was assisted by Sulla and Titus Didius. Unfortunately, Lupus was an ineffective general and, after several mistakes, was killed in action. Marius, seizing the opportunity, took the overall northern command. Strabo, after being defeated near Mt Falernus, had some success in his siege of Asculum. Another siege at Aesernia, which was a key fortress and a link between the north and south, resulted in its surrender.

The Samnites had success in the south; under C. Papius, they were able to capture the city of Nola (near Naples) along with other towns in the area. Later, however, L. Caesar was able to secure their defeat. News of this victory was received with great relief in Rome, but the Samnites continued their thrust across Italy, seizing Aesernia. Although they had tried to also take Pinna (modern Penne), this city remained loyal to Rome.

Areas closer to Rome were also under threat. One of the Italian leaders, Papius Mutilius, was able to win over many towns in southern Campania, while other leaders led raids into Apulia and Lucania. Drusus' old enemy, Q. Servilius Caepio was defeated and executed by the forces of Poppaedius Silo after leaving a secure position. Even Marius had an indecisive skirmish with Silo, as the former refused to be drawn into a full-scale battle. The following year would see continued mixed results, but gradually the Romans were successful in stopping the Italian threat.

One setback of 89 BCE was the unfortunate death of the consul L. Porcius Cato in battle, but the other consul of the year – Strabo – had a decisive victory and was able to systematically destroy the Italian army, while the city of Asculum finally surrendered. There was also an attempt by the Italian forces to encourage a revolt in Etruria, but this again was defeated by Strabo. Marius, however, was forced to retire due to his ill-health. Therefore, it was Strabo who controlled and resolved the Italian resistance in the north.

In the south, Sulla had good results as well. He had captured and destroyed Stabiae, defeated the Samnites near Nola, subdued the Hirpini, invaded Samnium and captured Bovianum, while the Romans also captured Herculaneum and besieged Pompeii. It was a ruthless, well-organized campaign that showed Sulla's military strength and abilities to their best. As Livy notes, Sulla then 'proceeded to Rome to run for consul, having achieved more than most people achieve before their consulship'.[18] Both he and Strabo were easily elected consuls for the year 88 BCE. As the year continued, most of the Italian forces were overwhelmed and destroyed, thereby bringing an end to the conflict, although there would still be some isolated resistance from the Samnites in the beginning of 88. Ultimately, the capital of Italica – Corfinium – surrendered, while the praetor Metellus Pius defeated and killed Poppaedius Silo near Apulia. The Social War was over.

During his consulship in 90, L. Julius Caesar had proposed a *lex Julia*, which offered full citizenship to the Italians and Latins who had not revolted. It meant that whole communities had to pass the law, not just individuals; the Romans felt that this was 'in preference to giving it to them as a body when their own strength was still unimpaired.'[19] According to Appian, the allies were 'enrolled in separate tribes of their own, like those who had been granted citizenship earlier, in order that they might not, by being mixed up with the older citizens, vote them down in elections by their strength of numbers.'[20] A further *lex Papiria Plautia* in 89 was a concession that granted citizenship to any Italian who immediately stopped fighting and went to a magistrate to enrol. These two pieces of legislation did a great deal to stop the war, by giving the Italians pretty much what they had fought for, even though they had lost in the field.

THE WAR IN THE EAST

The internal problems in the Italian peninsula had consumed most of Rome's attention from 91 to the beginning of 88, but while the Romans had been occupied, Mithridates VI of Pontus, a region on the Black sea (modern Turkey), had been making forays into Anatolia, with great success. An alliance with Nicomedes III of Bithynia (northern Turkey) partitioned several areas between the two leaders, but Mithridates seemed to be beginning to worry about Nicomedes' increasingly anti-Pontic stance, as the latter appealed to Rome when an argument arose between them about Cappadocia (an inland area of Asia Minor/Turkey). Twice the Romans intervened in 95 and 92 in favour of Nicomedes. In 89, Nicomedes, perhaps emboldened by this support, invaded Pontus, but this time Mithridates himself sent a representative to complain to the Roman envoys in Asia about Nicomedes' aggression. That representative – Pelopidas – complained that 'Mithridates, who is your friend and ally, calls upon you as friends and allies (for so the treaty reads) to defend us against the wrong-doing of Nicomedes, or to restrain the wrong-doer'. The Romans, however, responded that it was Mithridates, and not Nicomedes, who was to blame.[21] It seemed inevitable that war would occur between Rome and Pontus.

Regardless of his earlier appeal to Rome, Mithridates had already been very successful; his generals had defeated Nicomedes by the river Amneius, then the Romans abandoned Bithynia after the defeat of the consular legate Manius Aquillius, one of Marius' most loyal followers. Unfortunately for Manius, the inhabitants of Mytilene, in an effort to curry favour, delivered him to Mithridates. First, Mithridates led him around 'bound on an ass, and compelled him to introduce himself to the public as a "maniac," . . . finally, at Pergamon, Mithridates poured molten gold down his throat, thus rebuking the Romans for their bribe-taking.'[22]

Unfortunately, the rivalry between Marius and Sulla needed to be dealt with first before there could be any attempt to stymie Mithridates. The conflict between the two would result in civil war, fighting in the city of Rome, with violence and bloody prescriptions. While the first part of the decade may have started with an Italian desire for citizenship, the decade would end as one of the most bloody and violent in its history.

CIVIL WAR IN ROME – THE FIRST WAVE

It was perhaps predictable that Sulla would be elected consul for 88 BCE, but a difficult choice nevertheless confronted the senate: who would lead the campaign against Mithridates – Sulla or Marius? The senate decided ultimately on Sulla, but the assembly had another idea – prompted by the tribune Rufus, Marius was appointed. It was an interesting choice. Although Marius had had to retire from the last months of the Social War due to ill-health, Plutarch records that he made a regular routine of exercising in the Campus Martius and 'showed that he was still agile in arms and capable of feats of horsemanship, although his bulk was not well set up in his old age, but ran to corpulence and weight.'[23] The people were divided in their amusement and pity for the old man, but using the time-honoured tradition, Marius was able to convince them – through the mechanism of a tribune – that he deserved one final shot at victory and immortality.

Sulla ignored the assembly, leaving Rome and travelling to the waiting army in Nola. Able to persuade his legions to accept him as their rightful leader, the representatives from the assembly were stoned when they tried to intercede. It was at this point that Sulla, frustrated by the Marian influence, gathered six legions together and began his fateful march on Rome itself.

This action was unprecedented, forbidden by law and by tradition. The senate sent two praetors to plead with Sulla, but his soldiers 'contented themselves with breaking their fasces, stripping them of their senatorial togas, insulting them in many ways, and then sending them back to the city.' When they returned to the city, the two announced that 'sedition could no longer be checked, but must run its course.'[24] Near Pictae, another commission from the senate approached

Sulla, with news that the senate had reaffirmed his rights and to beg again that he reconsider coming with an army into the city of Rome. Although Sulla gave every indication that he had listened to the impassioned pleas, he sent two individuals, Bascillus and Mummius, towards Rome, where they seized the city gate and the walls of the Esquiline hill. Perhaps it is best to turn to Plutarch for his lively, colourful account of what happened next:

> Then he himself followed hard ... with all speed ... (the men) burst into the city and were forcing their way along, when the unarmed multitude pelted them with stones and tiles from the roofs of the houses, stopped their further progress, and crowded them back to the wall. But by this time, Sulla was at hand, and seeing what was going on, shouted orders to set fire to the houses, and seizing a blazing torch, led the way himself, and ordered his archers to use their fire-bolts and shoot them up at the roofs.

> This he did not from any calm calculation, but in a passion, and having surrendered to his anger the command over his actions, since he thought only of his enemies, and without any regard or even pity for friends and kindred and relations, made his entry by the aid of fire, which made no distinction between the guilty and the innocent. Meanwhile Marius, who had been driven back to the temple of Tellus, made a proclamation calling the slaves to his support under the promise of freedom; but the enemy coming on, he was overpowered and fled from the city.[25]

Although Sulla and his supporters in the senate passed the death penalty on Marius, Sulpicius Rufus and some others, the violence seems to have been curtailed with only a few men executed. Rebuking the senate, Sulla set about strengthening his position. Appian remarks that 'at daybreak, they summoned the people to an assembly and lamented the condition of the Republic, which had been so long given over to demagogues, and said that they had done what they had done as a matter of necessity.'[26]

Marius and Sulpicius were then outlawed. Marius was able to escape, but Sulpicius was captured and killed. An almost supernatural journey of escape through forests and swamps, repeated assassination attempts (and failures) with pursuit by Sulla's supporters colours Plutarch's *Life of Marius*, but in the end, he was able to escape by boat. Marius attempted to land near Carthage, but he was expelled; later, he sought and found refuge in Numidia, where he had had great successes the previous decade. He began to plot his return by gathering together his friends and supporters. Marius was determined to have his seventh consulship as the eagle had preordained when he was a small boy.

In Rome, Sulla proposed that all legislation must have the previous support of the senate, thereby significantly curbing tribunate agitation. From the Gracchi to Saturninus to Rufus, powerful tribunes had been able to bypass the senate in order to present their popular legislative programmes. Started by Tiberius Gracchus, a loophole of some 40 years appeared to have been effectively ended, an aspect that had characterized Roman politics. Sulla also interposed several more severe restrictions on the tribunate, which in turn undermined its usefulness, whether by manipulations by the tribune himself or by manoevres from other political figures such as consuls. Sulla, although annoyed with the senate, nevertheless considered it the fundamental agency and representative of the Roman *res publica*. He then enrolled 300 of 'the best citizens' into the senate, which had the benefit of not only replacing those who had died, but also to shore up his own support within that august body. Another measure was the annulment of any and all of Sulpicius' tribunate legislation, including Marius' command over Sulla in the east. The ensuing elections for 87 nevertheless showed the strongly defined sentiment in the city of Rome as one consul – Gnaeus Octavius – was a supporter of Sulla, while the other – L. Cornelius Cinna – supported Marius. Although some of Sulla's opponents were elected to other political offices, his appointment in the east was nevertheless reconfirmed. Taking his troops out of Rome, Sulla then hurried eastwards.

Appian notes with disdain that:

> Thus the seditions proceeded from strife and contention to murder, and from murder to open war, and now the first army of her own citizens had invaded Rome as a hostile country. From this time the seditions were decided only by the (use) of arms. There were frequent attacks upon the city and battles before the walls and other calamities incident to war. Henceforth there was no restrain upon violence either from the sense of shame, or regard for law, institutions, or country.[27]

A dangerous precedent had been set.

CIVIL WAR IN ROME – THE SECOND WAVE

Fighting soon broke out between the supporters of the two consuls. Cinna attempted to redistribute the new Italian allies throughout all of the Roman tribes, contrary to previous legislation in 90 and 89, but his consular colleague, Octavius, expelled him from the city. Other political business soon came to a halt. Rome was about to be under attack again.

Hearing that Cinna was raising an army among his supporters in the Italian towns, Marius, along with his son, then returned from exile in Africa with the army that he himself had raised. These two, along with other exiles such as Carbo and Sertorius, surrounded Rome with their forces. Pompeius Strabo had been called 'to the aid of his country' and encamped near Cinna.[28] At this point, Marius captured and sacked Ostia – Rome's most important port. This resulted in Marius now having control of all shipping, including the important grain-supply to the city.

Cinna was able to capture Arminum and Placentia in northern Italy, but it appears that Pompeius was able to establish a colony at Comum (north of modern Naples) and a first attack on Rome itself was repelled. Unfortunately, Pompeius died – whether by a bolt of lightening or by a plague that was afflicting his army is unclear, but due to his excessive greed, few appear to have mourned him. In fact, Plutarch comments that as the body 'was on its way to the funeral pyre, [the people] dragged it from his bier and heaped insults upon it.'[29]

In the end, the senate sent envoys to Cinna and Marius, finally agreeing to them entering Rome. They ousted Octavius, the other consul, and were able to take control of the city. Some of his soldiers, in unrestrained pandemonium, ran through the streets, killing some of the leading supporters of Sulla, including Octavius. The heads of several of those killed adorned the Forum but, after five days, Cinna appears to have put a stop to the chaos. He simply ordered his troops to kill any renegade Marian soldiers. A brief respite came with the possible threat of Sulla's return 'as if the change of wind were coming on, messengers arrived from all quarters with reports that Sulla had finished the war with Mithridates, had recovered the provinces, and was sailing for home with a large force', but it was to no effect.[30] Without any elections, Marius and Cinna declared themselves consuls for the following year. After the senate passed a law outlawing Sulla, with all of Sulla's legislation and reforms rendered invalid, Marius was appointed the new commander in the east, but his luck had finally run out. Securing that seventh consulship for 86, Marius died in early January. Cinna took sole control of Rome for a short time, but a suffect consul – L. Valerius Flaccus – was appointed.

One of Flaccus' first measures called for the wide-scale cancellation of debts. This was a particularly popular, but also essential, move. The effects of the Social War, just a few years before, had been particularly difficult on the economy of the Italian peninsula. Many towns had been attacked, some destroyed, and rural agricultural practices had had little time to repair themselves. The broken landscape was a continual reminder that towns had been attacked, lands destroyed and people displaced. The economy would take a generation to recover among Rome's newest citizens, and with the additional threat of civil war, it was a smart decision by Cinna and Flaccus to appear to be doing something to offset the economic ruin and deprivation that now dotted the countryside.

Flaccus was also appointed commander in Asia, replacing Sulla, who was travelling through Macedonia. The Asian cities refused to allow him within their walls and he was forced to remain on the outskirts. His subordinate, C. Flavius Fimbria, had other ideas and Flaccus was murdered, placing his army now under Fimbria's control. He was to take his fight straight through to Mithridates in 85. Cinna had declared himself consul again without an election that year. Much like the year before, Cinna appointed Gn. Carbo as his colleague for the consulship.

In the East, Sulla was having great success over Mithridates and during 85, was able to agree peace terms at Dardanus in August. Previously boasting that he preferred to meet with Flaccus, Mithridates for the moment had to be satisfied with Sulla as they thrashed out a treaty. Mithridates was to return all of his acquired properties and retreat back to Pontus, which Sulla magnanimously allowed him to keep.

Flaccus' replacement, Fimbria, had great reason to fear Sulla. Victorious over Mithridates, Sulla immediately turned to this renegade general. He ordered him to give up his illegal command, but Fimbria jokingly remarked that Sulla himself did not hold a lawful command.[31] After drawing a line in the sand, many of Fimbria's supporters fled to the safety of Sulla's camp. With increasing desperation, Fimbria went through the remaining soldiers, begging and pleading for their assistance, but many more, seeing the situation was dire, deserted to Sulla. Appian records that in the first instance, Fimbria instructed a slave to assassinate Sulla, but when that failed, Fimbria begged Sulla for an audience. Sulla sent his legate as an open insult to Fimbria. Fimbria then went into a temple and stabbed himself, but seeing that the wound was not deep enough, ordered his slave to finish the job. Sulla gave the body to some of Fimbria's freedmen and the body was accorded a proper burial, Sulla perhaps resisting the opportunity to further agitate Cinna and Carbo.

Following this and having re-established Nicomedes back as ruler of Bithynia, he set his sights on home. Sulla was on his way back to Rome.

THE CIVIL WAR – THE THIRD WAVE

Cinna and Carbo declared themselves consuls again for 84 BCE. Aside from the approaching threat of Sulla, another, more insidious, danger began to plague the inhabitants of Asia and the Aegean – pirates. Throughout the next few decades, these would become a major problem, with several notable individuals taken captive, but it would not be for another 15 years or so that it would create significant economic problems for Rome. Nevertheless, individual skirmishes would occupy various generals throughout this area, as well as in the Mediterranean. Also in 84 a census was completed at Rome which counted a total of 463,000 citizens, but whether this also included the newly enfranchised Italian allies is not clear.

As the year began, the self-appointed consuls Cinna and Carbo began their preparations for war against Sulla. Sulla wrote to the senate, recounting what he had done in Africa against Jugurtha as a praetor in Cilicia during the Social war, and as consul. He focused on his victories against Mithridates, arguing that he had recovered many territories for the Romans, but now found himself 'declared a public enemy by his foes, his house had been destroyed, his friends

put to death, and his wife and children had with difficulty made their escape.'
Sulla continued that:

> He would be there presently to take vengeance, on behalf of themselves and of the entire
> city, upon the guilty ones . . . and assured the other citizens, and the new citizens, that he
> would make no complaint against them.[32]

Messengers were sent to reason with him. Cinna and Carbo were told to stop
recruiting soldiers until Sulla's reply was received but, according to Appian, this
is when the two proclaimed themselves consuls, travelled across Italy collecting
soldiers and then grouped at Liburnia (along the Adriatic coast in modern
Croatia), which was to be their base against Sulla. It was not long before Cinna
became the first casualty as he was murdered in a mutiny, while Carbo decided
to withdraw his troops, bringing Cinna's along with his.

In Rome, elections were postponed due to thunderstorms, but the atmosphere
remained tense, awaiting Sulla's demands – he had met with the various messengers and they were now returning to Rome with his terms of settlement.
Meanwhile, Sulla spent the time travelling around Greece as a tourist. He visited
the hot springs on Euboea (an island), acquiring artworks and even a collection
of Aristotle's works, but unfortunately lost some on the return trip to Rome.

Carbo, increasingly desperate, ignored a senatorial resolution to disband all
armies and continued to cause havoc among the Italian cities. He planned to
seize hostages, but was stopped by the senate. He was further undermined by
the desertion of his quaestor, Verres, who decamped over to Sulla with a sizable
amount of money. Time was running out for Carbo but there was still enough
opposition to Sulla that it would not be easy for the victorious general to conquer
Rome.

THE FOURTH AND FINAL WAVE – 83–2 BCE

The son of Pompeius Strabo, Gnaeus Pompeius, better known to us as Pompey,
was busy raising an army in Picenum, where his father had a large following.
After defeating L. Junius Brutus, Pompey then joined with Sulla. Other senators
began to support Sulla, who was slowly making his way down to Rome. In July
83, a serious fire destroyed many of the buildings on the Capitoline hill. While
some attributed this disaster to Carbo, others to Sulla's agents, the evidence was
not clear. The omens were not good.

Sulla was making some progress as he moved through Italy. In Rome, although
not of the appropriate age – he was not yet 20 – Marius' son was elected consul,
along with Carbo. The two concentrated their efforts on recruiting more troops,
certain of the showdown that would occur once Sulla had consolidated his own

troops and support. Along with Sulla, there was Pompey and Metellus Pius, who were waiting to confront Carbo and C. Marius.

The year 82 began with Sulla establishing a treaty with the Italian allies. He sent Pompey to join Metellus in northern Italy, while Sertorius – long a supporter of the elder Marius – took his protest to Spain. With the main contestants in place, the battle for Rome was about to begin.

It was a complete disaster for Carbo and C. Marius. Pompey and Metellus strolled almost leisurely through Italy, with the hope of welcoming deserters from Carbo's army; at the river Aesis, Pompey was able to withstand a three-sided attack with great success. Sulla, perhaps fearing that the young man was in trouble, hurried to the area, but when he found Pompey's troops jubilant over their victory, it is reported that Sulla called him 'Imperator,' and forever afterwards, had a special regard for the young and brilliant military man.[33]

Sulla was able to destroy C. Marius and forced him to take refuge, while Pompey finished the job at Senae; the young man then committed suicide. Sulla then turned his attention to Carbo, but an indecisive battle followed. Carbo fled to Africa, but his army was crushed by Pompey. The Samnites, who had never reconciled with the Romans following the Social War, decided to march on Rome. What must the people of the city have thought with this new threat? Plutarch records their response – 'there was a tumult in the city, naturally, and shrieking of women, and running hither and thither, as though the city were taken by storm,' but 'riding up at full speed with seven hundred horsemen,' Sulla arrived.[34]

After a few hours delay, Sulla routed, defeated and destroyed the enemy. He then ordered the massacre of at least 3,000 prisoners, with the screams filling the city. Undeterred, Sulla calmly addressed the senate, which 'gave even the dullest Roman to understand that, in the matter of tyranny, there had been an exchange, but not a deliverance.'[35] Sulla was now supreme ruler of Rome. He had vanquished his enemies and, with a benevolent air, awarded those inhabitants in Spain, Gaul and Sicily, among others who had remained faithful to him, Roman citizenship. Circus games were presented to the people, while a golden statue of Sulla on horseback was displayed. Sulla, however, was not happy with his legal status. Leaving the city momentarily, he ordered that he was not a tyrant, but should instead be declared dictator. L. Flaccus accordingly passed a law, which formally appointed Sulla as dictator with absolute control. Thus, the defender of senatorial pre-eminence became legally its dictator.

There were still some areas of resistance to Sulla, but they were short-lived. Pompey was able to curb the problems in Sicily, with the final humiliation of Carbo, who was brought in chains before Pompey and put to death on the island of Cossyra. It was the end of any active opposition to Sulla, but many who went into exile were dissatisfied with the result. In Spain, Sertorius, furious at Sulla's victory, welcomed many of them. He had a particular gift for dealing with people and the locals supported his efforts to recreate a psuedo-Roman governmental structure in the province, with its own senate, elected officials and even a school that taught Latin, with Roman dress and practices. For some six years, until the mid-70s, he held sway over this area. It was a mini-Rome of sorts, but the original city did not concern itself with this off-shoot at the moment, as there were more pressing concerns as Sulla began Rome's rehabilitation. If the ordinary Roman believed that peace and security would now be Sulla's immediate objective, they were wrong.

SULLA AS DICTATOR

On 28 January 81 BCE, the city of Rome watched with amazement as Sulla finally celebrated his delayed triumph over Mithridates, with a magnificent feast to follow – 'his provision for them was so much beyond what was needed that great quantities of meats were daily cast into the river, and wine was drunk that was 40 years old and upwards.[36] Although 'the masses (may have) needed a breathing-spell and recreation after their toils,' Sulla's actions illustrate clearly his awareness that he needed to placate the urban masses quickly. There had been over a decade of instability, urban and rural confusion, along with constant threats to the Roman governmental structure. It was indeed time for a rest, and while Sulla may have shown his benevolence to the Roman people, the retribution to his enemies was anything but. One wonders what the ordinary person on the street thought after the drunken glory of January led to the retaliation, violence and bloodshed to the rich and political victims that followed in the next months.

Another objective to this great show was that Sulla was able to assuage his own personal vanity and, basking in the admiration of Rome, he began perhaps to feel that he had achieved the greatest goal of his career. He had fought and defeated some of Rome's great enemies – Jugurtha and Mithridates; he had saved the city of Rome from popular movements, re-enforcing senatorial tradition and ultimately, had returned home triumphant. He was dictator of Rome and it was time to finally defeat his enemies.

He began to punish those who had remained Marian: the inhabitants of Praeneste and the Italian towns who had supported his opponents were swiftly and cruelly dealt with. In Praeneste, those who were Roman, Samnites and local were divided into three groups. The Romans were pardoned, but Appian records that all the men in the other two groups were killed, while their wives and children allowed to go free. The city was plundered, while a neighbouring town – Norba – realizing that the same fate awaited them, killed themselves, by falling on each others' swords or strangling themselves with ropes, burning the town and its riches to the ground.

Sulla took away the hard-fought-for Roman citizenship as well as their lands. It was not just individuals who had displeased him, he:

'took vengeance on whole communities. He punished some of them by demolishing their citadels, or destroying their walls, or by imposing fines and crushing them by heavy contributions. Among most of them, he placed colonies of his troops in order to hold Italy under garrisons, sequestering their lands and houses and dividing them among his soldiers, whom he thus made true to him even after his death.'[37]

It was, however, his political enemies in Rome that angered Sulla the most, and it was these individuals who suffered the most in what could be categorized as akin to the French 'Reign of Terror'; but this was no revolution, it was Sulla and his supporters dealing with their obsession for revenge. Unlike the French, it was mainly the aristocracy, in particular the political (and financial) elite, who would suffer in the infamous proscriptions.

THE PROSCRIPTIONS

Originally, the proscriptions were lists of individuals who had been declared public enemies due to their opposition to Sulla, but the whole process quickly got out of control. In the first wave, it is estimated that some 40 senators were killed (and approximately 1,600 equestrians) and their property confiscated, but it escalated until the Forum was quite literally running with blood. Sulla published a list of those who were proscribed, but 'not even those whose names were not inscribed . . . were safe' as 'the names of many, some living and others actually dead, were added to the lists so that the slayers might gain immunity; thus, in this respect the procedure marked no new departure, yet equally by its terror and its strangeness, it angered absolutely everyone.'[38]

There was no 'safety at all for any one outside of Sulla's circle' as many were betrayed by their associates and 'consequently, as a result of this state of constant expectation of death, not only those whose names were inscribed suffered, but the rest also in equal measure.'[39] Those who ventured outside saw the heads of the slaughtered brought to the Forum and exposed on the rostra while additional names were being added to the lists. There was more:

Nor was vengeance wreaked upon those alone who had borne arms against him, but on many innocents as well. In addition, the goods of the proscribed were sold, and their children were not only deprived of their fathers' property but were also debarred from the right of seeking public office, and to cap the climax of injustice, the sons of senators were compelled to bear the burdens and yet lose the rights pertaining to their rank.[40]

Those who took refuge in temples were killed, others were thrown at Sulla's feet and killed, while many fell victim to the mob, killed by the bloodthirsty crowd. Any that managed to flee were hunted like animals and destroyed. It was unbridled mayhem and massacre and Sulla seemed to delight in its vengeance and vehemence. Sulla's allies eliminated their rivals, confiscated their property and the blood ran. Sulla did nothing to stop the wave after wave of violence. It was not a good time to be in Rome.

Many did escape, among them the young Julius Caesar. He had a precarious position – his aunt Julia had been married to Sulla's greatest foe, Marius, while his wife, Cornelia, was the daughter of Cinna. Even though Sulla had confiscated her dowry after Caesar's refusal to divorce her, he did not immediately order Caesar's death. Although ancient sources argue that Sulla saw the danger that Caesar posed, this appears to be a much more modern interpretation. It is suggested that Caesar's mother and other relatives, who were Sullan supporters, interjected on his behalf. The truth is probably more mundane than that. Caesar was still in his late teens (or 20, depending on date of birth) and perhaps no threat at all.[41] By hiding, Caesar was literally out of sight and to finish the cliché, effectively out of mind.

Another young man, who had served with military distinction under Pompeius Strabo and was a strong Sullan supporter, namely L. Sergius Catilina, or Catiline, remained in the city and participated in the proscriptions, including the cruel murder of an ex-praetor M. Marius Gratidianus (an expert on coinage), which later was used as evidence of Catiline's early designs for violence by senatorial colleagues in order to discredit him in the mid-60s BCE. Others, who remained in the city, would remain forever scarred and mindful of the high price that dictatorship and ruthless ambition cost their families, communities and the *res publica* itself. The young Marcus Porcius Cato apparently had to be restrained from voicing his threats against Sulla, querying why the crowd cheered Sulla as he passed them – his tutor replied that 'men fear[ed] him more than they hate[ed] him, but the 14 year old begged 'why didn't you give me a sword so that I might slay him and set my country free from slavery?'[42] Perhaps this is a later invention, but nevertheless, the sentiment expressed characterized a generation that would grow to fear another Sulla. As a later historian was to cry 'Sulla wielded with unbridled cruelty the powers which former dictators had employed only to save their country in times of extreme danger. He was the first to set the precedent for proscription – would that he had been the last![43]

His retribution had been swift, but there was one more thing that Sulla had to do. He dug up the body of Marius and removed his monuments (later to be restored by Caesar). He ordered his soldiers to destroy the body of the once great military leader, finally ending their rivalry under his terms and conditions. Sulla was indeed ruthless against his enemies.

SULLA'S REFORMS

Sulla was more than a mere butcher. The uncertainty and confusion of the proscriptions ended within weeks, and Pompey celebrated a triumph for his successes in Africa, where he had been instrumental in stamping out most of the opposition to Sulla. It was now time for Sulla to take control of the *res publica*, imposing his vision of senatorial dominance on the politics and governmental structure.

He settled numerous veterans at colonies throughout Italy, such as at Capua in Campania (north of Naples), Aleria (on Corsica) and Arretium (central Italy). Minor legislation dealing with the falsification of wills and a sumptuary law, limiting private expenditure on feasts, were also introduced. He also set about rebuilding the city, even to extending the ancient pomerium – or city boundary of Rome. However, Sulla's greatest reforms were to the political system itself. He enlarged the senate, increased the number of various offices, with praetors increased to 10, and quaestors to 20, while a *lex annalis* set a fixed sequence of magisterial office-holding so that those embarking on the *cursus honorem* had to follow age restraints and time separation from holding the next office.

Sulla went further. A *lex iudicaria* transferred the juries back from the *equites* to the senate and set up special courts to deal with murder, extortion, treason and bribery, which would be overseen by senatorial figures, with juries comprised only from the senatorial class. Immediately after securing the dictatorship, Sulla had raised heavy taxes from their provinces and now he introduced a *lex cornelia de provinciis*, which was a long-overdue programme of reform regarding the conduct of provincial governors.

Sulla saved his bitter vengeance, however, for the office of the tribunate. He perhaps felt that it was the actions of popular tribunes, such as the Gracchi, Saturninus and, in particular, Sulpicius Rufus – who had illegally proposed Marius for the Mithridatic command over the senatorial appointment of Sulla – that had caused so many problems to the stability and importance of the senate. Perhaps he felt that most of the problems could be attributed to public involvement in political events, where the senate was ignored by rebellious individuals using the tribunate to further popular agendas, rather than listening to and being guided by the august members of the senatorial class.

He stripped the tribunate of any and all of its effectiveness. All legislation had to go through the senate first, thereby curtailing the method that the Gracchi and others had utilized. His biggest reform was proposing that anyone holding the tribunate should be barred from holding any further political office, meaning any ambitious individuals could no longer rely on the tribunate to gain popular support. These reforms meant that the tribunate was now dead, its new role was a complete rejection of its original purpose – to protect the rights and wishes of the people. Appian, writing 200 years later in an Imperial Rome where the tribunate had long since lost its bite, amusingly notes that he was 'not able to say positively whether Sulla transferred this office from the people to the senate, where it is now lodged, or not.'[44]

After serving as dictator for 81 and part of 80, Sulla re-established consular government, and served himself as consul for 80 with Metellus Pius. Now a private citizen, Sulla retired and withdrew to his country estate near Puteoli. As a young man, he had enjoyed the company of actors and musicians, gaining a somewhat disreputable reputation; now in his retirement he surrounded himself again with such merry company, writing his memoirs and intervening only slightly in political events. He died in 78 BCE and his funeral was on a scale never seen before:

> Sulla's body was borne through Italy on a golden litter with royal splendour. Trumpeters and horsemen in great numbers went in advance and a great multitude of armed men followed on foot. His soldiers flocked from all directions under arms to join the procession . . . while the crowd of common people that came together was unprecedented, and in front of all were borne the standards and fasces that he had used while living and ruling.
>
> When the remains reached the city . . . they were borne through the streets with an enormous procession. More than 2000 golden crowns which had been made in haste were carried in it, the gifts of cities and of the legions that he had commanded and of individual friends. It would impossible to describe all the costly things contributed to this funeral . . . The entire senate and the whole body of magistrates attended with their insignia of office. A multitude attended with their peculiar decorations, and, in their turn, all the legions that had fought under him. They came together with eagerness, all hastening to join in the task, carrying gilded standards and silver-plated shields, such as are still used on such occasions. There was a countless number of trumpeters who in turns played the most melting and dirge-like strains. Loud cries of farewell were raised, first by the senate, then by the knights, then by the soldiers, and finally by the plebeians.
>
> The body was shown where public speeches are usually made, and the most eloquent of the Romans then living delivered the funeral oration, as Sulla's son, Faustus, was still very young. Then, strong men of the senators took up the bier and carried it to the Campus Martius, where only kings were buried, and the knights and the army marched past the funeral fire.[45]

3

The Up and Coming Generation: Rome in the 70s BCE

As Sulla's dictatorship began to fade from memory, the mood of the following years was decidedly different from the civil wars of the 80s. It was to be a decade of senatorial pre-eminence again, with only external troubles bothering Rome, and all boded well for the new generation that began to make itself felt in politics, the military and society in general. At least, that was what Sulla had hoped. The reality was rather different.

The 70s were, in fact, the decade where greed, luxury and personal desire ran rampant through the now unchecked senatorial classes, pirates ravaged the coastline and economic problems and slave uprisings became the norm. It was the decade when senators passed luxury laws, but entertained themselves at sumptuous banquets; a decade when the rights of the people had been destroyed by the ineffective tribunate, but they cried out for relief from debt, poverty and starvation; and, essentially, a decade where Rome faced not only a resurgence of Mithridates' power in the east, but internal threats more dangerous and insidious than the civil wars – the slave revolts would terrify Rome more than a rebellious general ever could. It was the decade where senators partied, but Rome was coming apart at its foundations.

THE CONTINUED INFLUENCE OF SULLA?

In the consular elections, a sworn enemy of Sulla – Lepidus – was elected as consul for 78 BCE, while the pro-Sullan Catulus joined as his colleague; this was a problem as 'they hated each other bitterly and began to quarrel immediately, from which it was plain that fresh troubles were imminent.'[1] It appears that Lepidus wanted to restore back to the Italians the land taken by Sulla, but Catulus strongly opposed this measure. After a speech criticizing Sulla, Lepidus began to propose legislation trying to undo Sulla's laws, but again, Catulus refused. The senate was worried. It made Catulus and Lepidus swear not to fight, but perhaps its next move – sending Lepidus to administer Cisalpine Gaul – was not thought through. Before leaving, Lepidus announced that anyone sent into exile by Sulla would find a welcome with him. After raising support in his province, Lepidus stated his intention to stand for re-election as consul, but he refused to return to Rome for the elections. The situation was becoming fraught with danger, and the senate along with the consul Catulus no doubt feared a repetition of Sullan proportions, but Lepidus was no Sulla.

The following year saw Lepidus declared a public enemy with the senate recalling him back to Rome, albeit with his army. Catulus did the same and the two men, with their armies, met in battle near the Campus Martius (outside of the city boundary). It was a decisive battle for Catulus, who forced Lepidus back to Etruria. Rome itself was safe, as Catulus reasserted senatorial control over the city. New consuls (for 77) were elected and business continued almost as if Lepidus had never existed, as first Pompey was appointed to lead the government forces against Lepidus' supporters in Cisalpine Gaul and then, after a defeat at Cosa, Lepidus committed suicide. One rumour was that Lepidus was distressed by separation from his wife, but whatever the reason, he was dead.

Pompey was not entirely successful, as the remnants of Lepidus' army made their way towards Spain under the command of Marcus Perpenna Vento. Perpenna also belonged to the anti-Sullan camp, so that when Sulla came to power, he had fled Rome with a substantial sum of money and an army. In fact, with a following of Roman nobles, he made his way towards Spain and Sertorius – the other rebel leader.

The proconsul Quintus Sertorius had gone to Spain in 83 BCE. Although the Roman officials there did not recognize his authority, he was able to quickly assert his dominance – even to creating a quasi-Roman governmental structure with its own senate. There had been a minor revolt, which he had dealt with swiftly, even killing several children who had attended his school and selling others into slavery. He was an absolute ruler, but Sulla had had no time to deal with him. Q. Metellus Pius (cos. 80) was finally sent to deal with Sertorius, but to defeat him would take time. In 78, Sertorius had ambushed and defeated one of Metellus' legates and in the following year, Sertorius, a master of guerrilla warfare, was able to wear Metellus down and with subsequent successes, it appeared to be a losing battle.

At this point, Pompey demanded that he be given proconsular *imperium* in order to go to Spain, but as Pompey actually had not been consul yet, it made the request somewhat premature. Things, however, worked out in Pompey's favour – Metellus, a most able general with experience in the Social War and under Sulla, had had no success and with Sertorius gradually increasing his stronghold in the area, the senate had no option but to appoint Pompey to the task.

Although Pompey was able to subdue some unrest in Gaul on his march to Spain, Sertorius had the first laugh as he was able to ambush and destroy a legion of Pompey's army, along with its leader. When word of Pompey's march through the Pyrenees filtered down to Perpenna's men, they demanded that either he take them to Sertorius, who was winning victories against the Romans, or they would leave him to Pompey's mercies, determined to abandon him. Perpenna had no option but to join forces with Sertorius, but he employed nefarious methods to undermine him by trying to cause discontent and unrest among the native tribes under him.

Initially, Pompey had little success. He was outmanoeuvred by Sertorius, who was able to capture Lauro, while Pompey was forced to winter among hostile tribes in Spain. Metellus had some success in 75 and Pompey followed up with a decisive victory against Perpenna near Valentia, but he was defeated by Sertorius, who, in turn, was then defeated by Metellus. The three men continued to circle one another, with some successes on both sides, but nothing was definitive. Pompey wrote to the senate to complain about his lack of money and supplies, but it was Sertorius who took a bold step. He was able to negotiate an agreement with Rome's eastern enemy, Mithridates, that the two would join together to attack Rome itself.

Metellus had other ideas, initially offering a reward for the assassination of Sertorius but, after celebrating his victory at Segontia, he retreated back into Gaul. In early 74, the senate finally agreed to Pompey's demands, agreeing to send money and two more legions to Spain. Yet it was not enough. Perpenna was able to capture Cale, while a surprised Pompey was forced to retreat from Palatina. Even when both Pompey and Metellus joined forces at Calagurris, Sertorius was still able to defeat them both. Winter again saw Pompey and Metellus unable to stop Sertorius, with the former wintering in Gaul, while Metellus, taking refuge in further Spain, caused some criticism with his luxurious lifestyle. Seventy-three would pass with no decisive victories on either side.

It was not until 72 that any resolution came, but not in battle. Perpenna, who had been jealous of Sertorius' power and who had instigated many minor revolts that caused some resentment among the native tribes, decided to have a feast to which he invited Sertorius. Disgusted by the vulgar displays, Sertorius indicated his disapproval by moving his position on the couch. This was the signal that Perpenna was waiting for and Sertorius was murdered:

> The suppers at which Sertorius was present were always marked by restrain and decorum, since he would not consent to see or hear anything that was disgraceful ... On this occasion, however, when the drinking was well under way, the guests, seeking a reason for a quarrel, openly indulged in dissolute language, and pretending to be drunk, committed many indecencies, with the hope of angering Sertorius. But he, either because he was vexed at their disorderly conduct, or because he had become aware of their purpose from the boldness of their talk and their unwonted contempt for his wishes, changed his posture on the couch and threw himself upon his back, as though he neither heard nor regarded them. But when Perpenna, after taking a cup of wine in his hands, dropped it as he was drinking and made a clatter with it, which was their signal. Antonius, who reclined above Sertorius on the couch, hit him with his sword. Sertorius turned at the blow and

Pompey the Great

would have risen with his assailant, but Antonius fell upon his chest and seized both his hands, so that he could make no defence even, and died from the blows of many.[2]

Although Perpenna now held overall command, with the death of Sertorius the war in Spain against Rome was pretty much over. A final attempt by Perpenna to rally the remnants of Sertorius' army was unsuccessful as he was taken prisoner by Pompey. Although he gave Pompey some important letters and documents that appear to implicate many notable Romans, Pompey burned them and ordered the death of Perpenna. With the deaths of both Sertorius and Perpenna, the province was easily overtaken, reorganized and brought back under Roman control.

PIRATES

Throughout the decade, there had been numerous problems caused by the increasingly bold pirates. In 81, the consul Murena had faced problems with pirates, but it was not until later in the 70s that real difficulties arose. In 78, P. Servilius Vatia had been sent to deal with pirates in the eastern Mediterranean, based in particular in Cilicia along with their allies, the Isauri, but this was only a temporary measure. Pirates continued to plague the Romans and, in some instances, even captured and kidnapped Roman citizens. In fact, one particular young Roman aristocrat, Caesar, seems to have had an amusing adventure when he was captured in 75. This episode from Plutarch illustrates how ingenious he was:

To begin with, then, when the pirates demanded twenty talents for his ransom, he laughed at them for not knowing who their captive was, and of his own accord agreed to give them fifty . . .. for eight and thirty days, as if the men were not his watchers, but his royal body-guard, he shared in their sports and exercises with great unconcern. He also wrote poems and sundry speeches which he read aloud to them, and those who did not admire these he would call to their faces illiterate barbarians, and often laughingly threatened to hang them all. The pirates were delighted at this, and attributed his boldness of speech to a certain simplicity and boyish mirth.

For all of his charm and casual manner, Caesar also demonstrated just how ruthless he could be:

After his ransom had come . . . and he had paid it and was set free, he immediately manned vessels and put to sea . . . against the robbers . . . their money he made his booty, but the men themselves he lodged in the prison at Pergamum, and then went in person to Junius, the governor of Asia . . . [who] kept saying that he would consider the case of the captives at his leisure, [so] Caesar left him to his own devices, went to Pergamum, took the robbers out of prison and crucified them all, just as he had often warned them on the island that he would, when they thought he was joking.[3]

The year 74 saw continued problems with the pirates – M. Antonius was given *imperium infinitum* to deal with them, but again, it was ineffective. The following year, in 73, pirates attacked the coast of Sicily. The provincial governor, Verres, had put Cleomenes of Syracuse in charge of several ships, which again was only a temporary relief. In 72, M. Antonius led an attack on the Cretans, whom he accused of aiding the pirates, but the problem still remained. The difficulty was that the Romans appear to have used the same tactics as the pirates in that these spot attacks removed the momentary threat, but without a systematic and widespread campaign by the Romans, the pirates would merely move to another area where they could continue their activities. For the rest of the 70s, pirates would continue to threaten the Roman economy and its individuals, but the time would come when the people, tired of the constant piracy, would demand that the senate take more definitive action.

WAR IN THE EAST

After the death of Nicomedes of Bithynia in 74, tensions began to increase in the east. Although Nicomedes had left his kingdom to Rome, Mithridates of Pontus had other ideas. The natives of Bithynia were not pleased with the idea of Roman rule, and Mithridates, who had entered into an agreement with Sertorius, started encroaching on nearby territory and led a bold invasion into Bithynia. Later that year, the senate appointed the consul Lucullus to the eastern command.

Lucius Licinius Lucullus had served under Sulla during the civil war as well as during the eastern war during the 80s. Elected aedile in 79 along with his brother, they had given splendid games that were the talk of Rome. A favourite of Sulla's, the dictator dedicated his memoirs to him and, following his death, made him guardian of his son, Faustus, favouring him over Pompey. Although Plutarch notes an amusing tale of Lucullus learning how to be a general on his way to the east, there is no doubt that Lucullus was a skilful and energetic individual who had already learned well from Sulla.

Mithridates' generals were able to defeat the Romans under the provincial governor Cotta near Chalcedon in a particularly gruesome encounter:

> Cotta did not go out to meet him because he was inexperienced in military affairs, but his naval prefect, Nudus, with a part of the army occupied a very strong position on the plain. He was driven out of it, however, and fled to the gates of Chalcedon over many walls which greatly obstructed his movement. There was a struggle at the gates among those trying to gain entrance simultaneously, for which reason no missile cast by the pursuers missed its mark. The guards at the gates, fearing for the city, let down the gate from the machine. Nudus and some of the other officers were drawn up by ropes. The remainder perished between their friends and their foes, holding out their hands in entreaty to each.[4]

Lucullus was, however, on the way. He assembled his army nearby, imposed strict discipline and waited. Although Mithridates held the superior position, Lucullus was able to best the enemy by persuading him to allow the Romans to move camp. Perhaps news of Sertorius' death had prompted Mithridates to open secret negotiations with Lucullus, but his decision to trust the Romans was foolhardy. Now Lucullus was in the better position strategically, while Mithridates found himself cut off. Lucullus was able to rescue Cotta, but Mithridates was not deterred and decided to push ahead. At Cyzicus, he developed an elaborate plan:

> As he had plenty of soldiers he pushed the siege in every possible way. He blockaded the harbour with a double sea wall and drew a line of circumvallation around the rest of the city. He raised mounds, built machines, towers, and rams protected by tortoises [military formation]. He constructed a siege engine 50 metres high, from which rose another tower furnished with catapults discharging stones and various kinds of missiles. Two quinqueremes joined together carried another tower against the port, from which a bridge could be projected by a mechanical device when brought near the wall.

The Cyziceans were more than equal to the task:

> The Cyziceans were at first dumbfounded by the novelty of the device and gave way somewhat, but as the rest of the enemy were slow in following, they plucked up courage and thrust the four over the wall. Then they poured burning pitch on the ships and compelled them to back out stern foremost with the machine.

In short, they left nothing untried that was within the compass of human zeal. Although they toiled most perseveringly, yet a portion of the wall, that had been weakened by fire, gave way toward evening; but on account of the heat nobody was in a hurry to dash in. The Cyziceans built another wall around it that night, and about this time a tremendous wind came and smashed the rest of the king's machines.[5]

Mithridates was ultimately unsuccessful, and Lucullus was able to step in to rescue the city. After an assassination attempt, things were not going well for Mithridates and his army, as they suffered from starvation and plague around Cyzicus. Luck, however, was still on his side as he was able to slip away and make his way to the nearby town of Parium. The city of Cyzicus was handsomely rewarded by Lucullus for its loyalty, given more territory and would enjoy preferential treatment by the Romans, who would favour its independence.

Mithridates continued his attacks, but under the command of Lucullus, the Romans were able to capture towns within Pontus itself. Following close on Mithridates' heels, Lucullus invaded Pontus. Cotta, who had had to be rescued earlier by Lucullus, was able to advance to Heracleia and besiege the city. The year 71 began with continued skirmishs between the Romans and Mithridates with treachery apparent in both camps.

Lucullus was defeated in several minor incursions, while one of Mithridates' allies, who apparently deserted to the Romans, allegedly then tried to kill Lucullus, but as Lucullus was sleeping, he was unable to enter the room. In frustration, Olthacus struck at the servant and took flight back to Mithridates.[6] Mithridates sent a force to attack Lucullus' supply convey, but it was defeated with heavy losses. When word came that Lucullus was on his way to Pontus, there was panic and chaos in Mithridates' camp:

Accordingly [Mithridates] fell into a panic and contemplated flight, and at once communicated his purpose to his friends in his tent. They did not wait for the signal to be given, but while it was still night each one sent his own baggage out of the camp, which made a great crush of pack animals around the gates.

When the soldiers perceived the commotion, and saw what the baggage carriers were doing, they imagined every sort of absurdity. Filled with terror, mingled with anger that the signal had not been given to them also, they demolished and ran over their own fortification and scattered in every direction over the plain, helter-skelter, without orders from the commanding general or any other officer. When Mithridates heard the disorderly rush, he dashed out of his tent among them and attempted to say something, but nobody would listen to him. He was caught in the crowd and knocked from his horse, but remounted and was borne to the mountains with a few followers.[7]

Although Mithridates sought refuge with Tigranes of Armenia, the king refused to meet him, but allowed him residence at his estates. Despairing completely, Mithridates sent an order back to his own royal palace, sending 'the eunuch

Bacchus to his palace to put his sisters, wives, and concubines to death as he could. These, with wonderful devotion, destroyed themselves with daggers, poison, and ropes.'[8]

Lucullus was able to capture various other strong-holds and fortresses and, early in 70, sent an envoy to Tigranes to demand the surrender of Mithridates, but he still eluded the great general. As the decade ended, Mithridates was still on the run, many of Lucullus' soldiers were starting to get angry about the constant marching, and there appeared no resolution in sight. Mithridates and the east would continue to occupy Roman foreign policy for another decade.

SPARTACUS

While Rome was engaged in dealing with Sertorius in Spain and Lucullus was on his way to the east to deal with Mithridates' seizure of Bithynia, in 73 BCE a slave by the name of Spartacus escaped with a band of over 70 fellow gladiators from a training school at Capua. It is believed that Spartacus was of Thracian descent, and had actually served in the Roman army but had fallen on hard times. He had deserted, was captured and then sold into slavery, being sent to a gladiatorial school in Capua.

Spartacus brought his gang near Vesuvius, and hundreds others soon joined in, but it was mayhem with his followers plundering and attacking local farms. Although he apparently tried to restrain them, he was unable to control the mob. Spartacus had been joined by thousands of men – freedmen, slaves, the poor and even tribes in Gaul – and it was becoming a major threat to the security of the region and to Rome itself.

One praetor, Claudius Glaber was sent out with a hastily organized force of 3,000, but Spartacus was able to lead his men down the mountain and easily routed the ill-equipped recruits. Although two more commanders were sent out, Spartacus was able to defeat them and slip away to safety when the praetor P. Varinius confronted him with a larger army. Nevertheless, Spartacus later defeated him, increasing his own troops by his impartial division of plunder. The Romans had underestimated him as they 'did not consider this a war yet, but a raid, something like an attack of robbery.'[9]

It is estimated that Spartacus had gathered a large army of about 70,000 slaves at this time, and to defeat him would take time. Spartacus dealt another blow by defeating the consul Lentulus as well as the governor of Cisalpine Gaul. He celebrated another victory over the combined Roman forces in Picenum, but announced he would not march on Rome – he wanted to lead his men north through the Alps and to freedom. However, he was still within the Italian peninsula with Rome itself starting to see the threat he posed – escape would be near impossible. Although he was able to capture Thurii and was able to provide new weapons for his army, things were about to change.

The senate, finally realizing the seriousness of the Spartacan revolt, appointed the former praetor Crassus – one of Rome's richest men – to deal with the uprising. Crassus was given six legions, but foolishly one of his legates with two legions decided to attack Spartacus. It was yet again another Roman disaster, and Crassus dealt with the insubordination by decimating what he considered the most cowardly men. Crassus attacked and decisively destroyed Spartacus' troops, chasing him to a peninsula near Rhegium. Although Spartacus tried to cross to Sicily, he was betrayed by the Cilician pirates and was unable to leave Italy. Spartacus tried to fight his way out, hoping to take his remaining men to Brundisium, but Lucullus was on his way back from Macedonia with his troops, while Pompey had been recalled from Spain.

In 71, Spartacus was able to break out through Crassus' siege works and slowly made his way towards Brundisium. The large group divided into two armies. Spartacus separated from the mainly German cohort, and it was the second group, under the leadership of Castus and Cannicus, which was completely annihilated by Crassus, who killed over 30,000 slaves. Although Crassus had written to the senate, requesting additional assistance, it was not now necessary. Crassus was determined to take Spartacus and the remaining slaves under his control, hopefully before Pompey could make his way there. Although they had had minor success against Crassus, it was almost the end:

> This . . . was the ruin of Spartacus, for it filled his slaves with over-confidence. They would no longer consent to avoid battle, and would not even obey their leaders, but surrounded them as soon as they began to march, with arms in their hands . . . Crassus . . . pressed on to finish the struggle himself, and having encamped near the enemy, began to dig a trench. Into this, the slaves leaped and began to fight with those who were working there, and since fresh men from both sides kept coming to help their comrades, Spartacus saw the necessity that was upon him, and drew up his whole army in order of battle.

> In the first place, when his horse was brought to him, he drew his sword . . . then pushing his way towards Crassus himself through many flying weapons and wounded men, (but) he did not indeed reach him . . . finally, after his companions had taken to flight, he stood alone, surrounded by a multitude of foes, and was still defending himself when he was cut down.[10]

There were so many dead that Spartacus' body was never found. As for Crassus, he took some 6,000 slaves and crucified them along the via Appia from Capua to Rome. A remaining 5,000 or so tried to escape, but Pompey was waiting with his army on his way back from Spain and captured them. Thus, Spartacus and his army were finally destroyed.

There were indeed repercussions to this event. On one hand, Crassus was awarded only an ovation for his successes over Spartacus, as it was considered just a fight against slaves; Pompey was awarded a triumph. This was for his successes against Sertorius in Spain, but Crassus argued that Pompey was trying to take all the glory of the Spartacan victory for himself. It was an ominous sign as the two men were to seek the consulship for 70 BCE. On the other hand, Spartacus and his followers illustrated a fundamental flaw to the Roman system. Far from being the Marxist hero of the twentieth-century, with his subsequent glorification in modern cinema, Spartacus never tried to overthrow the Roman government; he wanted freedom. He and his men had ravaged the countryside, which caused numerous economic problems for its inhabitants less than 20 years since the Social War, but there was more. Spartacus' revolt illustrated the superior numerical advantage that slaves had over Romans. While it is difficult to ascertain how many slaves there were, estimates can be illuminating. Around the time of Augustus, it believed that for a population of about 900,000 citizens in Rome, there were about 300,000 slaves. Following this same line of thought, it has been further argued that out of a population of some six million, there were over two million slaves – thus, every one in three people were slaves. It was never far from Romans' minds that another slave revolt could occur at any time.[11]

LIFE IN ROME IN THE 70S

Meanwhile in Rome, the city was developing a taste for luxury and extravagance. In September 79, magnificent games with bulls and elephants fighting one another were staged by the brothers Marcus and Lucius Lucullus in their roles as aediles. In 78, the consul Lepidus proposed a *lex cibaria* to restrict the spread of luxuries although, throughout the 70s, the senate themselves appear to have ignored this. In 73, a senator was regarded as extravagant for serving a whole boar for a banquet, while in Spain, the consul Metellus had been criticized for his luxurious lifestyle, but perhaps the greatest example of Roman corruption, vice and profligacy was a man called Verres.

VERRES

Gaius Verres is considered one of the most infamous individuals in Rome, his career was one of bribery, extortion and provincial mismanagement on a scale perhaps never before seen. Throughout the 70s his behaviour caused consternation and disgust among the locals. He was greedy, opportunistic and cavalier with his favours. He was willing to overlook most transgressions, particularly if the price was right, and Verres demanded huge amounts to satisfy his greed.

Verres had originally supported Marius but seeing the way the situation was going in the 80s, quickly allied himself with Sulla, who rewarded him with a tract of land and dismissed charges of embezzlement. By 80, he had secured a quaestorship under Dolabella, then governor of Cilicia, and the two appear to have treated the province as their own personal mint, plundering the natives, seizing artworks and causing trouble to the local economy.

It was Dolabella who was ultimately had to stand trial in 78, and with the evidence of Verres, who had secured a pardon, Dolabella was convicted. A few years later in 74, Verres was able to secure the city praetorship and sought to increase his personal wealth by thwarting several legitimate inheritance claims and attempting to make a profit on temple and building restorations. For his efforts, Verres was rewarded with the rich pickings of Sicily, sent as provincial governor in 73.

Sicily had been secured by the Romans as early as the third century BCE and, with its fertile grounds was a prosperous province, serving as a trade base and providing much needed grain for the hungry masses in Rome. Verres, however, descended on the island with his greed unchecked. He continued his old tricks, sending individuals to prison on false charges, refusing ratification of wills and even extorted additional corn. As many of Sertorius' army made their way to Sicily, seeking refuge from Pompey, Verres may have illegally punished them.[12] As his governorship extended into 71, Verres became much bolder. According to Cicero's later prosecution, he subverted the local censors, altered the terms of the *lex Hieronica,* which regulated the traditional taxation of produce, and increased the corn tax impositions on other towns within Sicily. Verres seized the possessions of many Sicilians, he took artworks and statues for his own collection and generally plundered the island with such abandon that the grain shipments to Rome appear to have been under great threat. Sometime in December 71, Verres returned to Rome with a huge fortune, while L. Metellus was sent out as his replacement (the trial will be discussed in greater detail on pp. 75–7).

The Sicilians were furious about Verres' behaviour and immediately appealed to the senate. The year 70 would see Verres brought before the people and tried for his crimes, eventually fleeing into exile. It was to make the reputation of one young man, Cicero, while illustrating to the people that such unbridled greed would not be allowed in the *res publica*.

THE UP AND COMING GENERATION

In 73, a young Sullan supporter – Catiline – was brought to trial for adultery with a Vestal Virgin, Fabia, but Catulus testified in his favour and Catiline was ultimately acquitted. The fate for both individuals would have been death – the virgin would be punished by burial alive with a few days worth of food and water; while the man would have been whipped to death. Later that year Catiline married Orestilla, after allegedly murdering his own son to please her, but this is most likely a fabrication by the later author Sallust, whose *Bellum Catilinae* had a anti-Catilinarian approach. Catiline was later elected praetor in 68 and sent to Africa, but he would loom large in the next decade.

Meanwhile, Caesar, following his capture by pirates in 75, came back to Rome, and was elected military tribune in 71. Caesar appears to have involved himself in the law courts during the intervening years, but it is not clear if he played any military role during the Spartacan uprising. In 70, he was elected quaestor for 69.

Pompey had had an excellent decade. From the quashing of Lepidus' revolt to his successes against Sertorius in Spain to wiping up the remnants of Spartacus' army, Pompey had become one of Rome's most distinguished and effective military figures. He also showed a moderation in victory, with fair and moderate terms imposed on Spain and southern Gaul as he set about reorganizing the province – a distinct contrast to Crassus' punishing regime. When faced with cowardice or disobedience, Crassus had resorted to decimation of troops (killing every tenth soldier). As the decade came to a close, it was Pompey who was the public's darling, not Crassus, in spite of Crassus' success against Spartacus.

The young Cato had volunteered to fight alongside his half-brother Q. Servilius Caepio who, as military tribune, was serving in the consular army of Gellius against Spartacus. Cato was later commended by Gellius for his bravery. He made his first public speech, trying to protect the Basilica Porcia and married his first wife, Atilia, during the last years of the 70s.

Barely known at the beginning of the decade, the young Cicero had won a significant court case in 80 defending Sextus Roscius on the charge of parricide, but following this victory, Cicero left Rome along with his brother Quintus and Servius Sulpicius Rufus due to fears about Sulla. Cicero had returned by 75, where he was elected to the quaestorship and served in Sicily. It was there that his reputation for integrity and honesty would later encourage the Sicilians to call upon the young orator and lawyer to bring charges against the mismanagement and embezzlement by the provincial governor Verres.

Lucullus was off in the east, winning glory and victories against Mithridates. The two main senatorial figures, Catulus and Hortensius, were considered above reproach and were leading the *res publica* back to safety following the threats of

Lepidus and Sertorius, not excluding the Spartacan uprising as well. Although piracy still caused problems, Rome was perhaps finally living up to Sulla's vision. The senate was still in control, but as the decade ended, things would abruptly change. Sulla's reforms from the beginning of the decade were about to be revisited.

THE CONSULSHIP OF POMPEY AND CRASSUS – 70 BCE

With armies outside of Rome, both Crassus and Pompey decided to put their animosity to one side and together, decided to seek the consulship for 70. Crassus had already held the praetorship and had shown remarkable military skill and success in dealing with Spartacus; but Pompey was another story. He was only 35 and had never held a major political office; yet the senate gave way and allowed him to stand for the consulship, against the *lex Annalis* of Sulla. Pompey celebrated his triumph, then he and Crassus were elected for their first joint consulship.

It was not an easy time for either man. They despised each other and the year was characterized by their infighting. In two public displays, the consuls were begged to reconcile. The first appears to have been early in the year as both still held their armies outside of Rome:

> The people . . . implored them with lamentations and the greatest dejection, reminding them of the evils produced by the contentions of Marius and Sulla. Crassus yielded first. He came down from his chair, advanced to Pompey and offered him his hand in the way of reconciliation. Pompey rose and hastened to meet him. They shook hands amid general acclamations and the people did not leave the assembly until the consuls had given orders in writing to disband their armies. Thus was the well-grounded fear of another dissension happily dispelled.[13]

However, things did not run smoothly, as 'when once they had assumed office, they did not remain on this friendly basis, but differed on almost every measure, and by their contentiousness rendered their consulship barren politically and without achievement.'[14] Although Plutarch despaired of their cooperation, their first consulship in 70 was in fact quite advantageous for the *res publica*. This was the year when the major restraints placed by Sulla were swiftly and efficiently thrown out. The tribunate was restored, the courts underwent yet another reform while other legislation provided for the rehabilitation of the censorship. There were agrarian and other economic measures proposed as well as a recall of those who had supported Lepidus the previous decade. Plutarch may like to characterize this year as 'barren', but the fact remains that it was a pivotal year in the Republic.

Pompey, as consul designate, had declared that there were several issues that he intended to deal with, among them the courts and the tribunate. In the matter of the courts, the praetor L. Aurelius Cotta introduced a law that reformed the composition of juries. Where Sulla had limited participation only to the senatorial class, Cotta proposed that the juries be comprised of senators, *equites* and *tribuni aerarii*.[15] Other measures proposed during the year were two *leges Plotia*. One was an unknown land bill, although it has been suggested that it may have dealt with the resettlement of Pompey's veterans; while the other apparently authorized the return from exile of L. Cinna and other supporters of Lepidus.[16] The censorship, another area where Sulla had stymied its effectiveness, now came back into its own. All its rights were restored and the first census in a decade occurred. Elected as censors, Gellius and Lentulus did a systematic recording and expelled some 41 senators, which overturned one of Sulla's reforms. Even Pompey showed up to be counted:

> At this time, then, the censors Gellius and Lentulus were sitting in state, and the knights were passing in review before them, when Pompey was seen coming down the descent into the Forum, but leading his horse with his own hand. When he was near and could be plainly seen, he ordered his lectors to make way for him, and led his horse up to the tribunal. The people were astonished and kept perfect silence, and the magistrates were awed and delighted at the sight. Then the senior censor put the question: 'Pompeius Magnus, have you performed all the military services required by law?'

> Then Pompey said with a loud voice: 'I have performed them all, and all under myself as *imperator*.' On hearing this, the people gave a loud shout, and it was no longer possible to check their cries of joy, but the censors rose up and accompanied Pompey to his home, thus gratifying the citizens, who followed with applause.[17]

The most pressing matter was perhaps the tribunate, which was restored in all its glory and problems during the year.

THE RESTORATION OF THE TRIBUNATE

Throughout the 70s, there had been an increasing number of calls to restore the tribunate. One of Lepidus' main policies had been its restoration. As early as 75, the restriction against its holders taking further political office had been removed and in 73, a young tribune, Licinius Macer, had attacked the government, arguing that the powers of the tribunate should be brought back. By 70, it had become a rallying cry for the masses as Pompey found when consul-elect:

> When [Pompey] first delivered an address to the people... [he] mentioned that he would restore the power of the tribunes, a great shout was raised at his words, and grateful murmur pervaded the assembly.[18]

This was the only legislation that Pompey and Crassus appear to have worked together on. Their law provided for the full restoration of tribunician power, including the right to veto legislation and to propose their own measures. Once again, another Sullan law had been overturned and the tribunate would again become the agitator for public demands. Sulla had seen the tribunate as a major disruptive force and not all senatorial figures were convinced of the necessity of its return and nor were they at ease. While the 'fabric of the state might be merely shaken by a Gracchus, a Sulpicius or in time a Clodius,' how the tribunate had been used by ambitious figures such as Marius or Sulla illustrates the real danger that the tribunate posed when in conjunction with ambitious military and political figures.[19] It may be easy to read more into its restoration, particularly in light of later political events in the 60s – with tribunes agitating for extraordinary commands which benefited Pompey specially – but for the moment, the traditional rights of the people had been honoured and restored, for good or bad.

THE TRIAL AGAINST VERRES

The issue of provincial management was one of the most important matters during 70 BCE and the trial of Verres would make some reputations, destroy others and signal to the people a refusal by some senatorial individuals to allow the mass pillage and plunder of Rome's provinces. Although Pompey had mentioned provincial affairs in his pre-consular address, no legislation was apparently forthcoming during this year. Perhaps it was enough that one of its most infamous governors was about to see the repercussions of his actions.

Pompey was particularly experienced in provincial matters – his reorganization of Spain and Gaul following Sertorius' rule had given Pompey a reputation for tolerance and compassion. In 72, the consuls Gellius and Lentulus passed legislation allowing for Roman citizenship to be granted in various areas in Spain, in particular to those who had supported Pompey. Yet, with the Verres trial, Pompey was apparently uncommitted. He had condemned provincial corruption and had a number of supporters among the Sicilians, but his interest in this matter cannot be properly measured. Nevertheless, it was the trial of the year and, perhaps, the decade.

When Metellus had arrived in Sicily, taking over from Verres as provincial governor, he found a province bankrupt, economically deprived and broken. He overturned many of Verres' policies and in doing so, began to remedy some of the wrongs. In 73, a *lex Terentia Cassia* had been passed to deal with problems with the grain supply in Sicily, when Verres had commandeered much of the available corn. His governorship of the province had ruined its economy and a number of leading individuals had had their wealth and goods stripped by his greed. There had been interference with the tax rolls, as well as with the contracts with the wheat growers and, generally, a sense of frustration had permeated in the province. With encouragement from Metellus, a number of leading Sicilians approached Cicero – the young, honest quaestor – to represent their claims against Verres. Previously Verres had been quaestor under Dolabella in Asia Minor. The latter had been condemned for his pillage of that province, but Verres had been given a pardon due to his testimony. He was not so lucky this time around.

Cicero, overcoming a challenge from Q. Caecilius, who had been a quaestor under Verres and was appointed a prosecutor. He went to Sicily to collect evidence against him – by August Cicero was ready to proceed. Verres did have some supporters; his defence was to be conducted by one of Rome's great orators, Hortensius.

A number of charges were levelled against Verres, most involving his actions in Sicily. First, was the charge of extortion during the war against Spartacus. Far from using money to assist in the campaign, Cicero alleged that Verres had accused the slaves of many Roman citizens of being in league with Sertorius. Only by paying huge bribes were these individuals released. He had ordered the seizure of numerous ships as being under Sertorius' command, taking the valuable cargo and throwing the crews into prison, later executing them as traitors. Furthermore, he had ordered the scourging of an elderly Roman citizen who had dared to criticize him; the man later died. The main charge was that of embezzlement, where Verres had allowed one city to pay off its naval requirements and had entrusted Cleomenes to protect the city with insufficient ships, later resulting in pirates attacking the harbour of Syracuse in 73.

It appears that Verres did not attend court on the first day, but Cicero's first oration addressed him nevertheless. He continued, blackening Verres' name and reputation 'for he has done many impious and nefarious actions both against the gods and men; by punishment for which crimes he is now disquieted and driven out of his mind and out of his senses.'[20] According to Cicero:

> We have brought before your tribunal not only a thief, but a wholesale robber; not only an adulterer, but a ravisher of chastity; not only a sacrilegious man, but an open enemy to all sacred things and all religion; not only an assassin, but a most barbarous murderer of both citizens and allies; so that I think him the only criminal in the memory of man so atrocious, that it is even for his own good to be condemned.[21]

The speech continued much on the same vein, with Cicero attacking Verres. Cicero brings up the jury composition – applauding that the corruptible ones favoured by Verres and his counsel Hortensius had been removed. Noting that it is up to the judges to demonstrate to the Roman people that they will not be influenced by the esteemed defence, Cicero begs that only a conviction will persuade the Roman people that such outrageous behaviour as demonstrated by Verres was not acceptable. Further complaining about backstage manoevres to adjourn the trial so that a more favourable praetor might be found, Cicero argues that no delay is necessary – he is ready to proceed and conviction is the only result that he expects.

Passing over Verres' early life, Cicero focuses briefly on Verres as quaestor under Dolabella and his shameful acts. He recounts Sulla's own reluctance to deal with Verres and then turns to his conduct in Sicily. Earlier, the defence had argued that they had had little time to conduct their investigations, but Cicero refutes that. He notes that if he had sufficient time, having gone in January, then the defence, who were aware of the charges, also had enough time. Cicero recounts further extravagances in Asia and then returns to his main topic – Verres in Sicily. Numerous anecdotes colour Cicero's speech, rebuking him:

> When among foreign nations you have injured the reputation of our dominion and our name by your infamy and your crimes – when you have with difficulty saved yourself from the sword of the friends of the Roman people, and escaped from the fire of its allies, do you think you will find an asylum here? You are mistaken – they allowed you to escape alive that you might fall into our power here, not that you might find rest here.[22]

Lingering over Verres' illegal actions, a dramatic portrait of corruption at its most extreme and most damning was presented to the people. As published, the entire prosecution was clever, inflammatory and made Cicero's reputation. After the first speech – where Cicero had outlined the charges, pandered to the judges and commented on the problems he had had in bringing this prosecution, Hortensius urged his client to plead no contest and to seek voluntary exile. By the end of year, having forfeited his estate, Verres was living in Massilia where he remained until the end of his life.

There were two immediate benefits to Cicero – in the first instance, as the successful prosecutor, he was able to seize Verres' estate, but even more importantly, able to assume Verres' rank as an ex-praetor in the senate. The second was that Cicero had been able to establish himself as a leading orator and lawyer, perhaps even eclipsing Hortensius. Cicero would work hard throughout the next decade to consolidate his limited power base and his ambitions would reach fruition in a consulship during one of the most contentious years in Roman history.

The decade ended with most of Sulla's reforms having been cancelled or ignored. Pompey, without holding any other political office, had secured his first consulship. The tribunate, the composition of the juries and the censorship had had all previous restrictions removed. Yet, the senate could pride itself on its accomplishments – legally recognized (and senatorially approved) commands had resolved the threats of Lepidus, Sertorius and Spartacus. Sicily was in the process of rehabilitation, while Lucullus was gaining against Mithridates. The senate and people of Rome had every right to be optimistic and hopeful as the 70s ended. Even Pompey and Crassus appear to have again reconciled towards the end of their joint consulship, as Plutarch remarks:

> And when at last their term of office was closing, and they were addressing the assembly, a certain man, not a noble, but a Roman knight, rustic and rude in his way of life, Onatius Aurelius, mounted the rostra and recounted to the audience a vision that had come to him in his sleep. 'Jupiter,' he said, 'appeared to me and bade me declare in public that you should not allow your consuls to lay down their office until they became friends.'

> When the man said this and the people urged a reconciliation, Pompey for his part, stood motionless, but Crassus took the initiative, clasped him by the hand, and said: 'fellow citizens, I think there is nothing humiliating or unworthy in my taking the first step towards good-will and friendship with Pompey, to whom you gave the title of 'Great' before he had grown a beard, and voted him a triumph before he was a senator.'[23]

4

Hopes for the Future: Rome in the 60s BCE

By the end of 70 BCE, the newly-elected censors had expelled 64 senators, Cicero had won his first important trial against Verres, and there was the dedication of the rebuilt temple of Jupiter Capitolinus. It would appear that all the signs for the Republic were favourable following the first consulship of Crassus and Pompey. They had restored the powers of the tribunate, revived the censorships and presented banquets and games to the people. The praetor L. Aurelius Cotta carried a bill that changed the composition of the jury courts from senatorial control to a mix of senators, *equites* and the *tribuni aerarii*, so that power in the courts was more evenly distributed.

The census of 70–69 BCE had showed an increase in population, with new citizens and territories finally incorporated as a result of the Social War two decades earlier. At the same time, laws regarding excess wealth, magisterial corruption and electoral bribery were introduced. Rome appeared to be on the brink of a new and exciting phase of its history, having cleaned out the senatorial cupboard of its more corruptible individuals and laws having been introduced to curtail major excesses.

Senatorial control at this time was in the hands of a small, but vocal minority of conservative figures, led by Catulus and Hortensius. Catulus came from an extremely prominent family; his father had been consul with Marius in 102 BCE, and had dealt successfully with the Cimbric threat. Although his father later opposed Marius and eventually killed himself, the son had avenged the death. In a final irony, the dedication of the temple of Jupiter Capitolinus, originally reserved for Sulla, had instead been carried out by Catulus. Hortensius, his son-in-law, was a powerful and prominent orator and advocate who held the consulship in 69 BCE. Lucullus had assisted Sulla in the First Mithridatic War with notable success; he was later appointed guardian of Sulla's son Faustus, had served as consul in 74 (along with Caesar's uncle) and secured the command against Mithridates following his consulship. He had had numerous successes and was also highly regarded by the senate as well as by his soldiers.

In the midst of public contempt towards the senate, few men were considered by the populace to be above the fray, but in addition to Catulus, Lucullus and Hortensius, Pompey was extremely well respected and highly regarded as well. He had shown his military prowess and political abilities in Hispania over the previous decade, although he had showed some bad judgement in swooping in and resolving the threat of Spartacus in the waning days of the Third Servile war of 71, taking credit and celebrating a triumph, much to the annoyance of Crassus. This led to a charge that Pompey was particularly effective in mopping-up other generals' successes, a complaint that would be again levelled against him when he assumed command over the Third Mithridatic war, also infuriating the ex-consul Lucullus.

Although Pompey and Crassus had worked together on occasion, with the most notable example being the restoration of the tribunate, as the 60s continued, their mutual disdain would increase. However, the repercussions of their consulship of 70 were clear, as they had systematically dismantled Sulla's reforms: 'reactions to what was done in 70 BCE and speculations as to what Pompey intended in the future, were important themes in politics for the next few years at least.'[1]

In addition to the tribunate, another issue that continued to occupy Rome's attention was piracy. The pirates had cut off the valuable grain supply to Rome, which had caused great unrest, with inflationary and largely unaffordable prices for the urban plebs, while bribery and extortion among the ruling classes had been exposed to the people. The extraordinary commands given to Pompey in the mid-60s should be considered as evidence of his popular support, while the tribunician legislation around this time reflects continued attempts by the populace to curtail bribery, remove unsuccessful commanders and, generally, resolve pressing issues.

THE THIRD MITHRIDATIC WAR (75–65 BCE)

Having launched an attack through the East at the same time that Spartacus' servile revolt occupied the Italian peninsula, Mithridates had been virtually unopposed. Now that Spartacus had been defeated, the senate turned its attention back to the East. Lucullus was appointed commander, being sent to Pontus. Meeting up with several Roman legions in Asia Minor, he was able to immediately turn the tide against Mithridates, but the length of the campaign dismayed his soldiers and ultimately, the senate. The Romans had captured Pinaca, while Tigranes lost control of Syria, but Mithridates and Tigranes were quickly raising another army. Lucullus' army began to mutiny, while in Rome, the praetor L. Quintus passed a measure reassigning Asia to alternative commanders. Thus, the proconsul Metellus was sent to Crete in 68. Although he was unable to stop the threat of piracy, he captured both Cydonia and Cnossus. Lucullus, however, was not quite finished yet. He was able to stop Mithridates and Tigranes, but his army refused to go any further. Lucullus then turned to the city of Nisibis, which he began to besiege.

Other commanders were having less success. Re-entering Pontus, Mithridates secured much-needed support against the Romans and then defeated the Roman leader, M. Fabius. It could have been possible for him to have destroyed the Romans, but the aged Mithridates had been struck by a stone, and, fearing their leader's fate, the mercenaries stopped battle, which allowed the Romans to escape.[2] Rescued by Triarius, who was on his way to join Lucullus, the two men launched a counter-offensive against Mithridates. Even though his troops engaged the Romans for a lengthy period, a bridge collapsed, which caused Mithridates to once again retreat.[3]

Critics began to complain that Lucullus was ignoring the demands of his war-weary troops, refusing to allow plundering, and working with the *equites* who had sizable financial stakes in the area; finally, mutiny was on the horizon, but it would not be until early 67 that a full-scale mutiny would take place – thanks perhaps in part to Lucullus' brother-in-law, the young P. Clodius.

68 BCE

In Rome during 68, the consul Metellus died shortly after assuming office, leaving his co-consul, Q. Marcius Rex as sole leader. The main event of the year was the elections for the consuls for 67, where one candidate, C. Calpurnius Piso, was notorious for his massive open bribery. In an election characterized by its rampant corruption, the young Marcus Porcius Cato, running for the military tribunate, was said to be the only one who actively obeyed the canvassing regulations.[1] Another young patrician was also attempting to gain political office – in 68, Catiline was elected praetor and for the next two years was propraetorian governor for Africa.

The tribunician elections were no less interesting than the consular contest. Among those elected were P. Servilius Rullus (possibly with the support of Crassus and Caesar) and P. Sulla's half-brother, L. Caecilius Rufus. The tribunes-elect met regularly throughout the autumn, preparing their agenda for the following year, which was to include the joint questions of debts and land. One proposal was a redistribution of public lands, such as the *ager Campanus* and the *ager Stellas*, and with possible colonies abroad, giving of land to Pompey's veterans when they returned and resettlement of the urban plebs. The year to follow would be full of intrigue, riots and chaos as the tribunes attempted to propose their legislation with great popular support and vocal opposition to the *boni*, including those *boni* whom the tribunes respected.

By 67, Pompey may have felt somewhat apprehensive, with the elections of C. Calpurnius Piso and M. Glabrio as consuls; the former having achieved success with his extensive bribery. It was, however, two tribunes of the year that would

Crassus

bring Pompey back into the political arena. C. Cornelius and A. Gabinius may not have agreed with each other's measures or methods, but their proposals overall would greatly benefit Pompey.

LUCULLUS' COMMAND IN THE EAST

The situation with Mithridates in the East was one matter that came under scrutiny in the first weeks of the year. Having advanced into Armenia, Lucullus had some further success against Mithridates and his ally, Tigranes, but spreading himself too thin, the Roman faced insurmountable odds. His soldiers, many of them having fought for 20 years, were tired and restless. The year began with the young aristocrat, P. Clodius encouraging a mutiny among Roman troops in Nisibis. He then left Lucullus' troops and went to join his brother-in-law Marcius.

Mithridates waited for the approach of Lucullus, refusing to engage in any combat. Another Mithridates, the son-in-law of Tigranes, however, did inflict a serious defeat on the Roman army in Pontus.

Slowly and systematically, the areas under Lucullus' command were stripped away. The two tribunes, C. Cornelius and A. Gabinius, sought to remove Lucullus from his entire Eastern command, arguing that part of Lucullus' army should be demobilized and that the provinces of Bithynia and Pontus be transferred to the control of the consul M'. Acilius Glabrio. Cicero, however, records that Gabinius had a much more personal way of attack – he showed a picture of Lucullus' splendid and ostentatious villa to the assembled crowd and they voted Lucullus out of his command.

PIRATES

Although P. Servilius had been moderately successful in the 70s dealing with the threat of piracy to Rome, the scale of the problem had greatly increased. In the early 60s, there had been numerous attacks, including at Delos, which had been sacked, although the city's facilities were quickly restored. There were numerous raids in the Aegean sea, with further attacks along the Italian coast, including at Ostia. It was a severe problem, threatening the security of Rome itself.

By 67, even the corn supply to Rome was disrupted. Gabinius then proposed that one man be selected, with a fleet, legates and with the proviso to draw upon the treasury and resources available, to deal with the pirates. It was generally assumed that Pompey would be the man chosen, but Piso strongly resisted the proposal and threatened Gabinius, who left the Forum prior to any serious conflict. In fact, there was overwhelming senatorial opposition to Pompey's appointment. Gabinius then proposed an extraordinary three-year command to combat the pirates with full funding, supplies, troops and ships to be provided by the state. It was generally assumed again that Pompey would be chosen, but the consul Piso was adamant that he would not allow the bill to pass.

Further opposition from the senate was swiftly forthcoming. Although Gabinius publicly appealed to Pompey, the latter refused to take part at first, but eventually did speak to the crowd. Appearing hesitant, Pompey outlined his achievements, but proclaimed that it would not be hard to find another commander. Gabinius then emphasized Pompey's successes and begged him to do his duty. When one of the other tribunes, Trebellius, attempted to interject his veto, Gabinius demanded that he be immediately stripped of his tribunate, and it was not until 17 of the 18 necessary tribes had voted for his dismissal that he withdrew his veto. Roscius, yet another tribune, also tried to interject his disapproval but, threatened by the crowd, also left the area with a two-fingered gesture of frustration.

Both Hortensius and Catulus had spoken against the proposal. Catulus argued that it was wrong to invest such an extraordinary command onto one man, and if something happened to Pompey, who would take over? Enthused, the crowd responded by screaming: Catulus himself. Opposition then crumbled, with a second bill appointing Pompey and increasing the available troops, ships and monies that the commander could avail himself of.

Pompey made thorough preparations for the task ahead. He divided the Mediterranean into various sectors, assigning his legates to oversee each area. His main concern was to again open the links between Rome and North Africa, the main shipping channel for Africa's grain:

> With his forces thus scattered in all quarters, he encompassed whole fleets of piratical ships that fell in his way, and straightforwardly hunted them down and brought them into port; others succeeded in dispersing and escaping, and sought their hive, as it were, hurrying from all quarters into Cilicia. Against these, Pompey intended to proceed in person with his sixty best ships. He did not, however, sail against them until he had entirely cleared (the seas of pirates).[2]

Within 40 days, the pirates had been driven back to Cilicia, 'owing to [Pompey's] own tireless energy and the zeal of his lieutenants.'[3] Yet, Pompey did show compassion to some:

> Those pirates who had evidently fallen into this way of life not from wickedness, but from poverty consequent upon the war (in the east), Pompey settled in Mallus, Adana, and Epiphanea, or any other uninhabited or thinly peopled town in rough Cilicia . . .

The others were not so lucky:

> He took 71 ships by capture and 306 by surrender from the pirates, and 120 of their towns, castles, and other places of rendezvous. About 10,000 of the pirates were slain in battles.[4]

Although the seas were relatively free for the next few years, Pompey's claim to have completely destroyed the pirate threat was not necessarily true. There would be continued minor attacks, which resulted in the need for another grain dole in 62, illustrating that trade was being interrupted, although not to the extent seen previously in the decade.

Either during Pompey's sweep of the seas, or immediately afterwards, another Roman citizen was kidnapped. When serving as prefect to his brother-in-law, the proconsul of Cilicia Q. Marcius Rex, the young Clodius was kidnapped by pirates in 67, but whether he was ransomed or simply released due to fear of Pompey is not clear. Dio is adamant that there were some repercussions nevertheless:

> Now, Clodius, after being captured by the pirates and released by them in consequence of their fear of Pompey, came to Antioch in Syria, declaring that he would be their ally against the Arabians, with whom they were then at variance. There, likewise, he stirred up a sedition and all but lost his life.[5]

Later, Cicero was to imply that his release was due to his granting sexual favours to his captors, but in fairness to Clodius, Cicero was writing a rather damning portrait of him, bringing in every rumour, scandal and falsehood that he could invoke. His speech *De haruspicum responsis*, delivered in 57 BCE upon Cicero's return from exile – exile at Clodius' instigation – could hardly be construed as objective or reasonable.[6]

Difficulties with the pirates would perhaps never be as severe as during the 60s BCE, but Pompey's claim of having defeated them did have the benefit of reassuring the ordinary Roman that trade and grain supplies would flow more easily. Bringing stability to the business of the city cannot be overestimated, and Pompey indeed deserved credit for resolving, albeit not completely, the threat that piracy had brought to Rome.

OTHER MEASURES

Possibly with his colleague's assistance, Gabinius also tried to pass measures against the senatorial practice of lending money to embassies from abroad and continued his attack on the senate. He also tried to stop the reading of Cornelius' next bill, which proposed that no person should be exempt from the penalties of legislation without a popular vote. As the consul, C. Piso, protested about the abuse hurled at one of the tribunes, a small-scale riot broke out.

A more far-reaching effort, and perhaps directed at Piso himself, was legislation to deal with electoral bribery. Although Dio states that the legislation came from the consuls, it was actually the tribune Cornelius who proposed the measure in the first instance.[7] Piso was not pleased; the crowd less so:

> When a great uproar arose at this, since Piso and a number of the senators opposed (Gabinius), the crowd broke the consul's fasces to pieces and threatened to tear him from limb to limb. Cornelius, accordingly, seeing their voice, dismissed the assembly for the time being, before calling for any vote.[8]

In fact, Piso seems to have had numerous problems with the tribunes of the year, resisting many of their measures, and, in particular, the command given to Pompey to battle the pirates. He had also opposed the bribery law proposed by Cornelius, but was later forced to present a much watered-down bill of his own on the issue. The senate interceded when riots broke out and hastily approved a compromise that a quorum of 200 senators had to be present to deal with such changes prior to its ratification by the people.

Cornelius also argued for a ban on high-interest loans to foreign delegations, but the senate again rejected this. His co-tribune, Gabinius, appears to have been able to pass a similar bill. Other proposals were vetoed, but despite opposition, Cornelius was able to pass two other laws, one that restricted the power of the senate to grant immunity from legal restraints, while another forced praetors to confirm to the terms of their edicts.

One praetor, eager to gain support from the *equites*, passed a law reserving the front rows of seats at the theatre for them, but the populace was not amused:

> Marcus Otho was the first to separate in point of honour the knights [*equites*] from the rest of the citizens, which he did when he was praetor, and gave them a particular place of their own at the spectacles, which they still retain. The people took this as a mark of dishonour to themselves, and when Otho appeared in the theatre they hissed him insultingly, while the knights received him with loud applause. The people renewed and increased their hisses, and then the knights their applause. After this they turned upon one another with reviling words, and disorder reigned in the theatre.[9]

FROM 66–4 BCE

In 67, the consul Glabrio had been selected to take over the command against Mithridates, but he, like Lucullus, was unsuccessful. The following year, the tribune Manilius passed a law transferring the command against Mithridates from Lucullus to Pompey. The historian Robin Seager argues convincingly that the continued popular support for Pompey was gradually eroding the influence of the senate, but it is also clear that Pompey was a very successful general.[10] Furthermore, Pompey was already in Asia, as part of his strike against the pirates, where he was resettling some of them on available lands. There were those who protested against Lucullus' recall as they felt that Pompey was merely cleaning up and organizing the resettlement and treaties already established in Asia Minor, a charge that would be echoed in the later part of the decade as Cato and others sought to block ratification of Pompey's eastern settlement.

Despite the fact that both Hortensius and Catulus were vehemently opposed to Manilius' bill, Cicero spoke on behalf of the *lex Manilia* in his first speech to the people:

> I wish, O Romans, that you had such an abundance of brave and honest men, that it was a difficult subject for your deliberations, whom you thought most desirable to be appointed to the conduct of such important affairs, and so vast a war. But now, when there is [Pompey] alone, who has exceeded in valour, not only the glory of these men who are now alive, but even all recollections of antiquity, what is there that, in this case, can raise a doubt in the mind of any one?[11]

Cicero realizes some of the criticism:

> And will any one doubt that this important war ought to be entrusted to him, who seems to have been born by some especial design and favour of the gods for the express purpose of finishing all the wars which have existed in their own recollection?

In fact, Pompey is already there, so why not let him finish the matter? Cicero admonishes the people:

> You would have entirely lost Asia, O Romans, if the fortune of the Roman people had not, by some divine interposition, brought [Pompey] at that particular moment into those regions. His arrival both checked Mithridates, elated with his unusual victory, and delayed Tigranes, who was threatening Asia with a formidable army.

> And can any one doubt what he will accomplish by his valour, when he did so much by his authority and reputation? Or how easily he will preserve our allies and our revenues by his power and his army, when he defended them by the mere terror of his name?[12]

After rebuking both Hortensius and Catulus, Cicero turned the matter over to the people, who responded by voting overwhelmingly for Pompey. Pompey responded by entering into negotiations with Mithridates and making a pact with Phraates, the king of Parthia.

Lucullus had had since 73, over eight years, to resolve the problems in Asia Minor and defeat Mithridates, so it is not surprising that many members of the senate and the Roman people were tired and frustrated with his increasingly lacklustre performance. He had been successful in dealing with the crisis, but it had dragged on far too long, with no real and effective resolution. Lucullus had been strongly supported both by his soldiers and the senate in the first few years as he had been winning decisive victories, but over the past year or so, he had not been so lucky. Simply put, Lucullus was faltering and his resolve, along with that of his troops, was weakening. While it may be convenient to believe that Pompey manipulated the proposals of the tribunes for his own ends, it would have been ridiculous not to send a replacement, whether it was Pompey or not. The fact remains that in all other wars, unsuccessful generals, no matter how victorious in the beginning, were eventually replaced. This situation was no different.

While the extraordinary command could be construed as evidence of Pompey's increasing popularity with the urban masses, and also several of the tribunes, Pompey did have one extremely important attribute – he knew how to finish a war. Whether Crassus' criticism that Pompey took all the credit for resolving the Servile war is correct, or just mere jealousy for Pompey's triumph in recognition of his victories over Sertorius, Pompey was extremely effective in battle and in negotiating treaties with reasonable demands. Lucullus' vanity might be greatly bruised, but it was nevertheless time for a change of command in the East.

After meeting Lucullus in Galantia and taking charge of his army, Pompey invaded Armenia Minor, which forced Mithridates to retreat. In a night-time battle, Pompey was able to inflict a serious defeat:

> After exhausting their long-distance missiles, [the Romans] charged down upon them, [and] the outermost of the enemy were slaughtered, one blow sufficing for their death, since the majority were unarmed, and the centre was crushed together, as all by reason of the danger round them moved [together]. So they perished, pushed about and trampled upon by one another without being able to defend themselves or show any daring against the enemy. For they were horsemen and bowmen for the most part, and were unable to see before them in the darkness ...

> When the moon rose, the barbarians rejoiced, thinking that in the light they would certainly beat back some of the foe. And they would have benefited somewhat, if the Romans had not had the moon behind them and as they assailed them, now on this side and now on that, caused much confusion both to the eyes and hands of the others. For the assailants, being very numerous, and all of them together casting the deepest shadow, baffled their opponents before they had yet come into conflict with them. The barbarians, thinking them near, would strike vainly into the air, and when they did come to close quarters in the shadow, they would be wounded when not expecting it. Thus many of them were killed and fewer taken captives. A considerable number also escaped, among them Mithridates.[13]

Mithridates sought refuge with Tigranes but, being refused, he set off towards the kingdom of Bosporus. Meanwhile, Pompey founded the city of Nicopolis (in Cappadocia) on the site of his victory over Mithridates.[14] Tigranes' son deserted to the Romans, but was kept as a prisoner while his father and Pompey met near Artaxata. Tigranes was re-established as king of Armenia, but had to forfeit any other territories. Pompey then placed his troops in winter quarters near the river Cyrnus.

Back in Rome, however, it was chaos and confusion. Many senators, frustrated by Pompey's success, began to try to undermine those tribunes and individuals who they felt threatened the supremacy of the senate. The middle years of the 60s BCE were dominated by trials brought against various individuals with varying degrees of success. During 66, enemies of the tribune of 67, Cornelius, brought charges of treason against him, but a riot halted the initial proceedings and they were disbanded. Another prosecution was mounted for extortion against the praetor C. Licinius Macer, which gave Cicero another opportunity for a great rhetorical attack. The trial ended with the voluntary death of Macer following his conviction. The tribune Manilius himself was brought to trial at the end of his term (in late December), but the charges are unclear.[15]

Meanwhile, the electoral situation in 66 was again fraught with difficulties and disorder. The consular elections, which were held in the summer, were disrupted, with the results ultimately overturned. In the new elections, held to replace those disrupted, Catiline proposed his candidature, but the current consul, L. Volcanius Tullus, dismissed his request on technical grounds (as having not been one of the original candidates in the earlier election). Unfortunately for Catiline, the ugly reality of alleged provincial mismanagement resurfaced as a delegation from his province appealed to the senate about his behaviour. Those consuls originally elected for 65, P. Autronius Paetus and P. Cornelius Sulla, were condemned for bribery and a new election was therefore called. It was this further consular election that Catiline had wanted to participate in, but the presiding consul refused to allow his candidature due to the accusations of provincial corruption. In the end, Cotta and Torquatus were elected as consuls in the new election.

Bribery and extortion trials continued to be the theme of the political scene that year. There was also an attempt to prosecute those who had benefited from the Sullan proscriptions. These attacks were also directed against Lucullus, his brother Marcus (quaestor in 83) and Sulla's son, Faustus Sulla – but to no avail. The tribune Memmius tried to bring charges again M. Lucullus, but one of the praetors for 65 – Cicero – decided that tribunician power should not be used in such a manner as it would be too detrimental to the prosecution, and moved the trial to the 29th December 66 in order to defend him, noting that a new praetor might not be as sympathetic as he would be. The trial was, however, even further delayed into 65. Memmius also 'excited' the people against Lucullus and delayed his triumph. Lucullus, meanwhile, divorced his wife, accusing her of incest with her brother, the infamous Clodius, who had led a revolt against him back in the East – Clodius responded by trying to bring charges against his former brother-in-law. Never friendly, Clodius and Lucullus would continue to spar with rather amusing results.

Meanwhile, Lucullus waited outside Rome. Unfortunately, he, along with Q. Metellus and Q. Marcius Rex, were all refused triumphs. These refusals brought by tribunes appear to reflect both public disdain as well as continuing to demonstrate popular support for Pompey. The scholar Peter Wiseman has pointed out:

> The presence of these three nobles in the suburbs, tending their fading laurels and doubtless feeding as many of their loyal soldiers as might make a decent procession if ever their triumphs could be authorized, was a potent and humiliating symbol of the tribunes' power and the authority of the people.[16]

The people may have voiced their feelings, with the tribunes controlling the political arena at present, but the senate was about to enact its own type of revenge – with court cases, passage of laws and refusal to allow associations, such as those they suspected many of Cornelius' and Gabinius' followers had formed for more nefarious purposes.

65 BCE

At the beginning of the new year, there was an increased atmosphere of anxiety and intrigue. It has been alleged by ancient sources that with the trial of Manilius looming, the first so-called Catilinarian conspiracy was formulated, but modern scholars have convincingly argued against this. Contemporary sources, meanwhile, offer little concrete evidence as well. In a later letter to Atticus, Cicero was still considering Catiline as a viable political figure, possibly even as a consular colleague for 63, so it is entirely possible that the beginnings of the conspiracy were backdated to the events of 66 and 65.

A supposed plot had been formed to murder the new consuls on 1 January 65 and to replace them with Autronius and Sulla or Catiline. The ancient sources are rather vague about its details, or whether Catiline was actually involved in or even knew much about the aborted plan.[17] Although some sources credit the senate with issuing the consuls with breastplates (a device used by Cicero himself two years later), contemporary sources offer little concrete evidence. Neither Sallust or Asconius, drawing on Cicero, mention this first conspiracy, and as contemporaneous sources, are perhaps the most reliable. Furthermore, Cicero spoke of Catiline in positive terms in his surviving letters during 65–3, which further negates the idea of this first conspiracy. Even the later second century author Suetonius, who delighted in gossip, argues that it was Caesar, along with Crassus, Sulla and Autronius, who planned to overthrow the new consuls. There is no mention of Catiline in his account.[18]

In the aftermath, one of the alleged conspirators, Cn. Calpurnius Piso, was sent to Spain with praetorian *imperium*. This perhaps offers the clearest evidence that there was no serious threat perceived by the senate at this time. Although it has been suggested that Crassus and Caesar were behind the move to send Piso to Spain in an effort to counterbalance Pompey's own support in this region, others have dismissed the idea.[19] Seager, in his biography of Pompey, suggests that it might be a plausible tactic used by the senate, but while Piso 'was believed to be hostile to Pompeius . . . he did not survive long in Spain before he was killed by some native cavalrymen.'[20] Rumours abounded that these men may have been supporters of Pompey.

Force and riots characterized the beginning of the trial against Manilius, which was halted as a preventative measure. When it reconvened, the defendant did not appear and was therefore found guilty. Another trial resumed the attack against the ex-tribune Cornelius for his behaviour during his tribunate in 67. The charge of obstructing a tribune's veto was brought and Catulus, Hortensius, M. Lucullus and others brought their very considerable weight to the prosecution. Cicero defended Cornelius and argued that '[they] were trying to . . . humble the plebs and tarnish the whole concept of tribunician power.'[21] Whether Cicero actually believed in the democratic nature of the tribunate as espoused in the fragments of his *Pro Cornelio*, his defence demonstrated the importance of the tribunate and why there had been so many attempts to restore its potency following Sulla's reforms. Cornelius was acquitted with all ten tribunes of the year supporting him.

In the midst of this unrest, the young Cato returned to Rome to run for the quaestorship. Many modern scholars have put this quaestorship in 65, while it is more probable that it was in 64.[22] In 65 BCE, Catiline was again brought to trial, but received the support of many of the most distinguished men in Rome, including one of the current consuls for 65, Lucius Manlius Torquatus, while Cicero even contemplated defending Catiline.[23] Acquitted, Catiline then turned his attention back to the consular elections. This time, no technicality would stand in his way, but on this, his first legal attempt, he was unsuccessful.

During the same year, magnificent games were given by the aedile Julius Caesar. Unfortunately, the patrician Caesar had little money and was forced to rely on heavy borrowing, particularly from Crassus. Like many other aristocrats of the time, Caesar was eager to establish himself politically and had achieved public recognition by the elaborate games in honour of his aunt Julia (in 69) as well as his involvement in senatorial matters. In September Caesar, as aedile, spent a massive amount of money providing magnificent games, to the detriment of his other fellow aediles, among them L. Calpurnius Bibulus:

> [As] aedile, Caesar decorated not only the Comitium and the Forum with its adjacent basilicas, but the Capitol as well, building temporary colonnades for the display. He exhibited combats with wide beasts and stage-plays too, both with his colleague and independently. The result was that Caesar alone took all the credit even for what they spent in common, and his colleague Marcus Bibulus openly said that he was the fate of Pollux: 'For,' he said, 'just as the temple erected in the Forum to the twin brethren, bears only the name of Castor, so the joint liberality of Caesar and myself is credited to Caesar alone.'[24]

This was a charge that was levelled throughout their careers, unfortunately, as Bibulus was also a praetor (62) and consul (59) during the same years as Caesar, which did not bode well for any future cooperation. Indeed, there would be none on either side. Around the time of his aedileship, Caesar also restored Marius' monuments, while the praetor Murena provided 'a most splendid proof of his liberality' with public shows.[25]

The censors of 65, Catulus and Crassus, were unable to agree on anything. Crassus proposed that Egypt be turned into a Roman province, but Catulus (along with Cicero) opposed him. Egypt, which had become the 'bread basket' of Rome, was still independently run, and seeing the profit that could be made, particularly if Egypt was under Roman control, Crassus had turned his attention there, but was rebuffed. In fact, disagreeing over whether the Transpadanes (northern Italy, the area between the river Po and the Alps) should become Roman citizens, the two men resigned the censorship without achieving anything – no census took place.

Also in 65 a *lex Papia* passed, which challenged false claims of citizenship, while deporting foreigners from the city 'because they were coming to be too numerous and were not thought fit persons to dwell with the citizens.'[26] The signs were not good as the year ended – a statue of Romulus and Remus was struck by lightning. Later, Cicero was to remind his audience about the event:

> [Do you remember when] ... many towers in the Capitol were struck with lightning, when both the images of the immortal gods were moved, and the statues of many ancient men were thrown down, and the brazen tablets on which the laws were written were melted. Even Romulus, who built this city, was struck, which, you recollect, stood in the Capital, a gilt statue, little and sucking, and clinging to the teats of the wolf. And when at this time, the soothsayers were assembled out of all Etruria, they said that slaughter, and conflagration, and the overthrow of the laws, and civil and domestic war, and the fall of the city and empire was at hand, unless the immortal gods, being appeased in every possible manner, by their own power turned aside, as I may say, the very fates themselves.[27]

Regardless of these omens, ordinary business in Rome continued, but there was increased tension in the air. Always suspicious of organized groups, such as work guilds (*collegia*), and perhaps in light of the violence that had surrounded the trials of Cornelius and Gabinius, the senate began to restrict the guilds' activities. There were numerous types of groups, ranging from trade and religious associations to burial clubs. Most were innocent, but the senate was taking no chances. In their zeal to curtail tribunate agitation, such *collegia* were outlawed and large gatherings restricted, which would have repercussions on the activities of political candidates' followers as well.

At the same time, Cato (as quaestor) had begun his reorganization of the treasury. Cato's actions, and the subsequent prosecutions of beneficiaries of the Sullan proscriptions, should be viewed as part of the series of popular, anti-corruption moves seen in the 60s. His administrative zeal showed itself within the first weeks of assuming office. Cato began reassigning some of the scribes and clerks that he distrusted in the treasury. Two particular individuals came under great scrutiny: one was dismissed, while the other was brought to trial for fraud. Catulus himself came forward to defend the latter individual, but when he apparently tried to beg for an acquittal, Cato stepped in and remonstrated against his pleas, noting that 'it would be a shameful thing, Catulus, if you, who are the censor and should scrutinise our lives, were put out of court by our bailiffs.'[28] Although this scribe was eventually acquitted, Cato never used him again, even stopping his pay.

Cato also reviewed the recovery of debts owed to the treasury, seeking debts of long standing as well as those monies due to individuals as well. Turning his attention to those who had received money under the Sullan proscriptions, he demanded that they return the illegal funds. Following this, various people were prosecuted for murder as the 'issue was popular, with considerable notoriety.'[29]

Two particular cases illustrate that it was the lesser figures who were condemned: the virtually unknown and innocuous L. Luscius and L. Bellienus. The latter conviction had some consequence as Catiline was then implicated for his own role, but acquitted:

> This matter, then turned out contrary to most people's expectation, as did also the case of Catiline, who, although charged with the same crimes as the others (for he, too, had killed many of the proscribed), was acquitted. And from this very circumstance, he became far worse . . .[30]

POMPEY IN THE EAST

After spending the winter in Aspis, Pompey was able to finally organize Pontus as a Roman province, but Mithridates continued with his guerrilla tactics. Nevertheless, the end was drawing near. During 64, Pompey granted territories to neighbouring kings and forced others into submission. Received with enthusiasm at Antioch and Seleuceia, he would later refuse to re-instate the king of Syria, signalling the end of Seleucid rule there. Desperate at this point, Mithridates entered into new negotiations with Pompey, but a large earthquake devastated the area. Pompey continued with his reorganization, subjecting Aradus to Roman control, while Tyre and Byblus remained free. Slowly, he made his way towards Jerusalem. Meanwhile, his predecessor, Lucullus, remained outside Rome, awaiting his triumph.

ELECTIONS FOR 63

In the summer of 64 BCE, elections were held for the magistrates for the coming year, with Catiline again announcing his candidature for consul, along with the ambitious new man, Cicero, and several other individuals. Mudslinging, accusations and threats of violence characterized the elections. Although Cicero was a new man and the senatorial class may have disliked allowing such people into the tight-knit circle that was the consular club, they did recognize that the brilliant orator might be a beneficial ally as well as providing a clear alternative to Catiline. An important factor in this election were the claims of Catiline and Antonius that they were from the right background, and in Catiline's case, patrician – as opposed to Cicero's lowly status:

> However, Catiline wished to obtain first a strong base of operations, and therefore sued for the consulship; and he had bright hopes that he would share the consulship with Gaius Antonius, a man who, of himself, would probably not take the lead either for good or bad, but would add strength to another who took the lead. Most of the better class of citizens were aware of this, and therefore put forward Cicero for the consulship, and as the people readily accepted him, Catiline was defeated, and Cicero and Gaius Antonius were elected. And yet Cicero was the only one of the candidates who was the son, not of a senator, but of a knight.[31]

Cicero, as a *novus homo*, ironically came from Arpinum – the same birthplace as Marius – and as new men, neither were particularly trusted by the senatorial establishment. Cicero used his outsider status to great effect in his electioneering, as shown in a letter to his brother, but still tried to court his senatorial colleagues:

> Almost every day as you go down to the Forum you must say to yourself, 'I am a *novus homo*. I am a candidate for the consulship. This is Rome. For the "newness" of your name you will best compensate by the brilliance of your oratory.' This has ever carried with it great political distinction. A man who is held worthy of defending ex-consuls, cannot be deemed unworthy of the constitution itself. Therefore approach each individual case with the persuasion that on it depends as a whole your entire reputation . . .

> See that you retain these advantages by reminding these persons, by appealing to them, and by using every means to make them understand that this, and this only, is the time for those who are in your debt now, to show their gratitude, and for those who wish for your services in the future, to place you under an obligation. It also seems possible that a *novus homo* may be much aided by the fact that he has the good wishes of men of high rank, and especially of ex-consuls. It is a point in your favour that you should be thought worthy of this position and rank by the very men to whose position you are wishing to attain.[32]

It is probable that Caesar and Crassus supported Catiline, particularly in light of his support of the land reform bill that would occupy the senate in early 63, but the threats issued by Antonius and Catiline, which promised a radical attack on the state, backfired on them. As David Stockton in his *Cicero: A Political Biography* notes:

> The *boni* and the well-to-do rallied behind a candidate they felt they could trust to resist the revolutionary schemes of reform, and in the later stages of his campaign, [Cicero] came out publicly more and more strongly as defender of the established order against the frightening threat of Catiline.[33]

In the end, however, it was Cicero to whom the senate offered support. Whatever bribery or political manoeuvres unseen influenced the voters is not clear, but Cicero and G. Antonius were elected for the consulship for 63.

Whilst the 60s may have begun well, by the middle of the decade various problems began to plague the senate and the stability of Rome. While 67 had shown how popular support could overrule the wishes and desires of the senatorial class, the middle years of the 60s were dominated by trials brought against various individuals with varying degrees of success. The political arena was extremely tense during the second half of the 60s BCE. The strength of the masses had been instrumental in securing Pompey's extraordinary commands while weakening senatorial supremacy. Any additional threats to the *res publica* would have created an almost intolerable atmosphere of suspicion and fear, but were they real? The idea of conspiracies, such as the so-called Pisonian threat of 65 BCE, found great currency in Rome, particularly as the spectacle of civil war was still fresh in many peoples' minds. Yet the question needs to viewed within its context. The year 63 would find Cicero and Antonius established as consuls, but whether Catiline's threats would come to fruition did not occupy the senate and people at the beginning of the year. It was at first a most ordinary year – at least until the summer, when Catiline ran for the consulship again, and then Rome was to face its most serious threat since the civil wars of the 80s.

5

Rome in Crisis? The Catilinarian Conspiracy of 63 BCE

'In these circumstances, Catiline, finish the journey you have begun: at long last leave the city; the gates are open: be on your way.'

CICERO, IN CATILINAM I. 10.

On 1 January 63 BCE, the crowds in the Forum waited anxiously for the political business of the new year to begin. Perhaps those who went about their everyday business did not notice it so much, but there were, nevertheless, worrying signs, as Dio notes, 'many thunderbolts fell from a clear sky, the earth was mightily shaken, and human apparitions were visible in many places, and in the west flashes of fire darted up into heaven, so that any one, even a layman, was bound to know in advance what was signified by them.'[1] This year would not be a good one for the *res publica*.

The problems of debt, lack of available lands for rehousing the urban poor and poverty would all continue to create problems for the ruling elite. The consuls, Cicero and Antonius, began the year by looking at some of the possible solutions, but with Pompey overshadowing all political activity, it was not an easy task.

The first proposal was an agrarian law presented by the tribune Rullus. This legislation had been painstakingly formulated in the last months of 64 and its provisions would create a ten-man commission, who would oversee an extensive resettlement package. They would be empowered to purchase land in Italy as well as to found colonies. By a unique selection process, these men were to be invested with extensive powers, and the rank of praetor along with *imperium* was to be conferred upon them; indeed, Cicero characterized them as kings and was resolutely opposed to the bill. The lands under consideration for redistribution were the *ager Campanus* and *ager Stellatis* where some 5,000 of the urban poor were to be settled, and the remaining lands were to be purchased with monies acquired from the sale of public land. The commission was to decide what constituted public or private land, with a special proviso for the Sullan settlers, who were to be compensated for any lands lost under legislation created by Sulla. The extraordinary powers of the commission also included collection of revenues from provinces being currently organized by Pompey and, further, the commision would have control over all booty and monies taken by generals during the Mithridatic war. Considered a measure to curtail Pompey's effectiveness, another tribune – Rufus – was to support Cicero's attack on the bill and further informed Cicero that he would veto the bill if it came to a vote. Cicero remarked that:

> Which, in the name of the immortal gods, do these things seem to you – the designs of sober men, or the dreams of drunken ones? The serious thoughts of wise men, or the frantic wishes of madmen? See, now, in the second chapter of this law, how that profligate debauchee is disturbing the Republic, how he is ruining and dissipating the possessions left us by our ancestors; so as to be not less a spendthrift in the patrimony of the Roman people than in his own. He is advertising for sale by his law all the revenues, for the [ten man commission] to sell them; that is to say, he is advertising an auction of the property of the state. He wants lands to be bought, in order to be distributed; he is seeking money. No doubt he will devise something, and bring it forward; for in the preceding chapters the dignity of the Roman people was attacked; the name of our dominion was held up as an object of common hatred to all the nations of the earth; cities which were at peace with us, lands belonging to the allies, the ranks of kings in alliance with us, were all made a present of to the [ten man commission]; and now they want actual ready money paid down to them.[2]

This proposal was eventually rejected, after appeals to the people that a bill that supported the Sullans was detrimental to the wishes of the people and possibly also damaging to their idol and hero, Pompey.

There were a few other measures proposed by the tribunes, such as the cancellation of debts, which again Cicero was able to successfully oppose. He was able to persuade the senate to pass legislation prohibiting bribery in elections, but it appears to have little effect – one of the successful consular candidates, L. Licinius Murena, was later prosecuted by an unsuccessful competitor, Servius Sulpicius, with strong support from that stalwart of integrity – Cato.

A total eclipse of the moon on 3 May was interpreted as a sign that some sort of civil disruption was eminent, which overshadowed the events of the summer. The mood of the people was uncertain. A riot broke out after the praetor L. Roscius Otho entered the theatre, but Cicero intervened and following his impassioned speech to the plebs, they turned and applauded Otho on his next trip there.[3] Cicero was to propose legislation that the *equites* were to retain their special privileges. Yet the animosity of the urban masses was an indication of their state of unrest, which mirrored that of their rural counterparts to some degree. Economic deprivation would become a key component of the losing consular candidate – Catiline's – message to the people in the ensuing months.

It was also a year in which notable trials took place. Charges were brought against C. Rabirius for the death of the tribune Saturninus in 100 BCE. The tribune T. Labienus brought an accusation of *perduellio* against Rabirius, with Caesar and his cousin L. Caesar (cos. 64) condemning him by virtue of their appointment as special commissioners overseeing the case. The traditional penalty was to be flogged to death in the Campus Martius. Cicero and Hortensius attempted to defend Rabirius, but his appeal was ended by the rising of a red flag, which was the ancient symbol to indicate that the city stood under attack. Caesar also brought C. Piso to trial, but he was defended by Cicero. Although Cicero had lent his considerable talents to the Piso trial, it was the charges against the consul-elect Murena that would dominate his thoughts throughout the latter part of the year. The tribune-elect Cato had vowed that due to the rampant bribery during the consular election, he would prosecute the winners; one was his brother-in-law, the other, Murena. It was this trial, along with the increasing threat of Catiline, that was to concern Cicero the most.

Meanwhile, Caesar was successful against Catulus in the election for the office of Pontifex Maximus, in a contest that was characterized by its excessive bribery, with Plutarch not being very complimentary about Catulus especially:

> The favour of the electors appeared to be about equally divided, and therefore, Catulus, who, as the worthier of Caesar's competitors ... sent and tried to induce Caesar to desist from from his ambitious project, offering him large sums of money, but Caesar declared that he would carry the contest through even though he had to borrow still larger sums ... the day for the election came, and as Caesar's mother accompanied him to the door in tears, he kissed her and said, 'Mother, today, you will see your son either Pontifex Maximus or an exile.' The contest was sharp, but when the vote was taken, Caesar prevailed, and thereby made the senate and nobles afraid that he would lead the people on to every extreme of recklessness.[4]

Dio is even more ruthless when he discusses the election contest:

> Because [Caesar] showed himself perfectly ready to serve and flatter everybody, even ordinary persons, and shrank from no speech or action in order to get possession of the objects for which he strove. He did not mind temporary grovelling when weighed against subsequent power, and he cringed as before superiors to the very men whom he was endeavouring to dominate.[5]

THE SUMMER ELECTIONS OF 63 BCE

The day for the consular elections drew near, but Catiline was again unsuccessful in his attempt to become consul:

> When the day of the comitia came, and neither Catiline's efforts for the consulship, nor the plots which he had laid for the consuls in the Campus Martius, were attended with

Bust of Cicero

success, he determined to proceed to war, and to resort to the utmost extremities, since
what he had attempted secretly had ended in confusion and disgrace.[6]

There was more:

> After collecting a small band, [Catiline] attempted to slay Cicero and some others of the
> foremost men on the very day of the election, in order that he might immediately be
> chosen as consul. But he was unable to carry out his plot; for Cicero learned of it . . . and
> did not venture to enter the assembly alone, as had been his custom, but took his friends
> along prepared to defend him if any danger threatened; and partly for his own safety and
> partly to arouse prejudice against his foes, he wore beneath his clothing a breast-plate,
> which he was careful to allow people to see.[7]

Catiline had borrowed so much money and threatened such violence if he did
not win, in fact, Cato threatened to prosecute him for his actions. Cato, who was
furious, also announced that he would prosecute the eventual victors as he was
disgusted by the rampant bribery. The eventual winners were Decimus Junius
Silanus, who had lost the previous year, and Lucius Licinius Murena.

During that summer, Cato stood for election as a tribune. There have been
many conjectures as to why Cato ran for the tribunate. It might be considered
odd that Cato, long classified by modern scholars as an advocate and supporter

of the primacy of the senate's authority in Roman politics, would seek the tribunate, in particular, given the revolutionary nature of the position. Many modern scholars note that the primary reason, as suggested by Plutarch, was a desire to oppose the supposed Pompeian agent Metellus Nepos.[8] This may be entirely plausible, but it is worth considering to what extent Nepos really was an agent of Pompey's. The historian Robin Seager has noted that while Nepos may have acted on orders from Pompey, in reality, he did not need to rely on Pompey for his continued success: 'as long as it suited [his] convenience [he] might ride on [Pompey's] shoulders, but from [Nepos] he could expect no loyalty when he had served [his] turn. [Nepos] was able to secure the consulship in the early 50s BCE without too much concern about Pompey'.[9] However, both of Nepos' proposed bills do suggest a desire to assist Pompey: one, to recall Pompey to deal with the military threat of the Catilinarian supporters in Etruria, and the other to allow Pompey to stand for the consulship *in absentia*, but neither measure was allowed to pass. In fact, Nepos was not much help to Pompey at all.

There were several other reasons for Cato to assume the tribunate: family tradition on both the paternal and maternal side, a desire to curry popular favour, and finally, the very real power that the tribunate carried. As mentioned before, his maternal uncle Livius Drusus had been tribune in 91 BCE and, in fact, the Livii Drusii had provided another tribune during turbulent times: Cato's grandfather in 122 BCE (against Gaius Gracchus). His grandfather had presented legislation, most likely with senatorial backing, that had effectively undermined the younger Gracchus' plans. Again, the very real political power of the tribunate itself should not be underestimated as a viable reason for Cato to run for the office. Cato was already heavily involved in the political matters of the day, not simply because he was an ex-quaestor and, furthermore, it appears that he participated fully in senatorial matters. He was fast becoming one of Rome's most influential figures and with the tribunate he would be in an office where he could demonstrate that political officials and the senate could work together for the benefit of the state, and at the same time, use the power of the tribunate itself to assist in his own plans as he sought further political office. The tribunate was closed to patrician politicians such as Julius Caesar, but due to his plebian birth Cato was able to use the office for his advantage, and succeeded in establishing his political position and influence among the Roman *plebs*. Neither Crassus nor Cicero had held the tribunate, although at the time that they might have considered seeking the office it was still under the Sullan restrictions. It is curious that Cicero never tried to run for the office in 70 BCE, when it is believed that he ran for the aedileship, but perhaps the restoration of the tribunate came a year too late for him. Obviously, as mentioned, Caesar was excluded as a patrician, and Pompey was considered too experienced to run for lesser offices.

Cato was successful in his own bid for the tribunate, along with Pompey's agent, Metellus Nepos, while both Caesar and Bibulus were elected praetors for the following year.

CATILINE

One would think that after two attempts at the consulship, Catiline would have admitted defeat, but nevertheless, he was determined to try once again in the summer of 63 (for the consulship of 62). This time, however, his approach was more radical than his senatorial colleagues were comfortable with. In the first instance he proclaimed that if he were not elected, he would overturn the government, establishing his own rule of law over the *res publica*. When he failed for a third time to secure election, he began to preach revolution and violence. Conditions for both the dispossessed lower-classes and the luckless veterans were particularly harsh in this period. Debt, with all of its associated problems, in addition to the scarcity of grain, created a group of disgruntled citizens who were willing to listen to revolutionary talk and to support actions to remove the existing governmental structure. Catiline fully exploited the unstable political and economic conditions in his rhetoric, which included the usual problems with debt, hunger, poverty and a deep distrust towards the uncaring political machine. Therefore, by the autumn of 63, the age-old concerns of land and debt seemed to have found a new champion in the guise of the defeated consular candidate, Catiline, and there was increased unrest both in urban and rural areas.

Catiline found a willing audience among the urban poor and indeed, the artisan/middle-classes were also prepared to listen to his arguments. Plutarch comments that others were supporting him:

> It was the old soldiers of Sulla, however, who were most of all urging Catiline on to action. These were to be found in all parts of Italy, but the greatest numbers and the most warlike of them had been scattered among the cities of Etruria, and were again dreaming and plundering the wealth that lay ready to hand.[10]

In October it was clear that Catiline finally realized that he would be unable to gain the consulship legally, and he turned to the dissatisfied urban plebs of the lower classes to further his plans to overthrow the government. Letters were presented to Crassus that told of plans for wide-scale revolt and the massacre of leading senatorial figures in Rome, planned for 27 October. Crassus, in turn, gave the documents to Cicero, who demanded an immediate investigation. The *senatus consultum ultimum* (martial law) was passed on 21 October 63 BCE, which not only reflected Catiline's increasingly threatening rhetoric, but also that news had reached the senate that forces were beginning to collect in Etruria under C. Manlius. On the day itself, nothing actually happened in Rome, although there was a small riot at Faesulae.

A connection with Catiline may, however, be premature. He was still in Rome at this time, when Cicero gave his first speech against Catiline to the senate, where the man himself was present. According to Sallust, Catiline offered himself to the care of Cicero or Metellus (*custodia libera*) as a sign of his good faith, but both declined his offer. Also around this time, Cicero sent the quaestor P. Sestius to secure Capua.

Furthermore, the ex-consul Marcius Rex, waiting outside of Rome for a triumph, quickly dealt with the 'revolt'. Q. Metellus Creticus (cos. 69), who was also awaiting celebration of a triumph, put down a suspected slave revolt in Apulia. The discouraged masses who met with Marcius Rex begged for debt-relief and assistance from the commander, but in a rather arrogant manner, he recommended that they approach the senate in relation to their concerns. They did not act upon his advice, perhaps feeling that the senate would not answer their needs.

Meanwhile, news of the uprising at Faesulae had reached the senate around the same time that there was an attempt by conspirators to seize Praeneste (20 miles southeast of Rome), while L. Aemilius Paulus finally indicted Catiline under the *lex Plautia de vi* (for violence).

In the city, there was increased tension as an alleged attempt to assassinate Cicero was uncovered and, the next day, he delivered a second speech against Catiline to the people as Catiline left the city. Perhaps too much has been read into this second speech. Catiline was about to be forced to declare bankruptcy and was facing prosecution in the *quaestio de vi* as well. The honourable retreat in respect of such circumstances was usually exile, but he did not go to Massilia as he had announced, but made his way to Manlius and the troops in Etruria.

It was not until approximately a full week after Catiline had left the city, that both he and Manlius were declared *hostes* (enemies of the state) on 17 November. Catiline left neither as a result of Cicero's invective speeches nor having been declared a public enemy, but perhaps having realized that the mood in Rome, both among senatorial colleagues and the artisan/middle-classes, had shifted away from him. Indeed at this time, Rome turned its attention not to the threat of Catiline, but towards a prosecution against Murena.

In mid-November, Cicero was one of the three senatorial figures, the others being Hortensius and Crassus, who defended the successful consular candidate L. Licinius Murena on the charge of *ambitus* (bribery). This was as a result of Cato's declaration that, due to the excessive bribery of the electoral contest, he would prosecute the victors. Sulpicius Rufus, one of the defeated candidates, had also announced that he would join in a prosecution against Murena. Incidentally, Cato refrained from prosecuting his own brother-in-law D. Junius Silanus, who had also been elected, but turned his attention to the other winner.

Rufus, however, seems to have argued that the election of Murena as a *novus homo* was an affront to the aristocracy and his election was, therefore, evidence of corruption. It is interesting to note that the placement of Murena among the top two returning candidates was also a reflection of Cicero's own influence. As a new man himself, he naturally felt an affinity with Murena and defended him during his consulship – Cicero attacked Sulpicius' irritation in *Murena*. 15: 'you poured scorn on Murena's birth and exalted your own'. A brief summary of the *Pro Murena* will suffice to illustrate how Cicero's overall focus was more on the threat of Catiline and the instability of the *res publica* then a refutation of the actual charges against Murena; within this, Cicero's treatment towards Cato is particularly intriguing. Cicero gives several reasons for his defence, as it was uncommon for a consul to do such a thing – Cato claimed that he should not have taken the brief as it was inappropriate behaviour for a consul. Cicero argued that a serving consul should assist his legally elected successor and that he felt that the situation, particularly in relation to Catiline, absolutely necessitated the acquittal of Murena and that there should be no further debate about the consular elections. Cicero, furthermore, felt that it was his duty to resolve this in a timely fashion as the *res publica* was under threat by Catiline.

Cicero condemns Sulpicius' own behaviour prior to the elections and argues that he was responsible for his own lacklustre performance, but Cicero is much more concerned with Catiline. He reiterates the Catilinarian threat and its effect on the voting populace, but delays introducing the charge of bribery until much later in his defence. The actual charge against Murena is relegated to a minor part of the rebuttal, Cicero concerning himself mainly with showing how wrong this prosecution against Murena was in relation to current events. Cicero is also very complimentary about Cato, while acknowledging his youth and passion for politics, he states that this is simply not the right time for Cato to have brought this prosecution, regardless of his own personal and public condemnation of the electoral contest. Each insult about Cato's youth is counterbalanced by admiration for his integrity, his family connections, his abilities and his role as a leading member of the *boni*. According to Cicero, the entire survival of the *res publica* depended on resolving the case as quickly as possible. Murena was inauspiciously acquitted.

Cicero was then free to return to the business at hand – Catiline. Towards the end of November, there were minor disturbances in Gaul, Picenum, Bruttium and Apulia, which were quickly quelled. Only the band of supporters in Etruria remained a viable threat to the security of Rome itself. The conspirators had approached representatives of the Allrobroges, the Gallic tribe, who had appealed to Marcius Rex for financial assistance. They suggested to the Gauls that they create some sort of diversion, but instead the tribe turned to the senate for assistance regarding Catiline

By early December, those co-conspirators who had remained in the city had been arrested and examined. Various letters between Catiline and the Allobrogian Gauls were collected and the senate called all the various 'conspirators' together on 3 December 63, which included the ex-praetor Lentulus Sura, the senator C. Cethegus and the *eques* L. Statilius. Following the seizure of weapons at Cethegus' home, one of the conspirators, Lucius Vettius, gave evidence, adding more names and giving further evidence to the senate.

On 3 December Cicero delivered his third speech against Catiline to the people, informing them of what was happening and turned the matter over to the senate for consultation on 5 December. Cicero had made sure that the senate was aware of all aspects of this crisis. The praetor C. Cosconius had kept records of the evidence, Q. Pompeius Rufus went to guard the gladiatorial schools in Capua (with fears of Spartacus a decade earlier still present), C. Pomptinus and L. Valerius Flaccus had aided in the arrest of the Allobrogian envoys, C. Sulpicius had found the weapons in the home of Cethegus, while even the quaestor, P. Sestius was to join the co-consul Antonius, in Etruria. It would therefore appear that there was a real threat which was taken seriously by the senate.

The next day (4 December) continued the testimony. One L. Tarquinius attempted to implicate Crassus – while a tantalizing puzzle for modern historians, this was a side issue. An attempt to rescue the conspirators who were currently under house arrest was unsuccessful.

On 5 December, the senate met to discuss what punishment to hand out to the conspirators, with Cicero arguing for the death penalty. Both the praetor-elect Caesar and tribune-elect Cato spoke as well. Caesar argued that life imprisonment was the best option, and for a time, other senators appeared to agree with him. It was, however, Cato that spoke convincingly of the death penalty, in that treason planned was treason realized. He was able to give the senate the moral justification to agree on the death penalty. Lentulus was forced to resign as praetor before he and the other conspirators were strangled, while Cicero made a brief speech to the crowd before a triumphal escort home.

By mid December, there were massive desertions in Catiline's army, while Q. Metellus Celer blocked Catiline's efforts to leave Etruria. The issue of Catiline dominated the rest of the month as the newly elected officials, including Caesar as praetor and Cato, along with Metellus Nepos, as tribune. The custom of the tribunes assuming their position prior to the exchange of other offices was to Cicero's detriment as Nepos forbade Cicero the usual address to the people when he completed his consulship at the end of December.

Nepos compounded this insult by proposing that Pompey be recalled to deal with the Catilinarian threat, but this was vetoed and there was rioting in the city itself. Cicero's co-consul, Antonius was sent to deal with Catiline's troops. Although Antonius may have been sympathetic towards Catiline and delayed his attack, Metellus Celer demolished Catiline, his troops and the threat to Rome.

There can be little doubt that proper senatorial procedure was followed, and that all senators, once they had agreed, felt that their decision was legal and just. A later letter from Cicero to Atticus shows that the proper rules had been adhered to; his recitation of those speaking only included two praetor designates, Caesar and Q. Cicero (Cicero's brother, Quintus), but all others were either ex-consuls or consuls designate: Catulus, Servilius, Lucullus, Torquatus, Lepidus, Gellius, Silanus and Murena.[11] The fact remains, as Cicero later acknowledged, that Cato got his desired result – the Catilinarian conspirators were executed. However, one issue that has bothered modern scholars is the legality of such an execution.

Under legislation passed by Gaius Gracchus in 122 BCE, no Roman citizen could be put to death without a trial. Under the passage of the *senatus consultum ultimum*, however, such a legal requirement could be interpreted in a different manner. As the five senatorial conspirators had freely admitted their involvement, the niceties of Gracchus' law were not essential – as by admitting their guilt, a trial was therefore not necessary. This would, however, be the bugbear that would haunt Cicero for the rest of his political career; indeed, Clodius was to focus legislation specifically against Cicero on this point. In that time and place, however, the senate itself felt that Catiline did pose a very serious threat against the *res publica* and no matter what would happen in subsequent months, the senate looked at this as something that needed to be resolved immediately.

There has been considerable modern debate about the whole event. Was there really a conspiracy, a real threat, or had Cicero actually misled the senate? A few points should perhaps be noted in defence of Cicero. Once the urban threat had been dealt with by the executions, only in rural areas was there any reason for concern. Catiline did fully exploit 'the unstable political and economic conditions' in his rhetoric and there is some reason to believe that there was a threat as discussed above, but when Catiline began to preach wide-scale destruction, many of his more respectable followers abandoned him.[12] There would have been serious economic repercussions for the artisan middle class, who, although eager for the abolition of debt, would have been extremely wary of Catiline's revolutionary talk.

What was also of major concern was the inclusion of slaves in Catiline's forces. The fear of another Spartacus, in addition to recent slave revolts in Sicily that had stopped some of the necessary grain shipments to Rome, would be in people's minds. It is entirely possible that there was no political threat, but with the conspirators still alive in Rome, it is impossible to determine how serious whatever conspiracy there was might have been. There also quickly arose a military threat in early 62, but the fact that this situation was just as quickly dealt with can be interpreted in two ways. First, that the political threat was serious and the actions taken by the senate effectively ended that crisis; and second, unlike the Spartacan revolt which had taken three years to stamp out, this slave threat was swiftly resolved. The ease in which the crisis was put down should not automatically undermine the perceived seriousness in with which it was treated in December 63.

Another issue that has fascinated scholars is whether Caesar or Crassus were in any way involved in the affair. On the day of the debate, Caesar apparently received a personal note in the senate, but Cato, accusing him of corresponding with the conspirators, ordered that Caesar read the note aloud: it turned out to be a letter from Cato's half-sister Servilia, who was having an affair with Caesar at the time. Yet the accusations continued. In 62 a commission was set up to investigate the conspiracy and again, Caesar was accused of complicity. The informer Vettius argued that he could produce a letter written to Catiline in Caesar's own hand, but given that Caesar had personally warned Cicero of the plot beforehand, nobody believed him. Cleared of involvement, one of Caesar's accusers and one of the commissioners were actually sent to prison.[13] Perhaps Caesar and Crassus' earlier support of Catiline in 65–4 led to such speculation, but there is no clear evidence.

In mid-December Cicero gave the customary end of office oath that he had defended the Republic, but Nepos interjected before Cicero could address the people as was the usual practice. Cicero was quite annoyed as a later letter remarked 'a short time previously he had said in a public meeting that a man who had punished others without trial ought not himself be allowed the privilege of speech'.[14] Prior to the end of the year, both Nepos and Cato had assumed the tribunate, so Nepos was legally entitled to stop Cicero. It is quite possible that this was an attack against Cicero himself, rather than the senate, but it was, nevertheless, something that bothered Cicero personally for the rest of his life. The repercussions of the Catilinarian crisis, aside from Nepos' vindictive attack against Cicero, were felt throughout Rome.

When placed in comparison to other more serious problems, this Catilinarian conspiracy may have been nothing more than a brief military threat, but nevertheless shows how economic problems and the role of the people were integral to the political security of the *res publica*. Although Catiline may have been defeated, those concerns would overshadow politics throughout the next decade.

POMPEY IN THE EAST

While Rome was preoccupied with the trial against Murena and the Catilinarian conspiracy, Pompey was having great success against Mithridates. After Pompey had captured the Armenian capital in 65, Mithridates had escaped to the Caucasus. Although Mithridates was able to gather a small band of men together, he sought refuge with his son – unwilling to incur the wrath of the Romans who had reorganized his province, his son Manchares refused to recognize him. After killing his son, Mithridates took over his throne and ordered the conscription of thousands of Scythians, but his other son, Pharnaces II, soon organized another revolt against his father. It was the end for Rome's most formidable foe:

> Mithridates then took out some poison that he always carried next to his sword, and mixed it. There two of his daughters . . . asked him to let them have some of the poison first, and insisted strenuously and prevented him from drinking it until they had taken some and swallowed it. The drug took effect on them at once; but upon Mithridates, although he walked around rapidly to hasten its action, it had no effect, because he had accustomed himself to other drugs by continually trying them as a means of protection . . .

> Seeing a certain Bituitus there, an officer of the Gauls, he said to him, 'I have profited much from your right arm against my enemies. I shall profit from it most of all if you will kill me, and save from the danger of being led in a Roman triumph one who has been an autocrat so many years, and the ruler of so great a kingdom, but who is now unable to die by poison because, like a fool, he has fortified himself against the poison of others. Although I have kept watch and ward against all the poisons that one takes with his food, I have not provided against that domestic poison, always the most dangerous to kings, the treachery of army, children, and friends.' Bituitus, thus appealed to, rendered the king the service that he desired.[15]

By the sword, then, Mithridates finally died. Yet, the Romans were not cruel to him in death. His body, after being embalmed by his son, was sent to Pompey as proof of his death. Indeed, Pompey 'showed Mithridates no indignity, but, on the contrary, commanded that he be buried among the tombs of his ancestors; for, feeling that his foe's enmity had been extinguished with his life, he now indulged in no vain rage against his dead body'.[16] Pharnaces was granted the kingdom of Bosporus as his reward and was enrolled as a friend and ally of the Roman people. The war in the East was over, and Pompey was quick to settle rebellious areas. Soon, he would be on his way back to Rome.

THE REMAINDER OF THE 60S

In the beginning of 62, the praetor Caesar, as Pontifex Maximus, proposed that the responsibility for the reconstruction of the temple of Jupiter be transferred to Pompey. Initially, this rebuilding was to have been under Sulla and then later, Catulus, whom Caesar now accused of embezzling public funds. Although senatorial figures came to vote, the ensuing riot and demands for Pompey's presence, caused such an uproar that serious violence was narrowly averted.

The tribune Metellus Nepos kept up the pressure and, in particular, continued his attacks against Cicero due to the execution of the Catilinarian conspirators. The senate had closed ranks in relation to the executions by announcing immunity for those involved, but the people may have felt that 'no doubt [this] merely confirmed the justice of [Nepos'] complaint'.[17] Nepos also began to propose legislation to recall Pompey. The first measure was an effort to have Pompey deal with the military threat of the Catilinarian army in Etruria, while the other was to allow Pompey to stand for the consulship *in absentia*. However, the problem in Etruria was quickly resolved as noted above, rendering Pompey's presence unnecessary.

Cato, as a fellow tribune, suggested that Nepos reconsider the motion, but Nepos 'broke out in extravagant threats and bold speeches'. The two men argued, with Cato proclaiming that 'while he lived, Pompey should not enter the city with an armed force'. Another tribune, Q. Minicius Thermus, also opposed the measure, but as Cato and Thermus tried to assert their vetoes, Nepos took the document from the clerk and began to read the plebiscite himself. When Cato took it from him, Nepos began to recite from memory. Thermus placed his hand in front of Nepos' mouth to stop him from speaking, with the result that violence broke out. Cato then took refuge in the temple of Castor and Pollux with Murena's entourage offering protection.

Nepos continued reading the bill, but in the end, Cato was successful in breaking up the meeting, thwarting Nepos' desire to pass his legislation. The senate then met to discuss whether Nepos should be stripped of his tribunate, but Cato argued that Nepos should retain his position. Meanwhile, Nepos called a public meeting and denounced both Cato and the senate, but whatever further assistance Pompey might have relied on from Nepos came to nothing as the tribune fled from the city. Wiseman's comments is particularly apt:

> Nepos had to explain how, with much popular support, a favourable political climate and the help of a troop of gladiators, he had succeeded only in making himself a laughing stock and Cato a hero. It must have given Pompey food for deep thought on who his friends should be.[18]

Cato then turned to another fellow tribune, L. Marius, to secure passage of his own plebiscite requiring those who had requested triumphs to report the number of enemy slain as well as those Romans killed, in an effort to curtail abuses of the system of awarding triumphs for minor successes. Cato also introduced a *lex frumentaria*, lowering the price of grain, but recognizing senatorial approval for his actions, went through the customary procedure in proposing and passing his measure. This *lex frumentaria* has usually been attributed to senatorial influence, but such legislation was also a tribunate mainstay in currying favour. Indeed, 'after Cato's law, the number of recipients must have been virtually doubled by its measure. This means that Cato, perhaps surprisingly, should have a greater place in the history of corn distributions that he is normally accorded . . .'.[19]

Cato was quite conscious of how to utilize the tribunate for popular gain and, furthermore, illustrated that popular measures could be passed with senatorial approval. As well, his restraint against Nepos would have had a great effect on the populace: his 'refusal' to depose Nepos showed Cato's own unwillingness to present himself in the same light as Tiberius Gracchus. It has, however, been widely suggested that Cato's *lex frumentaria* was merely a senatorial attempt to curtail urban unrest, but there are plenty of other reasons for Cato to have passed his measure. Aside from his own popular support, there were still problems with the grain supply in Rome. For all of Pompey's boasts that he had cleared the Mediterranean of pirates, there 'was still a need for L. Flaccus to be diligent against pirates when he governed Asia in 62', illustrating that grain was still too expensive for the majority of the urban masses.[20]

The final remnants of the Catilinarian army were dealt with by the special appointment of L. Novius Niger as *quaestor* later in 62, which suggests that not all resistance had collapsed when the consul C. Antonius went to Etruria in January. The fact that there was some sort of continued resistance does not, however, lend too much weight to Nepos' proposal to recall Pompey, as it was in the early part of 62, not during the summer, that his measure had been announced.

As the year drew to a close, there were definite signs of an increasing shift in support away from the older *boni* to a younger generation. The five leading senatorial figures who had been active at the beginning of the 60s were now either inactive in senatorial matters, such as Lucullus or Hortensius, or in the cases of Metellus Pius, Lepidus and Catulus (in 61), they were dead. The new generation that came to prominence was also a small group, but its influence should not be underestimated.

This new crowd consisted of Cato, his son-in-law L. Calpurnius Bibulus, and his two brothers-in-law, L. Domitius Ahenobarbus (married to Porcia) and the consul of 62, Silanus, who was married to Cato's half-sister Servilia. Other lesser figures included M. Favonius and the future consul of 48, P. Servilius Isauricus, who married Cato's niece in 60. Two members of the older set still assisted: L. Licinius Lucullus, when he famously came out of retirement to protest against the ratification of Pompey's Eastern treaties, and, although not active in the senate, the orator Hortensius continued to assert his dominance in the law courts throughout the 50s BCE. The new *boni* were to occupy the consulship and other august offices, uniting against those who were trying to impose their own wishes on the state. Although perhaps somewhat simplistic in their approach, Cato's circle were trying to establish some sort of balance between the needs of the *res publica* and the individual. The real fear of this generation was that of another Sulla trying to secure power, and in 62 it appeared that this worry was centred around Pompey.

Cato's primary aim in the later 60s BCE seems to be a calculated effort at curtailing the ambitious plans of prominent individuals, in particular, Pompey. When Pompey did finally return to Rome in 62, he immediately dismissed his army and divorced his wife, Mucia, who was the half-sister of the ex-tribune Metellus Nepos, who had failed him. He established himself at his Alban villa, waiting for his eventual triumph and watching matters unfold in Rome.

Meanwhile, there were two issues before the senate: the request of the Asian tax collectors to reduce the amount owed and the ratification of Pompey's Eastern *acta* (settlements). Tax collectors routinely bid on the revenue that they would collect from provincials – they agreed an amount with the senate, and then went to the region to collect the monies. It was such a lucrative business, where fortunes could be made, that it was usual for individuals to band together and bid as high an amount as possible to secure the contract. In this situation, however, years of wars and drought meant that in Asia the revenues did not flow as easily and, supported by Crassus, the tax-collectors approached the senate for a reduction of the monies that they would have to give to the treasury.

Regarded by Cicero as 'a scandalous affair, a disgraceful request and a confession of foolhardiness', senatorial business had come to a stop with the matter of the tax collectors.[21] Cato, infamous for his filibustering, had monopolized the debate. Cicero's frustration (and Cato's effectiveness) is clearly illustrated by a subsequent letter, where he rages:

> It is now three months that he has been worrying those wretched tax-collectors, who used to be great friends of his, and won't let the senate give them an answer. So, we are forced to suspend all decrees on other subjects until the tax-collectors have had an answer.[22]

By June 60 Cato had resisted and carried the day. The tax collectors were rebuffed. Caesar, however, in his consulship of 59, would resolve the matter within the first days of office in favour of the tax-collectors, much to the pleasure of Crassus.

Around this time as well, Rome was gripped by the infamous Bona Dea scandal, where the young quaestor-designate and patrician P. Clodius Pulcher had gained entrance to the sacred rites of the goddess Bona Dea held in Caesar's household; as a female-only rite, his presence was taboo. Adding to the scandal, Clodius had apparently disguised himself in women's clothing, thereby ensuring that tongues would be wagging even more. The ensuing scandal 'dominated Roman politics throughout the first months of 61, largely eclipsing Pompey's homecoming, and it very nearly destroyed Clodius' career'.[23] The subsequent trial, of which the details are largely unknown, secured Clodius' acquittal. Plutarch, in his *Life of Cato Minor*, records Cato's annoyance and the story that Clodius fled from the city. While the first may be true, it is unlikely that Clodius did flee. Cato, as a *quindecemvir*, would have had reason to argue that charges be brought against the young patrician and did protest when the measure dealing with the composition of the jury for Clodius' trial was thwarted by manoeuvres in the senate, even 'slapping' the consul Piso, if, as Cicero remarks, 'one can say 'slap in the face' of an utterance full of dignity, full of authority, and full of saving consul'.[24] The acquittal followed extensive bribery on Clodius' behalf.

In the usual summer elections of 61 for the consuls of 60, there was again massive bribery, even though two decrees were proposed and passed by Cato and his brother-in-law L. Domitius Ahenobarbus regarding bribery agents. Even the tribune Lurco presented another measure, but as it was published during the time between the election notices and the elections themselves, it was disallowed.[25] L. Afranius, who owed his political success to Pompey's patronage, and Metellus Celer were elected consuls. Pompey was also finally able to celebrate his third triumph in September 61.

January 60 saw Pompey try to present his Eastern settlements, but Afranius was proving to be a dismal failure at acting in Pompey's interests, and while the tribune L. Flavius introduced an agrarian law to resettle Pompey's veterans, the senate remained suspicious. Cato, along with Lucullus, mobilized the *boni* regarding the issue of Pompey's Eastern *acta*. Both men refused to allow the treaties to be dealt with as a whole package. By June, the *boni* had again been victorious and both the Asian tax-collectors and the question of the *lex agraria* had been shelved, albeit temporarily.

It was during this time that Pompey approached Cato, saying that he was interested in marrying one of his nieces, but Cato rebuffed his offer. Furthermore, a wedge had been driven between the two men with Cato's continued opposition to his ratification of the Eastern *acta* and Pompey was driven to seek assistance elsewhere, particularly as the consul Afranius had proved so useless. In mid-60, the pro-praetor Julius Caesar returned from Spain, desiring both a triumph and possible candidature for the upcoming consular elections.

The senate, influenced no doubt greatly by Cato, refused to allow Caesar to announce his bid for elections while still holding *imperium* (military command). Caesar decided to forgo his triumph and presented himself in the city proper as a candidate for the consulship of 59 BCE. Was this when Caesar approached Crassus and Pompey in order to form an alliance? Whatever measures both Crassus and Pompey had presented to the senate, these had been completely rejected by the *boni*; the most vocal opponent was Cato, who was the leader of this influential circle.

It was following the debate on 5 December, that Cato had clearly 'emerged as leader of the [*optimate*] coalition that controlled the senate'. Leadership of the *boni* had been the domain of a small, select circle that had included Catulus and Hortensius, but both had seen their power corroded throughout the 60s, particularly in response to popular and public support for Pompey. Others, such as Lucullus, Metellus Pius and M. Lepidus, had also been pushed aside by Pompey and public demand. The decimation wrought by Sulla both during the civil wars and the subsequent proscriptions had manifested itself into a weaker senate as well as a paucity of eligible consular figures. Not surprisingly, there were no consuls from the 80s BCE who had survived into subsequent decades still politically active[26]. Furthermore, the very prestige of the senate itself had significantly decreased over the decade as well. Attacks by various tribunes against the pre-eminence of the senate and frustrated attempts by consular figures to control the urban masses had also had repercussions.

Simply put, Catulus was dead and neither Hortensius or Lucullus appear to have had the political acumen and influence that Cato enjoyed in this period. Cato was without a doubt leader of the *boni* element in the senate and his filibustering ways had become famous. He had introduced a *lex frumentaria* that had greatly resolved urban unrest and was trying his best to preserve traditional Roman practices. That he was unsuccessful in the late part of the 50s is an indicator of what was at stake, and how the combined efforts of Pompey, Caesar and Crassus were temporarily successful in achieving their goals.

One should consider how the 60s had begun, filled with such promise, but had been destroyed by the rampant bribery, corruption and mismanagement by the senate and provincial figures throughout the decade. The darling of the people, Pompey, was now having problems in passing his legislation, while Caesar realized that he had been unable to capitalize completely on his own newly acquired popular support. Crassus may have had the money, but lacked the political power to assist his supporters. Cato had, in fact, emerged as the moral and political leader of the *boni* in the senate, but his unwillingness to compromise could be construed as unrealistic and destructive. One could argue that it was the excessive demands of Pompey, Crassus and Caesar that would stretch the Republican system of government to its limit in the next decade, but they are not wholly to blame. On the verge of this new decade, Cato was one of the most influential and powerful figures in the senate who would compete against the triumvirs.

6

A First Triumvirate? Rome in the early 50s BCE

By 59 BCE, the stage was set for conflict. Neither Pompey nor Crassus had been successful in obtaining senatorial approval for their various schemes – Pompey for the settlement of his Eastern *acta*, while Crassus' patronage of the Asian tax collectors was in jeopardy as the senate, led by Cato, continued to resist their demands for a reduction in the amount of tax due. It was the young Julius Caesar who offered an alternative to the obstructionist senate by suggesting that the three men combine their talents to try and remove such obstacles. Together, it was assumed, they could circumvent any difficulties and get their legislation passed.

The term 'triumvirate' has been used a great deal to describe the relationship between the three men, but the difficulty is that it invites comparison with the later official, formal agreement in the late 40s/30s BCE that consisted of Augustus, Mark Antony and Lepidus as they sought to consolidate control in post-Caesarian Rome. This previous agreement was neither formal nor official, but instead was a loosely accepted alliance between Pompey, Caesar and Crassus to deal with the immediate impediments to their plans. It was an extremely fluid arrangement that shifted and changed over time and, ultimately, collapsed, at first with Crassus' death in 53 and later, with the gradual distrust between Pompey and Caesar from 52 onwards. It is perhaps better to describe this pact as *ad hoc* at best, with the term 'triumvirs' used to demonstrate its unofficial stance. That there was such an agreement is attested to by later authors such as Appian and Plutarch, who drew heavily on the contemporary historian, Pollio, who dated the beginning of his history of the late Republic (now lost) to 59 BCE. The allegiance was acknowledged by other contemporaries such as Cicero, who at first had congratulated Cato for his filibustering, but by 60/59 was increasingly wary of the alliance between Pompey, Caesar and Crassus, blaming Cato for driving the three together.

It was actually Caesar who had been the unknown quantity of 61 and 60 BCE. At odds with many of Rome's other senatorial figures, his tactics alarmed and frightened his colleagues: from the wide-scale bribery against Catulus in the contest for Pontifex Maximus to his disruptive praetorship, nobody was certain exactly what Caesar would do as consul nor how he would achieve his goals. There are examples of Caesar's predisposition towards gaining Pompey's favour: he had first sided with Nepos in 62 and later sought to transfer the restoration of the Capitoline temple to Pompey. With the refusal of the senate to agree to his candidature *in absentia* for the consulship in 59, Caesar had abandoned his triumph. He was not to accede to such senatorial requests again.

The elections for 59 had seen rampant bribery, but, in the end, Caesar and Bibulus were successful. Hopes that Bibulus might be able to restrain his colleague were, however, extremely short-lived. Cato's distrust of Caesar was well known even before the year began, but relations between the two men during this particular year were to result in imprisonment, riots and threats. Thus, there was a foreboding atmosphere of general unrest even before Caesar and Bibulus entered office. When the news of the informal arrangement between Pompey, Crassus and Caesar became known, there was chaos not just in the senate, but also in the street. The pro-Caesarian and anti-Caesarian forces, ironically personified by the split between the two consuls themselves, would remind Rome of the time of Sulla with all its uncertainty, confusion and disruption. It was not a happy memory.

THE YEAR 59 BCE: THE CONSULSHIP OF 'JULIUS AND CAESAR'?

The first legislation that Caesar introduced in early January 59 BCE was a *lex agraria*; both its presentation and its reception would be volatile, setting the stage for an extremely contentious year. Not just the threat of violence, but actual riots and violence in its passage, along with rejection of tribunate vetoes as well as his co-consul's own disapproval, would characterize not just this legislation, but all of Caesar's efforts throughout his consulship. Humorously nicknamed 'the consulship of Julius and Caesar', as opposed to the usual practice of listing both consuls' names, this moniker is particularly apt, but more damning of Caesar than his consular colleague.[1] Caesar may have wanted to appear benevolent and predisposed towards the masses, but his actions here illustrate his complete disregard for constitutional and accepted Roman political tradition and practice. His *lex agraria* itself illustrates this contradiction as it was usually a tribune, not a consul, who concerned himself with agrarian legislation.

The main provisions of the agrarian bill, however, were straightforward: communal lands (excepting Campania), along with lands purchased with the proceeds of Pompey's *acta*, would be redistributed to both Pompey's veterans as well as other urban dwellers. Although a commission of 20 men would oversee the resettlement, Caesar excluded himself from membership. On the surface, this legislation was not ground-breaking, but the disaster was in its attempted passage.[2]

Caesar initially sought approval from the senate but, almost immediately, opposition was led by his co-consul, Bibulus, who anticipated the vetoes of three tribunes in an attempt to try and block the bill.[3] Furthermore, Cato, with one of his usual filibusters, argued that there would be no innovation in this year. Furious, Caesar had Cato imprisoned, but when a number of other senatorial colleagues voiced their disapproval, as they followed Cato out, Caesar was forced to rely on a tribune to set him free.[4] It is quite clear that 'the majority distrusted Caesar and admired Cato; when Cato opposed the bill on principle ... they followed his lead'.[5]

Turning then to the people, Caesar threatened the use of Pompey's veterans and invited both Pompey and Crassus onto the rostra, so they could speak in support of his measure. The three tribunes attempted to interpose their vetoes at the same time that Bibulus came to the Forum, trying to speak against the legislation. His *fasces* were broken in the ensuing violence, symbolically destroying his consular power, while a basket of dung was thrown over his head. Throughout the jeers, Bibulus continued to protest, but was taken to safety in the shrine of Jupiter Stator. Meanwhile, Cato 'who always entered with zest into a fight in the assembly', also tried to speak against the measure, but was forced to take refugee inside the Temple of Castor and Pollux.[6] In this 'enforced absence of the opposition', the measure passed, but with a catch: an oath was added which required the senators to uphold its measures'.[7]

The bill's passage was condemned by Bibulus and others, who argued that it was in violation of the auspices as well as tribunate vetoes, but neither constitutional method of obstruction had been acknowledged by Caesar. While many continued to protest, particularly against the inserted senatorial oath, in the end, they were forced into agreement. Despite this opposition and the general resistance from the senate, Caesar had triumphed, but at what cost? In the first instance, Caesar had deviated from his plan to appear magnanimous, his reputation suffered greatly as a result of this legislative fiasco. Second, he had completely alienated his co-consul as well as Cato and other members of the senate. Finally, and perhaps most importantly, Caesar had clearly demonstrated that under duress, he would utilize the threat of violence to implement his measures. Essentially, Caesar had shown what he was capable of and that if the *res publica* would not facilitate *him*, he would be more than happy to disregard it.

Although Pompey may have supported Caesar's measure, he was particularly conscious of his own reputation. Cicero remarks several times on Pompey's unhappiness during this period, and it is clear that the ex-consul was unused to such public scorn and hatred.[8] If Caesar was worried about Pompey's loyalty at this time, one move that would cement their continued friendship was marriage

Bust of Caesar

between the two families: Pompey was to marry Caesar's daughter Julia. While there may have been political manipulation by Caesar in proposing such a marital contract, it is clear that the match was ultimately one of love. It indeed bonded the two families together, but at the same time, provided fodder and amusement as Pompey was enchanted by the young woman. The marriage also served another purpose, perhaps not envisaged at the time – Pompey was to increasingly absent himself from senatorial business, not just from disapproval at Caesar's actions, but also to spend more time at home with his young bride. At the same time, Caesar married Calpurnia, the daughter of Lucius Calpurnius Piso, who was to be elected one of the two consuls for 58 BCE, with Caesar's blessing.

There may have been some physical threats against Pompey at this time, but they do not appear to be very serious. In an effort to discredit the young Curio, who alone was voicing disapproval against Pompey and Crassus, some sort of plot to assassinate Pompey was revealed.[9] The informer Vettius, allegedly working for Caesar, became friendly with Curio and declared that the young man was threatening to slay Pompey. However, Curio told his father of these allegations, who in turn reported this to the senate. Vettius was brought before the senate. He repeated his allegations, but his incoherent ramblings accusing different individuals and assertions of asking Bibulus for a dagger to do the deed caused much amusement among those listening. In fact, as Bibulus himself had warned Pompey on 13 May to be 'on his guard against plots', any credibility that Vettius may have had was destroyed. Cicero remarks that Caesar brought Vettius back the following day to the senate, where the plot was again discussed, but with omission of the same names that he had been so sure of the day before. In the end, Vettius was himself prosecuted and suffered an ignominious end, dying in prison. Another even more ludicrous event took place on 11 August, when a slave of Clodius' was apprehended carrying a dagger; that he dropped it in full sight outside of the senate building worried nobody, but Pompey 'reacted remarkably', he went home and locked his doors for the rest of the year.[10]

It is alleged that the infamous Vettius affair was an attempt to isolate Pompey from the *boni*, thereby even further consolidating the relationship between Pompey and Caesar, as Pompey may have increasingly felt he could only rely on Caesar for his personal safety, while the latter event may have been staged by Clodius for maximum effect, as he was prone to exaggerate any measures for his own publicity. In fact, some scholars have argued that Clodius may have been responsible for both thwarted attempts, but it is quite clear, at least to Cicero, that Vettius was working for Caesar.[11] It may perhaps be a weakness of Pompey's to fear such physical attacks, but Caesar was more than happy to exploit it.

As mentioned before, it was this threat of violence amidst the continued attempts by Bibulus and others to reject other elements of Caesar's legislation that would characterize his consulship. The year 59 BCE continued as it had begun: Caesar's reputation would suffer as his senatorial colleagues continued to voice their opposition in different ways. In another effort to stymie Caesar's efforts, Bibulus announced in April or May that he would retreat to his home to watch the skies for omens, thereby technically invalidating all of Caesar's legislation; Caesar, however, paid him no attention and pushed on with his legislative programme, although he actually presented nothing to the senate after this first *lex agraria*. Instead, he went straight to the assemblies. These first few months saw Ptolemy's succession secured in Egypt with a sizable bribe of which one half was shared by the triumvirs; the contracts of the publicans had been revised and by April, the land commission had been elected, among those in charge was Pompey. Pompey's Eastern *acta* were quite possibly ratified sometime in May, while Caesar's post-consular provincial command was revised through the assistance of the tribune Vatinius. In this particular instance, the senate, however, did approve the additional province of Transalpine Gaul. This may have been an attempt to pacify Caesar but, unfortunately, it was to no avail.

While the opposition could not stop Caesar, it did not mean he had an easy time. Bibulus may have been at home, but he continued to issue edicts against his co-consul and soon there were numerous personal and public verbal attacks against the triumvirs. Fortunately, Cicero's letters are particularly enlightening about the placards, signs and graffiti that littered the Forum as well as the increasing public distaste for Caesar. During July, in fact, when entering gladiatorial games, the crowd cheered and roared for Curio, but when Caesar entered, their silence indicated their displeasure. Meanwhile, Bibulus was exalted while Pompey's reputation was shattered.[12] Pompey, appearing on 25 July, delivered a speech against Bibulus' edicts, but was greeted with scorn and derision. Bibulus, relying on his popularity, was trying to delay elections until October, which would be one of his months to control the consulship. Caesar tried to incite the people against his colleague, but was unable to get any support. His *contio* (public meeting) against Bibulus was not very well-attended and Caesar may have been surprised at the public demonstration of support for his co-consul, with strong negative feelings voiced for him and his own actions. In fact, Cicero remarks that '[the triumvirs] feel that they have lost the goodwill of all parties; and so violent action on their part is all the more to be feared'.[13]

However, it was not just Curio who spoke out against the triumvirs, others soon joined in, as the historian Wirszubski has noted:

> Varro launched against the triumvirate a pamphlet entitled *The Three-headed Monster* (*Tricaranus*). The elder Curio in his speeches assailed Caesar's private and public life . . .(while) the young C. Cato, in a public speech', called Pompey 'privatus dictator'.[14]

As the threesome watched their popularity decline sharply, the opposition found strength. Bibulus had tried to impede the *comitia* as early as April, and by May, regardless of the marriage between Pompey and Julia, Cicero was able to categorize Caesar as 'clearly setting up a tyranny'.[15] The people 'are now venting their opinion and their disapproval openly and loudly', but there was no remedy to be had.[16] As the summer continued, Caesar was unsure how to proceed 'being unused to unpopularity . . . he sees to advance is dangerous, to retreat a confession of weakness, nobody is his friend'.[17] Although Caesar wanted to be restored to his previous high position, he had no idea how to mollify both his critics and the public.[18] By the end of the year, the public had had their say against Caesar; he was universally denigrated and despised.

At the end of 59 BCE, the long delayed elections finally took place. Although there had been rumours of Pompey and Crassus possibly seeking the consulship, their own political positions were precarious. Instead two others were chosen – Caesar's new father-in-law, L. Calpurnius Piso and the Pompeian ex-tribune of 67 BCE, Aulus Gabinius. Although a prosecution against Gabinius for electoral bribery was mounted, it failed. Meanwhile, threats against Caesar for his illegal actions began to rise when Clodius was installed as tribune in late December 59. Joining with Clodius, two praetors-designate were soon to voice their own determination to bring Caesar to account for his unconstitutional behaviour. One was C. Memmius, while the other was the future consul of 54 BCE, L. Domitius

Ahenobarbus, who was also Cato's brother-in-law. Unfortunately, other members of the senate refused to involve themselves, but perhaps this reluctance may simply be because they wanted the year to end and for Caesar to disappear into his province. The old cliché 'out of sight, out of mind' may indeed apply here. There was an effort to prosecute the tribune Vatinius for his involvement, but this was ultimately unsuccessful.

Yet another newly elected tribune, L. Antistius, did step forward with charges against Caesar, but Caesar was untouchable – first, due to the *imperium* that he held as consul, and afterwards when he immediately assumed the provincial *imperium* that his five-year command in Gaul carried. Although Caesar remained outside the city of Rome for a few months, the speed in which he left the consulship and acquired his proconsular *imperium* does open the door to suggestions that Caesar was more afraid of retribution than he would later admit. His critics openly mocked Caesar for his flight, which saw him secure his command within hours.

Although the consular year ended with Clodius' refusal to allow Bibulus to make the customary end of term oration, this may have been a reaction against the conduct of the consulship rather than a personal attack against Bibulus himself, particularly as early in 58 BCE Clodius invited Bibulus to a public *contio* in order to present evidence regarding charges against Caesar. Both the reputations of Caesar and Pompey had emerged in tatters, while Bibulus and his father-in-law Cato were unscathed by the turmoil of the year. Caesar's consulship was to end in a complete rearrangement of both the *res publica* as well as political alliances. While the year may have ended relatively peacefully, 59 clearly illustrated how it was not just the threat of violence that was utilized by Caesar, it was instead an almost daily occurrence. Caesar's opposition could not resolve issues through the courts, but were instead forced to mount a publicity campaign against him.

THE YEAR 58 – CLODIUS' TRIBUNATE

The only real winner of 59 BCE was perhaps Clodius, as he had benefited by Caesar's support in seeking adoption to the plebeian registry, which in turn resulted in his being allowed to stand for the tribunate. Clodius effectively used both sides of the political divide as he utilized 'the propaganda of the Catonians themselves against the triumvirate' and 'railed against the legislation of Caesar as having violated the religious sanctions and constitutional traditions.'[19] Clodius, in effect, should be considered his own man, with his own ideas and his own agenda.

It is necessary to take a further, more detailed look at Clodius at this stage, because as tribune he had become a political force to be reckoned within his own right. It has been customary to characterize Clodius as a tool of the triumvirs, as one standard history claims 'the triumvirs next used Clodius to remove from Rome two men whose presence was embarrassing: Cicero and Cato'.[20] Yet, Clodius' behaviour following his adoption was anything but positive or supportive of Caesar and, in particular, his verbal attacks and threats against Pompey argue towards an entirely different interpretation of Clodius' relationship with the triumvirs.

Modern scholars fortunately have begun to view Clodius separately from the Ciceronian perspective, which has been extremely valuable.[21] The portrait that now emerges is that of an extremely ambitious, politically motivated and well-connected young man who relied on both the people and his own aristocratic contacts to achieve political office. This reappraisal of Clodius presents an interesting dichotomy. If a more moderate view of Clodius is gaining acceptance, then the conventional motivations for Clodius' actions and behaviour become more difficult to sustain. This opens up a whole new avenue for exploration and allows the modern scholar to view Clodius entirely differently, which in turn, allows for a new interpretation of his behaviour, his alliances and, ultimately, his tribunate.

The measure against *obnuntiatio* (observing the auspices, performed by Bibulus to prevent Caesar passing any legislation) was proposed by Clodius in early 58 BCE more to regulate its practice rather than a specific attack against Bibulus; its composition clarified how and when such methods could be employed. The public *contio* to which Clodius summoned Bibulus was not an attack against him, but more likely against Caesar.[22] This *contio* offered public proof that Caesar's legislation was considered invalid by a number of individuals, although in the event none were repealed. Ironically, Clodius appears more as a defender of the constitution than simply a rogue demagogue bent on the destruction of the state.[23] One aspect of his legislation was that any magistrate utilizing the practice of *obnuntiatio* had to announce their objections in person – not just through *servatio* (notices) – as Bibulus had. In 57, there was the amusing tale of the consul Metellus Nepos 'skulking' through the back streets to try and prevent Milo from reaching the aedilician elections to postpone them by *obnuntiatio*.[24] If Clodius had wanted to attack Bibulus, as he was to do with Cicero, he could have made the measure retroactive, but there is no mention of this.

Clodius embarked on various legislation at the beginning of 58.[25] His four main measures (including that against *obnuntiatio*, discussed above) also included limiting the censors' powers in excluding individuals from the senate to only when both censors were in agreement, introducing a free corn distribution for citizens and removing the ban on *collegia*. This last act would have serious repercussions as political figures could then legally recruit gangs of supporters, and such violence became even more commonplace not just during this year but throughout the rest of the decade. The corn dole, on the other hand, was a traditional tribunate gesture – Cato in 62 BCE had proposed a reduction in corn prices during his own tribunate – and Clodius' actions in this regard, while more substantive than previous corn measures, was neither unknown or unusual.

In February, charges were brought by Caesar's opponents, not against Caesar, who enjoyed proconsular *imperium*, but against the tribune of 59, P. Vatinius, who 'shared responsibility with Caesar for the tumultuous legislation' of this year.[26] Vatinius was, however, absent from the city as a legate to Caesar, but he dramatically waived his judicial immunity by returning to Rome to stand trial. The praetor C. Memmius then began preparations for the proceedings and Vatinius sought Clodius' assistance. It is argued that the ensuing violence and abandonment of the trial was evidence of Clodius' support of the triumvirs, but there is also another possibility, which allows Clodius to emerge unscathed from the 'triumvirs' agent' appellation.[27] Vatinius had been a legally elected popular tribune and if he was attacked for his actions during his tribunate, then the same charges could then be levelled against Clodius at any time following the completion of *his* tribunate. It was therefore imperative for Clodius to try and stop this prosecution. It was not out of any loyalty to the triumvirs, Clodius was instead looking after his own interests and should be considered as such. The trial never proceeded and Vatinius returned to Caesar, with perhaps a sigh of relief from both the ex-tribune and ex-consul; in essence, their legislation was safe. Clodius was then free to turn his attention to Cicero and Cato, but the relationships between Clodius and Cicero and Clodius and Cato could not be more distinct or different.

CLODIUS AND CICERO

Whether or not it is believed that the triumvirs had any influence on Clodius, one particular relationship of his does not need to reassessed: that with Cicero. It is remarkable how the negative relationship between Clodius and Cicero has coloured modern interpretation on Roman politics. It has created a complexity that is not necessary, which is quite misleading for a modern understanding of this period. Clodius' legislation and actions cannot be construed as merely behaviour of a rogue demagogue, regardless how Cicero might characterize him. This is of fundamental importance when reappraising Clodius and his political career. He did utilize gangs and the threat of armed violence, but he was a legally elected official. The fact that Cicero feared him cannot be used as the main criteria towards an analysis of Clodius' character.

It is clear that Clodius had despised Cicero since the latter publicly attacked his actions and behaviour following the infamous Bona Dea scandal in late 62, and it may have been this that led Clodius to seek revenge. His retaliation was a piece of

Clodius (coin)

carefully crafted legislation. He did not attack Cicero in the middle of the night, nor use illegal methods to destroy his enemy. His hatred was personal, but he was in the position as a tribune to act on his impulses. Perhaps that was the problem. Cicero is viewed by the modern world from a variety of perspectives, including that of a philosopher, but his incessant reminders of how he had saved the *res publica* grated on many contemporary nerves. He tried to impose a seniority that was neither appreciated nor recognized. Cicero thought he could mould politics with reason and logic, but the fact is that his moment of glory had passed. He might consider himself leader of the *boni* since Catulus' death, but it was Cato, not Cicero, who influenced this small but important circle of senatorial figures.

The problem was Cicero: he did not fit in anywhere. Caesar had recognized that Clodius posed a threat, offering Cicero a position on his staff, but Cicero had declined. He complained to Atticus of his fear about Clodius, to which Pompey had been sympathetic until Clodius' gangs began to focus on Pompey, but Cicero was unable to do anything. The *boni* simply did not trust Cicero and while they made the right sounds in relation to Clodius' legislation, they did not overturn his proposals. Cicero would have to suffer Clodius, not just because he was Cicero, but because there was no real popular support for the ex-consul. The execution of the five senatorial figures had been a stain on the *res publica*, and Cicero was to pay the price.

Personal vendettas were not unknown in republican politics. The animosity between Crassus and Pompey is legendary, while Cato's hatred of Caesar had its repercussions as well. The difficulty is how Cicero has been viewed in the modern arena and thus an attack by anyone, in particular Clodius, is suspect. In turn, Clodius then becomes the personification of Cicero's fears; in essence, Clodius is equated with Catiline. Clodius further is categorized as an evil entity and, as such, it is therefore easier to assign only nefarious intentions for all of his actions, but Cicero's reasoning *en masse* cannot be supported. Clodius was an intelligent and clever politician, he in turn could argue that his attacks against Cicero, while personally motivated, were nevertheless important to restore stability. After all, the legislation of the most famed tribune, C. Gracchus, had been ignored. It was Clodius who would reaffirm the Roman citizenship with one of its main attributes – freedom from execution – stressed and emphasized.

Clodius proposed a bill that outlawed anyone who had put any Roman citizen to death without a trial, but made it retroactive: it was aimed at Cicero. Again, the response of the senate is puzzling. The execution of the five alleged senatorial conspirators had been agreed by the senate and was under the umbrella of the *senatus consultum ultimum*, long recognized as a temporary measure of martial law. While there were murmurs of protest, perhaps it was easier to sacrifice Cicero for the moment in order that stability might be re-established in Rome.

Cicero went into exile immediately, without waiting for the law to be passed. He had feared Clodius throughout 59, as can be seen in his letters and appeals to Pompey, and perhaps Cicero felt in extreme danger, hence his flight. Clodius then confiscated Cicero's property, which burnt down prior to its auction. Having somebody else bid for the site, Clodius began to build a temple while Cicero could only hear of this with dismay. His recall in 57 would demonstrate a time when it was Pompey, not Clodius, who controlled popular support and the senate. Cicero, nevertheless, would continue to fear Clodius until the latter was killed along the *via Appia* in early 52 BCE.

CATO'S ANNEXATION OF CYPRUS

The other puzzling dilemma is the relationship between Clodius and Cato. If new analysis, particularly within the last 20 years, has rehabilitated Clodius, none have been complimentary regarding Cato. This poses a problem. The main assumption is that although Clodius should be viewed as a separate entity, it is still argued that it was with the triumvirs in mind that Clodius sought to remove Cato from the city and its politics. If, however, it is accepted that Clodius was *not* an agent of the triumvirs, there can be no real reason why then Clodius targeted Cato. Perhaps the simplest explanation is that Clodius felt Cato might pose a problem for him during his tribunate, particularly as Cato enjoyed strong popular support as a result of his *lex frumentaria* during his own tribunate in 62, and perhaps it was easier to remove Cato with an honorary command. With Clodius, however, the simplest and easiest explanation is not always the only reason.

Why exactly did Clodius propose that Cato be placed in charge of the annexation of Cyprus? It has been suggested that there were two main reasons for this measure: first, it would bind Cato to Clodius so that the latter could rely on Cato if there were any attempts to repeal or invalidate the Clodian legislation *en masse*, and second, that Cato himself would be out of the city, which would in turn allow the triumvirs to control Roman politics. Plutarch notes that Cato saw through Clodius' actions, but this may be a later interpretation, particularly given the Ciceronian colouring of Clodius. The difficulty with such a narrow interpretation is that it ignores a number of other factors and assumes an antagonistic relationship between the two men as well as characterizing Clodius as merely a tool for the triumvirs. Although Cicero later remarks that Clodius had shown a letter from Caesar congratulating Clodius for successfully removing Cato, this may not contradict the hypotheses that Clodius was an independent agent.[28] Caesar may indeed have sent a letter, but it is apparent that Clodius was working on his own agenda, not Caesar's.

If it is accepted that Clodius was not working on the instructions of the triumvirs, then a whole new avenue of possibilities opens up about the dynamics of 58 BCE. First, it is possible that Cato and Clodius could have been more closely related than has been previously explored; they were at the very least of a similar age and were of the same generation.[29] Second, while Cato and Clodius sparred on occasion, there is no evidence that there was any lasting animosity between the two men, regardless of Cicero's accusations in the mid-50s.[30] Furthermore, there is evidence that Cato and Clodius worked together as allies on a number of measures. Finally, throughout the 50s, while Pompey and, of course, Cicero, were targets for Clodius and his gangs, there is no information regarding any such attacks by Clodius towards Cato. In particular, their united distrust of Caesar is clear, as both threatened to prosecute him for his illegal activities – malpractice – during his consulship.

There are still perhaps difficulties in establishing the relationship between the two men, but this need not be a major problem. They may have fundamentally agreed on many issues, but were kept from real cooperation not just because of their opposing political views, but also because of the methods that each employed to succeed in the political arena. It is well known that Cato was disgusted with Clodius' behaviour following the Bona Dea scandal, and therefore, it is reasonable to suggest that the two men publicly disagreed, but nevertheless, a lasting enmity does not seem to have developed. Yet, why is this important? Does it really matter what Clodius and Cato's relationship was or is it more convenient to accept the traditional view?

It is actually quite important to re-evaluate both Cato and Clodius, both in relation to this year and their overall association. It is quite clear that Clodius was not a tool of the triumvirs as evidenced by his behaviour from mid-59 onwards; therefore, his proposal for Cato to annex Cyprus was not part of their overall plan. Other reasons must accordingly be recognized for Clodius' actions and mere animosity cannot be the simple explanation.

It is the *lex Clodia de imperio* that has great significance. This extraordinary command confirmed Cato as *pro quaestore pro praetore* in order that he might supervise the annexation of Cyprus. While on the surface this might be considered unusual in that this bill appointed an ex-quaestor to a more routinely praetorian honour, it should be remembered that Cato already enjoyed prestige as a priest, which is reflected in his standing in the senate where he could speak *in loco praetorio*. Thus, while to get such an appointment was an honour conferred by Clodius' legislation, it did not bestow *imperium*, but rather added to Cato's already assumed pre-praetorian status. It was a situation where Cato's acknowledged administrative abilities, as had been seen during his quaestorship in 65, would be able to shine.

There are also many other reasons why Clodius may have proposed such a command, and indeed, for Cato to have accepted. Cato was not yet eligible for the praetorship and, with Caesar out of the city, Cato perhaps needed something significant to do during this time. He would have found himself, not of the *pedarii* (those senators without a magistracy) as such, but nevertheless, without a political office or function. Cato could have turned to the law courts, but Clodius was able to present an alternative. The two may have discussed some sort of role, but a military one might not have been welcome as Cato himself had had little military experience, but an administrative one would have been perfect for him. Cato may have accepted such a command that Clodius was offering in that it would not only utilize his considerable financial skills, but also in that it would have conferred great honour and prestige on him; furthermore, Cato was shrewd enough to recognize this. Far from removing Cato from the city as was the desired wish of the triumvirs, it was a position that he would have welcomed.

Given that there were few reported disagreements between Cato and Clodius, the idea of Clodius wishing to offer his own support to Cato is not entirely implausible. If it is accepted that the two men were not enemies, then this command should be construed as being of mutual benefit to each man. Although Cicero may have damned this appointment as a ploy by Clodius, this is not necessarily the reality. In no speeches post 55 BCE (Cato's return to Rome), is there a link between Cato/Cicero versus Clodius, which should be taken as a clear indication that Cicero had mistaken their relationship completely. If the basic facts are analysed and agreed, such as Clodius' independence from the triumvirs, then a whole new motive must be considered. Cicero is not our most reliable interpretative source as far as Clodius is concerned, and, therefore, this command must as a matter of course be viewed as a benefit to Cato as well as Clodius. It should also be remembered that such a command would confer immense influence on Cato's subsequent political career in Rome, and to assign a negative motive by Clodius is to undermine his intelligence. Clodius was not stupid and while Cato may have left the city for 18 months, he would return.

In the meantime, Cato took his command and went to Cyprus along with his nephew Brutus to coordinate and conduct the annexation of the province. This would not have been an easy task, particularly given the difficulties in both Cyrene in 74 and Crete in 66. Following attempts to reconcile Ptolemy with Egypt, Cato went to Cyprus. The end result may have greatly benefited the treasury, but he fell out with his closest friend, Munatius Rufus, who took offence at Cato's somewhat harsh administrative actions, such as talking with the purchasers himself as he did not trust others to conduct such negotiations. The two were at odds until after Cato returned to Rome in mid-56.

POST 58 BCE

The situation in Rome did not improve much following Clodius' tribunate. The removal of the ban against 'political associations' resulted in gangs roaming the streets of Rome, with Pompey apparently their target. By 56, Pompey himself looked to another young man – and another of Clodius' enemies – T. Annius Milo, who organized another gang to counter Clodius. It is particularly interesting that these two men were, in fact, senatorial figures, not some rogue element of society bent on the destruction of the state and property, but individuals who had held and would hold some of the most important political offices in Rome. This is absolutely incredible. It was not on the streets of Rome that some cut-throat or assassin stalked the ordinary people, it was the elected officials who promulgated such violent disorder. Corruption and bribery, long mainstays of electoral contests, were reaching into the hallowed senate itself, with fears among many about their own personal safety. While this is indeed remarkable, does it in fact argue towards a particularly unsafe city? Or rather, was the violence isolated against selected individuals, such as Pompey? Can one argue that this violence was not reflective of society overall, but restricted to the political arena?

Lintott, in his superb *Violence in Republican Rome*, argues convincingly that the main struggle was between Clodius and Pompey, and, therefore, whatever armed gangs roamed the streets were controlled by Clodius. He continues that 'he used limited violence (not a *coup d'etat* as the Catilinarians planned) to defeat and cow his opponents, and by adopting the forms of popular justice kept alive community solidarity among the new and heterogeneous citizens'.[31] There had been the implied threat of Pompey's veterans as Caesar passed his *lex agraria* in January 59, riots that disrupted the trial of Vatinius in early 58 and Clodius' own armed gangs, but as whole, it does not appear that anybody but Pompey and Cicero were Clodius' targets. There was the usual criminal element that changed day-time Rome to a fearful place at night, but other than isolated incidents relating to political events, the main threat apparently remained between Pompey and Clodius. Clodius was able to consolidate his own power among the urban poor who had benefited from the removal of the ban against *collegia*, his generous corn dole and those who also looked towards the senate for financial security and stability. This would be the same pool who would have supported Cato following his own *lex frumentaria* in 62 as well as, hopefully, also supporting Pompey. Clodius' manoeuvres therefore are not necessarily violence for its own sake, but rather a concentrated and deliberate attempt to marshal popular support for him and his agenda. Pompey was the most obvious individual that Clodius attacked and thus these criminal gangs were utilized for political advantage, not just random strikes against the masses. The poor and lower artisan class enjoyed the benefits that Clodius' legislation provided, and if the crowd were fickle, they were swayed to whomever promised and delivered the most. Clodius could not rely on them indefinitely, as he was to realize, when Pompey struggled to regain his own popular and senatorial support. One difficult instance, much to Clodius' fury, was the return of Cicero.

In August 57, the *comitia centuriata* finally passed a consular bill to recall Cicero. It is clear that regardless of the violence in the political arena, Pompey had finally been able to assert himself politically and have Cicero back on his side, much to the senators' distaste. In Rome there was a severe shortage of grain and Cicero approached the ex-consul, on the suggestion of various senatorial figures, regarding Pompey's taking command of the corn supply. Although Cicero may have had little overall senatorial support, nevertheless, on such an assignment Cicero would have been ideal, particularly given his friendship with Pompey. A law was drafted giving Pompey complete control of the corn supplies for a period of five years, with 15 legates to be appointed to oversee the practicalities. A tribune, Messius, however, suggested an amendment that Pompey also receive financial control of the project, a fleet and an army to assist him in this task. In the end, the first measure passed, but it did not carry *imperium*, so there were no restrictions on his remaining in Rome at any time. Two of the legates were known to be Cicero and his brother Quintus, but it would appear that only the latter performed outside the city, serving in Sardinia. By the time 57 ended, Pompey again enjoyed political and popular support, but this was not evident in the first few months of 56. His popularity seems to have come and gone as events and individuals fought for pre-eminence.

When Cicero returned from exile in 57, he delivered a number of speeches, both to the senate and the people, thanking them for recalling him from exile. In September, Cicero argued that the destruction of his house and the building of a temple by Clodius in his absence was illegal. In his speech *de domo sua*, Cicero made a scathing attack on the *res publica*, the character of Clodius and what had happened in Rome while he was away. He aligned himself with Cato and berated Clodius for his attack on Cato, stating that the Cypriot expedition was an underhanded attempt to remove Cato from the political arena. Cato's own thoughts are not known as he was not in Rome at the time.

Clodius also had further problems in 57 as the tribune T. Annius Milo started attacking him. In late November of that year, Cicero noted that Clodius was threatening the city with violence if the elections for 56 did not take place, as he was running for the aedileship. One of the consuls of 57, Lentulus Marcellinus, in turn threatened to prosecute Clodius for violence, but, of course, if Clodius secured the aedileship, he would be immune. Clodius' supporters filibustered the session, while Milo published Marcellinus' *sententia*. The matter dragged on for days, but since the elections had not taken place, there were no other officials such as praetors who would oversee such a trial in place, and therefore, no trial could be held against Clodius. Clodius was finally elected to the aedileship on 20 January 56, returned at the top of the polls.

THE YEAR 56 BCE – CATO'S RETURN AND THE ELECTIONS FOR 55

The year began without any elected officials in office, but by 20 January, as noted above, some elections had finally taken place. The first issue that concerned the senate was the infamous Egyptian question, which dominated politics in the first few months of the year. The background is simple, but its consequences in 56 were not. The fate of Ptolemy Auletes had apparently been agreed in 57, when it was proposed that Lentulus Spinther, who would be the next governor of Cilicia, was to restore the king to his throne, but Ptolemy himself refused. He wanted Pompey to return with him in order to secure his position, but there were numerous problems with this proposal. Auletes came to Rome and set about bribing anyone he thought might assist him in getting Pompey to take up his cause, but in the first instance was unsuccessful. Cicero himself was uncertain as to who deserved his support, as Spinther had been one of those who had pushed for his recall from exile, but Cicero had already shown his support for Pompey, serving as one of his legates on the grain committee. This matter continued to press for conclusion, but as February was the customary month for receiving foreign embassies, it was shelved momentarily.

Pompey, however, lost interest in Ptolemy's restoration as he turned his attention to supporting the ex-tribune Milo against charges brought by Clodius for assault. The trial, which was originally scheduled for 2 February 56, ended up taking place on the 6th. As Pompey began to speak, Clodius' gangs began shouting and generally disrupting the proceedings to such an extent that the trial had to be postponed until later in the month, most likely 17 February. A distant relation of Cato's, a C. Cato, launched a violent attack against Pompey, and it appears from Cicero's account that Pompey made charges against Crassus. Others, such as Bibulus and Curio, gave their support to the agitators – not in support of Clodius – but rather to show their contempt for Pompey himself. Cicero remarked that:

Pompey is criticized for his ingratitude to Lentulus and is really a shadow of his proper self. His patronage of Milo gives some offence to the degraded dregs of the populace, whilst the *optimates* find as much fault with what he does as what he fails to do.[32]

One really has to feel for Pompey here. In late 57 and in charge of the corn supply, Pompey is applauded, admired and respected, while just a few weeks later he is attacked both by his senatorial colleagues as well as by the general public. This is something that Pompey had to deal with throughout the decade and it does not appear that he was ever easy with his public persona, nor how to appeal to the masses. However, events in the law courts do not necessarily mean a loss of political power, and perhaps such observations by Cicero should be limited to a particular situation rather than an overall analysis of how Pompey was viewed. It is difficult using Cicero as a source in that we appreciate the immediacy of his correspondence, but an objective perspective is lacking.

In late February, a trial against the ex-tribune of 57, Sestius, occurred. The former tribune was charged on two counts: *de ambitu* (bribery) during his candidature for the tribunate; and, the use of force which violated a *lex Plautia de vi* dealing with excessive violence. As tribune, Sestius had worked with Milo for Cicero's restoration and it is fitting that the ex-consul would appear for the defence. His *pro Sestio* is a clever political speech. In it, he uses his usual legal techniques, but also addresses the concerns of the state, again attacking Clodius. Cicero had hoped that by going into voluntary exile, his actions would have avoided bloodshed and violence, but in his absence the state was ruined by Clodius (*pro sest*: 53–68). He recounts Sestius' difficulties in proposing legislation for Cicero's return and notes that without such support, Cicero himself would not have returned (69–96a). Cicero further defines the *boni* and aims to instruct the youths of Rome about various senatorial figures. He also attacks Vatinius (Caesar's tribune of 59), while appealing to the jury for compassion. With men such as Sestius, the damage to the state could be repaired. The speech had the desired effect: an acquittal was secured on 11 March 56.

It was a triumph for Cicero and the other figures who defended Sestius, such as Hortensius, Pompey and Crassus, showing that in some matters Pompey and Crassus could put aside their differences. The actuality was that the relationship between the two men was at its lowest point. It was following Sestius' trial, in the middle of April, that Caesar, Pompey and Crassus had their famous meeting at Luca. Although the 'details of what was determined at this conference are unknown ... the certain and most important result of it was an agreement between these three men to cooperate in a closer political alliance to secure certain political ends'.[33] There was some fear by the triumvirs that if L. Domitius Ahenobarbus reached the consulship in 55, he could possibly remove Caesar from his military command, which was due to expire that year; Domitius had announced that he would. Therefore, it was decided that Crassus and Pompey would run for the consulship.

However, all was not clear when the two men returned to Rome. There was a great deal of suspicion surrounding the meeting at Luca, which was increased by the evasive answers given by the two when confronted by the senate upon their return. Although only a few months elapsed between the Luca 'conference' and their announcement of running for the consulship, it was an issue that was the talk of the town at that time. The repercussions of their meeting were not only felt in the consular elections, but they also thwarted the *boni*, as Ahenobarbus was denied his consulship and the returning Cato did not get elected for the praetorship.

Another consequence of the renewed alliance between the three men could be seen as Cicero repeatedly spoke in the senate on Caesar's behalf, suggesting a renewal of his command with ten additional legates and more monies; this ultimately proved successful for Caesar, but not for Cicero himself. While Cicero might have the power and support of the triumvirs behind him, he was characterized by the *boni* as selling out. Increasingly, and to Cicero's dismay, the *boni*, among them Cato, were to distance themselves from him. The city was filled with violence and disorder, and Cicero, with his best intentions, was helping to fuel the disunity that the triumvirs inspired.

In the midst of all this, Cato triumphantly returned to Rome either in late spring, or at the latest in the early summer of 56. He had accumulated a sizable amount of monies with his integrity in financial matters intact. Plutarch's *Life of Cato Minor* may have its limitations, but it is:

> plausible in its picture of Cato's punctiliousness in realising Ptolemy's estate and transporting it to Rome. This was the task imposed on him by the senate and for the state's benefit ... Cato's command of Cyprus can be seen as an affirmation of the principle that the profits of empire should belong to the people as a whole, and that private profiteering is unacceptable; he was, moreover, remarkably efficient in raising revenue.[34]

Plutarch notes that Cato did not land to meet the assembled consuls and praetors, but 'swept past [them] on a royal galley of six oars ... and did not stop until he had brought his fleet to anchor'.[35] Some may have thought Cato ungracious, but as the treasure began to be removed from the ships, people forgot his rudeness and cheered him. Cato's account book had been lost, but he was nevertheless awarded honours by the senate, which he refused. He also asked the senate to bestow freedom on Nicias, the steward of the royal Cypriot household, which was agreed. The presiding consul for 56 was Cato's father-in-law, L. Marcius Philippus, which would have conferred additional benefit to him in trying to re-establish himself in the political arena.

The only real difficulty arose with the naming of the slaves (they would usually be called Cyprii, but Clodius, 'anxious to receive his share of the credit for Cato's successful mission, proposed that they should additionally be named Clodiani, in his own honour')[36] and Clodius began to threaten a prosecution in relation to the lost accounts, but this was probably not in earnest, as nothing came of it. It may have been nothing more than a momentary problem between the two men, as such a disagreement might have been the result of the desire of both men to achieve honour for the command. Perhaps Clodius felt that Cato was taking all of the credit for the mission to the detriment of Clodius' action in proposing him. After all, the treasures paraded through the streets of Rome would be utmost in everyone's mind, and who had brought them back, not who had sent Cato, would impress the people most. That this was a minor argument can be seen soon enough as Cato aligned with Clodius against Cicero's demand to revisit Clodius' legislation.

One criticism modern scholars have levelled at Cato is that of self-interest, in that if Clodius' legislation was annulled, then Cato's own provincial annexation of Cyprus would also be revoked. There is nothing to suggest that Cato feared such a move. Cicero may have complained on Cato's supposed behalf while Cato was away in Cyprus, but once he returned, it appears that Cato actually sought to disassociate himself from Cicero's vindictive rhetoric; at the very least, the two men were no longer linked together publicly by Cicero. Cato had achieved great honour and prestige from the Cypriot command, which would have further cemented his own political position as leader of the *boni* in the senate. Clodius, by reflection, would also gain great senatorial support as well as a secure alliance with Cato. Again, it must be noted that while there were numerous attacks against Pompey and Cicero by Clodius' gangs, there is little evidence that any were directed against Cato. Although this may be a minor point, if true, it lends further evidence to the idea of a much more amicable relationship between Cato and Clodius throughout the decade.

With Cato's reputation at an all-time high, he was determined to run for the praetorship, but there were continued problems and delays, particularly from Crassus and Pompey. The official date for handing in the nominations for the consular elections had actually passed when Pompey and Crassus finally announced their candidature, and the presiding consul, Marcellinus, refused to accept their bid. In the midst of this, one already announced consular candidate, Ahenobarbus, continued his own campaign, with notable additions to his cortege. Plutarch records that an ambush was planned against him. As the torch-bearer was slain, so were many of his supporters, with only Cato and Ahenobarbus remaining.[37] Even though Cato tried to persuade his brother-in-law to fight for his rights, Ahenobarbus finally retreated, much to the dismay of many.

THE YEAR 55 BCE – THE SECOND CONSULSHIP OF CRASSUS AND POMPEY

An *interregnum* (period without consuls) ensued in early 55 due to the disruption surrounding the elections, during which period Pompey and Crassus were eventually elected to a joint consulship, but Cato still would not yield. He decided to run for the praetorship, but was outmanoeuvred by the two consuls and was unsuccessful. There had been, as usual, extensive bribery surrounding all the elections, but an effort by an Afranius to introduce further bribery legislation, to which the senate tried to add an amendment that 60 days were to elapse between election and taking office (allowing prosecutions for electoral bribery), was rejected by Pompey and Crassus. It may be that the two consuls were trying to re-establish a normal government, but this argument does not seem credible in light of their further manipulations of the elections and proposed legislation during their consulship.

Pompey and Crassus immediately set about administering all the other elections in favour of their own candidates, to the detriment of Ahenobarbus, Cato and other members of the opposition. The following year, however, would see both Ahenobarbus elected as consul and Cato becoming praetor, which suggests that the voters, at the very least, resented and disliked the behaviour of the consuls, regardless of the sumptuous games that surrounded the dedication of the Theatre of Pompey, which opened that year.

The year 55 also saw a variety of proposed legislation, including a law on bribery in elections and another on the composition of juries, both suggested by Pompey. This second law limited juries to men who were to be taken from the highest rating of the census, i.e. the first five tribes. Crassus also proposed legislation about bribery and the use of *collegia* (which Clodius had re-legitimized in 58) in canvassing for political office. It is ironic that the two were prepared to take whatever measures they felt necessary to secure their own power, but imposed constitutional and legal restraints on others.

A *lex Trebonia* was also passed amidst violence, riots and Cato's protests, which established both the consuls' provincial commands, to be taken up after they left office. Much like Caesar had been able to manipulate his proconsular command for his own benefit in 59, Crassus and Pompey sought extended and prestigious appointments. Although the bill did not specifically mention Parthia and the two provinces of Spain, Parthia was the province Crassus was able to secure, even if it meant the recall of the consul of 58, Gabinius. Pompey's choice of Spain was 'more significant' and suggests that this may have been done in anticipation of a possible need for increased *cliens* (literally clients, or dependents) and support, particularly given Caesar's own sizable resources.[38] This is mere conjecture, particularly given that Pompey already had numerous supporters in Spain, due to his earlier involvement against Sertorius and his equitable and reasonable reorganization of the province.

It is certainly not clear that Caesar posed a serious threat to Pompey or the Republican system of government itself at this time, and the fact that Pompey later relied on the Spanish troops to assist him in the civil war (49–6 BCE) should not be superimposed on the events and decisions in 55. What is more probable is that Pompey needed a province and Spain offered something comparable to what Caesar and Crassus would have under their control; the triumvirs' efforts to secure equal portions would be the main concern by the three men at this point.

There was again a great deal of opposition to the *lex Trebonia*, with two tribunes trying to veto the legislation. The most vocal opponent in the senate was Cato, along with Favonius, but it was Cato who spoke in his usual filibustering manner for almost two hours. Plutarch records that he was pulled down from the rostra by an official, but continued speaking against the measure. The same official then tried to throw Cato out of the Forum, but once released, Cato again went towards the rostra, protesting and arguing to one and all, but the tribune Trebonius ordered him to be led to prison. As the crowd followed Cato, he was finally released. Over the course of the next few days, there was wide-scale bribery and even a riot, with Plutarch suggesting that Cato had been thrown out of the senate house; in spite of his efforts the bill eventually passed.[39]

The matter of extending Caesar's command in Gaul for another five years arose following this, but instead of protesting the matter to the people, Cato instead addressed Pompey himself, warning him to beware of his actions, but the latter ignored him. The year ended with Crassus leaving immediately for his province of Parthia, but Pompey remained to open his theatre. Although the plans made by the triumvirs at Luca had been achieved, it was at an extremely grave price to their popular and senatorial support, which decreased rapidly throughout the year. The annoyed L. Domitius Ahenobarbus had retreated when the threat of serious violence arose against him as a candidate for the consulship, but no doubt he, along with Cato, continued their attacks against the triumvirs. It was not just these two individuals who tried to hamper the two consuls' objectives; many others also resented and despised their cavalier attitude and their disregard for the usual political and legal practices exhibited in both securing the consulship and the proposals made during the year itself.

Even a group of poets, known for their new approach using ordinary events, emotions and political events, were to vent their anger. The poet Catullus apparently despised Caesar, as one of his poems notes that he 'was none too keen to wish to please you, Caesar' while several others poke fun at Caesar and his legate, Mamurra.[40] In poem 57 he argues that:

> They're a fine match, the shameless sods
> Those poofters Caesar and Mamurra
> No wonder. Equivalent black marks,
> One urban, the other Formian [Mamurra was from Formiae]
> Are stamped indelibly on each.
> Diseased alike, both didymous [twin]
> Two sciolists on one wee couch, [sciolists – pretenders to knowledge]
> Peers in adultery and greed,
> Rival mates among the nymphets,
> They're a fine match, the shameless sods

Later, Catullus was to apologize to Caesar for this and several other anti-Caesar/Mamurra poems and according to rumour was invited to dinner. Whether such a dinner ever occurred, however, is unlikely. As Caesar was in Gaul and Catullus appears to have died in 54 BCE, it suggests that it was a flattering story, perhaps to illustrate Caesar's forgiveness against such invective. Such political attacks in poetry were a revolutionary development in Latin literature, but to the modern reader, along with information about the placards and graffiti opposing Caesar, particularly in 59, it illustrates how politics permeated every aspect of Roman life. What it also shows is Caesar's continued unpopularity and the different types of slander – adultery, homosexuality, greed and stupidity – that were levelled against him.

Yet, Pompey's popular persona was improving. It is intriguing that Cato approached Pompey to try and stop the extension of Caesar's command. This could be construed as an increasing awareness by Cato and others that Pompey was the least to be feared among the triumvirs, but a full reconciliation between Pompey and Cato was not evident during this time. The *boni* were 'resigned, ready to make concessions, but unwilling to acknowledge Pompey's superior power as legitimate ... and however much large sections of 'good society' were troubled by the growing anarchy, corruption and violence, this was an argument against Pompey and his allies, not in their favour'.[41] Cato and his circle had no real need to do anything but make some conciliatory gestures towards Pompey. They may have recognized a weakness in Pompey, particularly in relation to his desire for public and popular respect, but 54 was to be their year.

7

Violence in Republican Rome: The Truth of the Late 50s BCE

The previous five years had seen an increase in the use of violence by political figures, both to aid the passage of legislation as well as in attacking and threatening others. While Caesar was safe in Gaul, Pompey continued to be harassed by Clodius' gangs and with the introduction of Milo's own armed agents, political violence was to become even more threatening. Although Cato may have eschewed any overt approaches to Pompey, the situation was to change dramatically as 54 continued, and it would appear that the *boni* were beginning to realize how much they would have to compromise in an effort to bring control back into a city that was once again plagued by violence and riots.

CATO'S PRAETORSHIP AND AHENOBARBUS' CONSULSHIP

The year 54 promised much for Cato and his circle. Cato had finally secured his praetorship, while Ahenobarbus was at last consul, after being thwarted by Pompey and Crassus the previous year. The *boni* immediately set about getting their revenge, bringing prosecutions against those who had benefited in 56 and 55.

The first prosecution was against a C. Cato – a distant relative of Cato the Younger – who as tribune in 56 had forced the postponement of the electoral *comitia*, which had resulted in the *interregnum* period that saw Pompey and Crassus elected as consuls for 55. Two counts were levelled against him dealing with the improper passage of legislation. Although the ambitious and youthful prosecutor (and later historian) Asinius Pollio tried his best, C. Cato was defended by M. Scaurus, one of Pompey's former lieutenants, and the young orator, Licinius Calvus, who had reconciled with Caesar after Luca. C. Cato was acquitted. Another young man, Sufenas, was also prosecuted, but also acquitted. He, along with C. Cato, had disrupted elections with corruption and violence, but the influence of the triumvirs came into play and the two were acquitted, to the dismay of the *boni*.

By midsummer, other elected officials from 55 came under scrutiny. The ex-aedile, C. Messius, had taken a post on Caesar's staff in Gaul, but came back into Rome to face charges under the *lex Licinia de sodaliciis*, with Cicero again speaking for the defence. Although there is no record of the trial or its verdict, C. Messius appears once again in 49, so it is probable that the verdict was favourable.[1] Next up was the ex-praetor P. Vatinius, who had been successfully appointed in place of Cato's own bid for office. Vatinius was perhaps not a particularly worthy individual, but the triumvirs were able to persuade Cicero to mount yet another defence, however, the speech was never published. Calvus, who had previously defended Scaurus, now aired both a personal and political grudge as he prosecuted the ex-praetor, but again, the influence of the triumvirs in the background secured yet another acquittal.

Meanwhile, Gabinius was prosecuted for illegally invading Egypt, but once again was acquitted through bribery with Pompey's influence resolving yet another attempt by the opposition to undermine the triumvirs. However, public support for Gabinius quickly turned against him as he was blamed for a flood. Dio records the event with excellent detail:

> The Tiber, either because excessive rains had occurred somewhere up the stream above the city, or because a violent wind from the sea had driven back its outgoing tide, or still more probably, as was surmised, by the act of some divinity, suddenly rose so high as to inundate all the lower levels in the city and to overwhelm many even of the higher portions. The houses, therefore, being constructed of brick, became soaked through and collapsed, while all the animals perished in the flood. And of the people all who did not take refuge in time on the highest points were caught, either in their dwellings, or in the streets, and lost their lives. The remaining houses, too, became weakened, since the mischief lasted for many days, and they caused injuries to many, either at the time or later. The Romans, distressed at these calamities and expecting others yet worse, because, as they thought, (the gods) had become angry with them for the restoration of Ptolemy, were in haste to put Gabinius to death even while absent, believing that they would be harmed less if they should destroy him before his return.

After delaying for a short time, he came to Rome and entered the city by night, remaining inside his house. He was acquitted having 'spent vast sums of money', but also 'the associates of Pompey and Caesar also very willingly aided him'.[2]

Although none of these prosecutions were successful, they should not necessarily be considered as evidence of support for the triumvirs *per se* 'by trumpeting in the public the misdemeanors of the triumvirs and forcing them to defend acts of dubious constitutionality, the *boni* strengthened their own moral and political position'.[3]

JULIA'S DEATH

It is believed that the sight of Pompey's gown sprinkled with blood following the violence that surrounded the aedicialian elections in 55 may have caused his pregnant wife Julia to collapse. In August of 54, she died in childbirth, with her infant child dying a few days later. According to Seneca, Caesar was in Britain when he heard of Julia's death. Although Pompey wanted her ashes to be placed in his Alban villa, the Roman people protested. Deciding that the ashes should rest in the Campus Martius, they approached the consul L. Domitius Ahenobarbus, who interfered and secured an interdict from the tribunes refusing this – in spite of this, the people had the last word as her urn was eventually placed in the Campus Martius. This death would have serious consequences for the triumvirs as Pompey, in genuine grief, retreated to his home and merely observed the events of the year unfold.

Although there had been an attempt over the summer to hold the consular elections, they were ultimately delayed to the end of the year. Domitius Calvinus, a strong supporter of Caesar, and M. Valerius Messalla Rufus were elected after the usual excessive bribery. Even for Rome, the elections this year caused a great scandal with their widescale abuses. It appears that Domitius Calvinus was prosecuted for his actions, but secured an acquittal. In November, the whole of Rome turned out for Pomptinus' triumph for his victory over the Gauls some seven years before, which no doubt gave some relief from the numerous trials as well as the disastrous flooding earlier in the year.

In the end, the year 54 was an extremely successful one for the opponents of the triumvirs, even if they had been unable to convict a number of figures who had great support from Pompey and Caesar. Their greatest prize was the conviction and subsequent exile of A. Gabinius, to the dismay of Pompey. The consul L. Domitius Ahenobarbus may have symbolized the resistance, but he had made a fundamental error in refusing the burial rites for Pompey's wife, which divided the people against the senate and, in particular, against Ahenobarbus.

THE SITUATION FROM 53 TO 49 BCE

The year 53 began with the conviction of Gabinius for extortion, but there were still no consuls. Pompey was requested to 'assist' in the elections. Rome again found itself at the mercy of armed gangs, with a tribune causing further riots by suggesting that Pompey be appointed dictator to deal with the unrest. Unfavourable omens, such as sweating statues and howling dogs surrounded political events.[4] It was not until July that Gn. Domitius Calvinus and M. Valerius Messalla Rufus were elected and assumed office. Clodius decided to postpone his

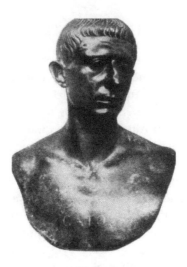

Cato the Younger

bid for the praetorship due to the delays in the elections and would set his sights on the electoral contest for 52 instead. Yet, there were again problems when the new consuls tried to sort out the elections for 52:

> They . . . did not appoint any successors, though they laid aside their senatorial garb and in the dress of knights, as on the occasion of some great calamity, convened the senate. They also passed a decree that no one, either an ex-praetor or an ex-consul, should assume a command abroad until five years had elapsed; they hoped that such men, by not being in a position of power immediately after holding office, would cease their craze for office. For there was no moderation and no decency at all being observed, but they vied with one another in expending great sums, and going still further, in fighting, so that once even the consul Calvinus was wounded. Hence no consul or prefect of the city had any successor, but at the beginning of the year [52], the Romans were absolutely without a government.[5]

It is interesting that while Calvinus is characterized as pro-Caesarian, this legislation, precluding any ex-praetor or ex-consul from assuming a provincial command for five years, in fact tries to stop the loop-hole that Caesar had used in 58 when, in the course of a few hours, he set down his consular *imperium* and almost immediately assumed his provincial *imperium*. It was not, however, retroactive, and thus, Caesar was relatively safe – for the moment.

Although domestic matters mainly concerned the people of Rome in 53, events from the east would also dominate politics. Early in the year, Crassus had seized treasures in Jerusalem. Marching towards Mesopotamia, Crassus ignored omens as he crossed the river Euphrates. Having possibly been led in the wrong direction by his guide, Crassus ended up with his forces being divided and coming out of the foothills and onto the plains.[6] On 9 June, the Parthian general Surenas led a charge against the Roman army that resulted in huge losses for the Romans. Although Crassus may have attempted to meet with the enemy to negotiate, he ended up being killed. His quaestor, C. Crassius, was able to take control of Syria, but Mesopotamia itself fell to Parthians. That left only Pompey and Caesar remaining in the trinumvirate; without Crassus as a balance, their relationship quickly began to deteriorate. The first break had happened with Julia's death, but the real repercussions of Crassus' demise would not felt until the following year.

Problems between Clodius and Milo, however, continued to escalate. Clodius argued that Milo should not be allowed to stand for the consulship for 52 as he had excessive debts. Cicero appeared in the senate in an effort to rebuff Clodius' claim, and Clodius was actually forced to retreat as one of the candidates for the quaestorship – Mark Antony – violently assaulted him. Cicero later noted, in a speech addressed to Antony:

> What would men have thought if [Clodius] had been slain at the time when you pursued him in the Forum with a drawn sword, in the sight of all the Roman people; and when you would have settled his business if he had not thrown himself up the stairs of a bookseller's shop, and, shutting them against you, checked your attack by that means?[7]

The death of Clodius would occur soon enough and the event would cause widespread looting, riots and public displays of anger and frustration, culminating in a dictatorship being offered to Pompey.

52 BCE

It was, however, the year 52 that would stretch and finally break the unofficial alliance between Pompey and Caesar, as well as bringing Rome to the brink of destruction – not by its politicians, but by its people. On 18 January, following uneasy warnings and portents, the praetorian candidate Clodius was ambushed and killed on the Via Appia on his way back from addressing potential voters south of Rome. Journeying on horseback and accompanied by two friends (and 30 armed slaves), he was passed by Milo's entourage on their way to Lanuvium. Both the later authors Asconius and Appian suggest that the meeting was accidental, but after a minor scuffle the two groups went to go their separate ways. A chance look back from Clodius appears to have angered one of Milo's gladiators, Birria, who hurled a lance which wounded Clodius in the shoulder. The situation then became crazed, chaotic and confused as the two sides went on the rampage. Having taken refuge at an inn at Bovillae (near Clodius' villa),

Clodius was finished off – his body thrown onto the Via Appia, ironically surrounded by the funeral monuments of his ancestors. In the melee, it is not clear whether Milo himself killed Clodius, but nevertheless, he was to be charged for the crime. Cicero's account argues that it was Clodius' fault that there was any incident at all:

> Clodius meets him unencumbered on horseback, with no carriage, with no baggage, with no companions, as he was used to, without his wife, which was scarcely ever the case; while this plotter, who had taken that journey for the express purpose of murder, was driving with his wife in a carriage, in a heavy travelling cloak, with abundant baggage, and a delicate company of women, and maidservants and boys. He meets Clodius in front of his farm, about the eleventh hour, or not far from it. Immediately a number of men attack him from the higher ground with missile weapons. The men who are in front kill his driver, and when he had jumped down from his chariot and flung aside his cloak, and while he was defending himself with vigorous courage, the men who were with Clodius drew their swords, and some of them ran back towards his chariot in order to attack Milo from behind, and some, because they thought that he was already slain, began to attack his servants who were behind him; and those of the servants who had presence of mind to defend themselves, and were faithful to their master, were some of them slain, and the others, when they saw a fierce battle taking place around the chariot, and as they were prevented from getting near their master so as to help him, when they heard Clodius himself proclaim that Milo was slain, and they thought that it was really true, they, the servants of Milo (I am not speaking for the purpose of shifting the guilt onto the shoulders of others, but I am saying what really occurred), did, without their master either commanding it, or knowing it, or even being present to see it, what every one would have wished his servants to do in a similar case.[8]

News travelled quickly, and some three hours later a crowd had gathered around Clodius' house in Rome. Clodius' widow made the most of his death, with the tribunes Plancus and Q. Pompeius Rufus joining in to inflame the crowd.[9] They paid no attention to Pompey's appeal for calm; the people convened an impromptu funeral pyre in the senate house, burning it and the *curia* down:

> So the populace, as a result of what it both saw and heard, was deeply stirred and no longer showed any regard for things sacred or profane, but overthrew all the customs of burial and burned down nearly the whole city. They took up the body of Clodius and carried into the *curia*, laid it out properly, and then after heaping up a pyre out of the benches burned both the corpse and the building. They did not do this under the stress of such an impulse as often takes sudden hold of crowds, but with such deliberate purpose that at the ninth hour, they held the funeral feast in the Forum itself, with the senate-house still smouldering.[10]

On 22 January, Milo sought an audience with Pompey, but Pompey refused to see him; subsequent days saw numerous public meetings, with Rufus on the 23rd accusing Milo of a plot against Pompey and around the 27th, with Milo arguing that Clodius had tried to ambush him.[11]

The crowd continued to bay for revenge, calling out for justice for Clodius, with the most vocal crying for Pompey to resolve the matter. There were rumours of a dictatorship being offered to either Pompey or Caesar, particularly as there had been no elections and no officials for 52 available.[12] Pompey was finally appointed sole consul in mid-February, but with restrictions. This was a temporary emergency measure and as consul, not dictator, his decisions would still be open to tribunician veto. The senate limited this sole consulship to six months, something that would hopefully keep Pompey in check and, furthermore, allow for magistrates to be elected and ordinary business to resume once the danger had passed. Meanwhile, the *senatus consultum ultimum* was passed in an effort to restore some sort of order, while the senate instructed Pompey to levy troops throughout Italy.

Plutarch notes that it was Bibulus who initially proposed in the senate (meeting in new surroundings due to the destruction of the *curia*) that Pompey be offered the consulship; then Cato rose up, to everyone's surprise, and approved the measure.[13] Cato advised that any government was better than no government at all, and he expected that Pompey would handle the present situation in the best manner possible and would guard the *res publica* when it was entrusted to him.[14] Although one scholar has mentioned that 'it must have been pleasant for [Pompey] to see Cato and Bibulus humble themselves in this way', their actions show, in fact, a clear desperation regarding the unrest, rioting and chaos in early January.[15] Cato's acquiescence to Bibulus' motion was a reflection of the great seriousness of the situation at hand; it must be remembered that the *senatus consultum ultimum* had been passed and the approach to Pompey illustrated that many, including the *boni*, wanted the matter dealt with quickly and efficiently.

One could argue that without Cato's approval, it is quite possible that the sole consulship would not have been offered; at least, it would have been without the support of the *boni*, which would not have had the same impact. With the whole senate agreed, Pompey could then address the major concerns of the day with their full support behind him.

It appears that Pompey then approached Cato, following the resolution of the senate, and asked him to be his counsellor and associate in the government, but Cato declined.[16] There are a number of ways to read this. Perhaps Pompey simply wanted to acknowledge the debt owed to Cato for suggesting his appointment, but there are several other tantalizing possibilities as well. Was Pompey suggesting that Cato take an official role, such as a legate, much like the *legati* that Pompey had as overseer of the corn supply, or as *magister equitum* as Mark Antony was to be under Caesar the dictator in 48; or, in fact, was Pompey asking Cato to be his co-consul? Whatever Pompey's intention, Cato refused. In private, Cato said that he would counsel Pompey upon Pompey's application to him, but in public would say what he thought best, even if he disagreed with Pompey.[17]

Pompey was swift to deal with the chaos, securing new legislation to deal with bribery and violence, although there was some delay due to tribunician resistance. A new *lex de vi*, which referred specifically to Clodius' murder and the ensuing rioting, was Pompey's first measure. Around this time, Pompey married Cornelia, daughter of Metellus Scipio, having first rejected Caesar's offer of his great-niece, Octavia, who was already married.[18]

It was the prosecution of Milo that was one of Cicero's darkest hours. Milo claimed self-defence, which Cicero seized upon as one of his main tactics. It is an interesting ploy. Cicero's strongest arguments were that the ambush took place near Clodius' villa, Milo had been on state business with his wife and retinue, and Clodius had approached on horseback. Cicero did not deny that Milo had murdered Clodius – even if one of his slaves or gladiators had done the deed, Milo would be responsible for their actions – but his overall thrust was that it was done in self-defence.

Milo's trial began in early April with the ex-consul of 54, L. Domitius Ahenobarbus as *quaesitor* (or instigator). Any mention of Clodius during the prosecution's case was shouted down by his supporters, there were threats of further riots and by the second day Pompey had armed troops and soldiers surround the law-court so the trial could proceed unhampered. By the time Cicero was able to present his defence, the atmosphere was thick with suspicion and fear. Cicero, never a friend to Clodius, brought up every negative action throughout his career from the infamous Bona Dea incident to his demagoguery and illegal actions.

Cicero suggests that Clodius was motivated by envy – Milo was seeking the consulship – and he sought to destroy his enemy. Milo is presented as a 'saviour of the people and state', Clodius having been so violent and malevolent that Milo had done a great service by ridding Rome of this travesty of a citizen. There were, however, three factors working against Milo: the crowd of Clodian supporters, who might be tempted to riot again; Pompey's influence on the judges; and the facts of the case itself. Cicero simply could not defend Milo adequately as numerous witnesses for the prosecution could attest to the hatred between the two men, Milo's own violent past actions and the uncertainty as to the actual details of what happened on the Via Appia.

In the end, Milo was condemned by 38 votes to 13. He went into immediate exile in Massilia. In his absence, he was also convicted of bribery and other lesser charges. When he later received Cicero's final polished version of his defence speech, Milo is said to have commented dryly that had Cicero delivered this version, he would not now be 'enjoying the delicious red mullet of Massilia'.[19] He was to later join in an uprising against Caesar in 48 during the height of the civil war, proving ultimately fatal, although actual accounts of his death vary.[20]

Other prosecutions followed as Pompey determined to purge the city of its violent elements. Cicero would successfully prosecute Plancus and Q. Pompeius Rufus for their actions in inciting the crowds to riot, but an action against Milo's henchman, M. Saufeius, failed twice. A certain Sextus Cloelius – considered one of Clodius' principal henchmen – was brought to trial and convicted. Pompey interceded on behalf of his new father-in-law Metellus Scipio to prevent an action against him for bribery, which was not well received.[21] The prosecution of Plancus saw Cato, as one of the potential jurors, argue that having Pompey as a character witness was untenable and although this resulted in Cato being dismissed from the jury, Pompey's influence made no difference to the outcome; Plancus was convicted and exiled. He made his way to Ravenna where he joined Caesar. Meanwhile, Mark Antony, who had been elected a quaestor, also rejoined Caesar in Gaul.

The big question now facing Rome was that of Caesar and, in particular, his interest in running for the consulship on his return from Gaul. As Caesar's command was due to expire in 50, it is surprising perhaps that this became important as early as 52. There is some method and reason behind why it became such a major issue: Cato was eligible for the consulship for 51 and there would be no way that Cato would allow Caesar to stand for the consulship in 50 if he himself was consul. It was under Pompey's control to resolve the question, yet his actions are somewhat convoluted and confusing.

In the first instance, the ten tribunes of the year joined together to pass a law that would permit Caesar to stand for the consulship *in absentia*, but Pompey overruled them, passing another law instead that compelled candidates for election to stand in person, which could be construed as a direct attack against Caesar. It is believed that Cicero may have met with Caesar sometime in mid-March to discuss M. Caelius Rufus' opposition to the *privilegium* of allowing individuals to stand for the consulship *in absentia*. There is some confusion about this: Dio argues that it was not a new law, but a revival of an older law, but Cicero notes that Pompey urged the tribunes to pass the legislation allowing Caesar to stand *in absentia*.[22] Syme, in his *Roman Revolution*, remarks that:

> Pompey sought by a trick to annul the law passed by the tribunes ... conceding to Caesar the right to stand for the consulship in absence. Detected, he made tardy and questionable amends. The dynast was not yet ready to drop his ally. He needed Caesar for counterbalance against the Catonian party until he made the final choice between the two.[23]

Cato was furious: he objected at length in one of his infamous filibusters, but was unsuccessful. Both L. Domitius Ahenobarbus and Cato announced that once Caesar entered Rome as a private citizen, they proposed to prosecute him for his illegal actions, not just during his consulship, but also for behaviour during his provincial command in Gaul, which Cato characterized as amounting to treason.[24]

Another measure proposed in 53 but finally passed in 52 was that a period of five years should pass between a magistracy and a provincial command, which would see both Bibulus and Cicero sent away from Rome in early 51–50 BCE, as the measure was made retroactive. Pompey's command in Spain was further renewed for another five years, but he continued to remain in Rome itself, ruling through his legates. By July or August, normal political functions had returned to Rome and Pompey chose a co-consul to assume power once his six-month period as sole consul was finished. He chose his father-in-law, Metellus Scipio, to the amusement of his colleagues. Scipio did, however, annul some of Clodius' legislation that had curtailed the powers of the censorship. The two ruled from September until the end of the year, when the new consuls would take over.

It was in September that the aediles Favonius and Curio sponsored various games and events, but most of the crowd packed into Favonius', where place of honour was given to Cato.[25] It is not clear when the elections for 51 actually took place. It may have been when Scipio finally assumed the co-consulship in mid-September, but whenever they were held, the end result was not to Cato's liking. He was defeated for the consulship, in favour of Servius Sulpicius Rufus, one of those defeated for the consulship for 62 (and who had brought unsuccessful charges against one of the victors, Murena) and Marcus Claudius Marcellus, who would agitate against Caesar's prolonged campaign and prove to be a staunch Pompeian supporter, both during his consulship and later in the civil war.

Plutarch records that Cato's defeat was due to the exasperation of the common folk, who were angry at his aloofness and refusal to partake in the usual bribery that surrounded elections. Cicero admonished Cato for his lack of action when the state clearly needed him, but his response was that while he had acknowledged the bribery rampant in the praetorian elections for 55 and had run again successfully the following year, he did not see the same situation in his failed bid for the consulship. Cato believed that he had given offence to the people, but he would not, however, change himself to accommodate them, and would not seek the consulship further. While the people may have applauded Cato for his moral integrity, in particular, at Favonius' games, this did not translate to votes for his consulship.

Cato had demonstrated that he was an implacable opponent of electoral bribery, and perhaps it was not in the interests of important voters to vote in favour of such a person. They could still applaud Cato in other situations and even admire him for his moral stance, but they did not have to take his side. Essentially, the most effective way to express their anger and dislike of his anti-bribery policy was by voting against him and this appears to be what Plutarch has suggested. There has been, however, another idea, proposed by Lily Ross Taylor, namely that Cato's defeat actually reflected the manoeuvres behind the scenes by Pompey and Caesar. As she states:

> Pompey had not completely broken with Caesar and he still distrusted Cato. Pompey, as well as Caesar's agents, probably contributed to the defeat of Cato for the consulship of 51. Pompey could have hardly wished to see the stern Cato in office and was doubtless the more opposed because his new father-in-law Metellus Scipio was Cato's bitterest enemy.[26]

While it could be argued that Pompey was influenced by Cato in the passage of the legislation that was aimed against Caesar, Pompey still did not trust him and it appears he would not assist Cato in securing the consulship. This could be due to Pompey's fear that if Cato was elected he would prove a formidable opponent, and also could effectively end the quasi-alliance with Caesar, therefore Pompey was anxious to prevent this from happening. If this hypothesis is correct, then it could be argued that Pompey's reasons for this course of action are as suggested, and this would further indicate Pompey's own indecision about whom to trust and whom to deal with. The evidence, however, is weak, as Taylor has based her argument only on Caesar's *Bellum Civile* 1.4, but offers no further documentation. It might, therefore, be a later modern interpretation rather than a reflection of the situation at the time. Plutarch's suggestion of the plebs' lack of support is the more plausible reason for Cato's defeat.

The historian Erich Gruen has argued that the significance of any concessions made in the legislation passed during Pompey's sole consulship have been overestimated and the events of this year should not be viewed as a victory by the *boni* or for Cato; but this argument cannot be fully supported by Gruen's assertions. He argues that 'narrow interpretation of the *lex Pompeia* as an anti-Caesarian move not only misjudges the politics of that year but seriously undervalues the scope and aims of Pompey's legislation',[27] but this is not immediately clear from the evidence. Furthermore, Taylor convincingly argues that Pompey's refusal to enter into another marriage contract with Caesar should be considered as one indicator of the breakdown between the two men and further notes:

> With the cooperation of the *optimates* [Pompey] made arrangements which strengthened his own position and weakened Caesar's. Pompey's command in Spain and Caesar's in Gaul were apparently to have expired together before the end of the year 50. The senate proceeded to lengthen Pompey's command by several years, and that meant that he would still have an army when Caesar had to give his up.[28]

Shotter further argues that 'it was a situation requiring, if conflict was to be avoided, a great store of goodwill between Caesar and Pompey; that commodity by 51 was in very short supply'.[29] While Pompey's views appears to be ambiguous, there is sufficient evidence that the *boni* were having some success in distancing Caesar and Pompey as the year came to its conclusion.

51 BCE

The year 51 saw the election of Ser. Sulpicius Rufus and, to Caesar's dismay, the ardent anti-Caesarian M. Claudius Marcellus as consuls. Thus, while Cato himself had not been elected, there was nevertheless an opponent to Caesar in the consulship. Dio notes that Marcellus introduced a number of measures in order to '[bring] about Caesar's downfall'.[30] The question of Caesar's successor in Gaul was proposed both by his co-consul Rufus and Pompey, but as the legislation was vetoed by the tribunes, it never passed. Marcellus further refused to acknowledge the citizenship bestowed by Caesar on the inhabitants of Novum Comum by flogging one of the magistrates; Cicero commented that it was 'a disgraceful performance'.[31] There was discussion about Pompey's Spanish command, but Pompey still remained in the city, allowing his subordinates to deal with his provincial duties. However, in July 51 BCE, the question of Caesar's possible recall was again mentioned, but the senate was unable to meet for several months in sufficient numbers. It was not until the end of September that a decree allowing Caesar to remain in his province until 1 March 50 BCE was decided. A number of measures were also proposed and passed on 30 September 51 BCE, a few of which were aimed at Caesar, namely that the question of Caesar's provincial command was to be shelved until March 50 BCE as well as a proviso that any of Caesar's soldiers who requested discharge should approach the senate. Caesar therefore remained in Gaul, dealing with pockets of resistance, but the main threat posed by the Gallic tribes had been resolved. His final decisive victory against the Carnutes effectively eliminated most resistance and Caesar was left to ponder his own worries about his eventual return to Rome.

Several trials also went forward in 51. Two of the tribunes from 52 were convicted on a charge of violence and expelled from Rome, while the orator Hortensius was able to successfully defend his nephew M. Valerius Massala against a charge of bribery. Although elections were able to take place apparently without any violence (but with the usual corruption), the consul designate C. Marcellus was prosecuted for bribery, but was ultimately acquitted. M. Servilius was prosecuted on two different charges of extortion, but was acquitted as well.

Cicero, in the meantime, had been sent as proconsul to Cilicia and was trying to deal with the threat of the Amanii tribe, in which he was successful, but his pleadings to be allowed to celebrate a triumph would later fall on deaf ears. Bibulus was sent as proconsul to Syria, arriving later than Cicero, although he was to claim victory for suppressing the Parthians, much to Cicero's annoyance.

The year ended much like the previous one – another general, Lentulus Spinther, celebrated a triumph for victories won as governor in Cilicia.

50 BCE

At the beginning of the year Curio proposed that an intercalary month should be inserted, in order to reconcile the calendar year with the seasons, which had become noticably out of sync; it was, however, unsuccessful. Nevertheless, he proposed several further laws in an apparent effort to gain popular support. Ordinary business continued in Rome, but on 1 March, the senate met again to try and resolve the Caesarian issue. The elected consuls demonstrated the influence of the *boni*, overseeing the election of L. Aemilius Lepidus Paullus and C. Claudius Marcellus as consuls for the following year. The debate over the provincial commands of both Pompey and Caesar again came under scrutiny: Pompey refused to leave Rome, while Caesar remained fearful of attacks if he returned to Rome without securing the consulship (and its immunity) first. Caesar canvassed for support, travelling through Cisalpine Gaul in celebration of his victories, and then retreating to Nemetocenna where he reviewed the army. Putting T. Labienus in charge, Caesar continued travelling around Gaul, believing that he 'would have no difficulty in getting what he wanted by the open votes of the senators'.[32] Caesar had hoped that bribery would assure the compliance of the two consuls, but only Paullus agreed not to take sides, after accepting monies that were used in the building and dedication of a basilica.

Meanwhile, Cicero was agitating for a triumph. He wrote numerous pleading letters to senators, among them Cato, but was unsuccessful. It is clear, however, that Cato did not advocate Cicero's claim during the senatorial meetings in May 50 BCE. Whilst a *supplicatio* (prelude to a triumph, but not an actual triumph itself) was ultimately decreed by the senate, a number of figures still actively opposed its passage. Initially, Hirrus – an enemy of Cicero's – threatened to obstruct the proceedings while the tribune C. Scribonius Curio also opposed the request, which has been attributed more to a need to free up comitial days rather than as a denial of Cicero's merit. Caelius proposed that any *supplicatio* would not be celebrated during 50, but rather delayed until the following year, which was agreed. Cato himself spoke in praise of Cicero's administration but did not recommend the *supplicatio*. Cato wrote to Cicero explaining the reasons why he had not supported him, adding that he had nevertheless given support for a complimentary vote and further encouraged Cicero to remain true to the ideals that the two share. Although Cicero heaps compliments upon Cato and notes that '[he] was well aware that such decrees of the senate are usually drafted by the greatest friends of the recipient of the honour', Cicero was privately furious.[33]

In subsequent letters to Atticus, he lets loose with his true feelings. In one he remarks that 'Cato's behaviour to me was shamefully spiteful. He gave me a character ... for rectitude, equity, clemency and good faith, for which I did not ask; what I did want, he denied me'. Furthermore, he is aware of Bibulus' success: 'Yet Cato voted Bibulus a twenty days' festival. Forgive me, I cannot and I will not bear it'.[34] Caesar himself had sent a congratulatory letter to Cicero discussing the meeting in the senate (although Caesar was himself not present), further commenting about Cato's disloyal behaviour and shabby treatment of Cicero. Although later Cicero was to join Cato during the civil war, it is not clear whether the two were ever truly personally reconciled.

Several trials came during the summer – Appius Claudius was prosecuted for his conduct in Cilicia, but was acquitted. The great orator Hortensius died sometime in June, and weeks later Cato remarried his wife Marcia, whom he had earlier divorced. Caesar was to comment widely that Cato had only divorced and remarried Marcia due to her increased wealth, but Cato refused to be drawn in – Plutarch notes the criticism, but points out that Cato was more worried about the protection of his household in the event of a possible civil war.

Cato continued to vent his anger against Caesar. When it was believed that the latter had attacked the Germans while there had been a truce, Cato denounced him. In retaliation, Caesar sent a letter to the senate with abundant insults and denunciations of Cato. Following its reading, Cato rose and noted that the accusations against him bore the marks of abuse and scoffing, and were childishness and vulgarity on Caesar's part. Meier argues that the situation for Caesar in 50 BCE was favourable, believing that the majority of the senate, along with the consul Paullus and the tribune, Gaius Scribonius Curio, were predisposed towards a decision supporting Caesar.[35] Yet, Meier continues:

> There were many who did not relish the prospect of his return, and they were by no means in favour of his being elected consul without laying down his command. Their reluctance to pass a resolution to replace him was no doubt due largely to their fear of him. To this extent their judgement was much the same as Cato's. The difference was that they did not want to risk a war. Caesar was not to be trifled with and must therefore be allowed to have his own way.

There was fear in April that the Parthians were threatening an invasion and the senate agreed with Pompey's proposal that two legions be sent: one from his own troops and the other from Caesar's. Young Appius Claudius was sent to Gaul to take over the legions and reported back that the soldiers were cold, tired and hungry and any move by Pompey to relieve their suffering and complaints could result in those men giving their allegiance to Pompey. However, Pompey was recovering from a lengthy illness and although he proposed laying down his command, there was no word from Caesar. The stalemate continued for a few more months. During the summer elections, Mark Antony was able to defeat L. Domitius Ahenobarbus for the position of auger; to Caesar's delight, and the fury of the *boni*, he was also elected tribune for the following year. The censors also had an opportunity to do a detailed census, even expelling several members of the senate for their behaviour; among them was the future historian Sallust.

However, all was not favourable for Caesar; the consuls themselves were not necessarily supporters. By the middle of the year Marcus Caelius was already speaking of a civil war. The debate about the commands of Pompey and Caesar was again raised in December 50 BCE. Most agreed that Caesar should be relieved of his command, but that Pompey should retain his, however, as Appian recounts, news had reached the city about Caesar:

> An unfounded rumour then suddenly swept round that Caesar had crossed the Alps and was advancing on Rome. There was great commotion and general panic, and Claudius [the consul] proposed that the legions at Capua should be mobilized against Caesar as an enemy of the state. When Curio opposed this on the grounds that the reports were untrue, Claudius retorted, 'If I am prevented by the vote of a public body from acting in the interests of the state, I shall act on my own authority as consul'. With these words, he hurried out of the senate to the suburbs, accompanied by his fellow-consul, and proffered a sword to Pompey, saying, 'I command you, I and my colleague here, to take the field against Caesar on behalf of our country; and for this purpose we grant you command of the forces which are now at Capua or elsewhere in Italy, and of any others you may wish to raise'.[36]

While the pro-Caesarian tribune Curio left the city to join Caesar, who had moved his army to Ravenna, Caesar himself was waiting to try and negotiate a settlement between himself and the senate, although his annoyance at the continued delays is evident. By the beginning of 49 BCE, it was clear that no compromise was forthcoming. Cato reminded the senate that it was clear that what he foretold was about to come true 'Now . . . those things are come to pass which I foretold to you, and the man is at last resorting to open compulsion, using the forces which he got by deceiving and cheating the state'.[37]

Plutarch notes further that outside the senate Cato could accomplish nothing as the people themselves were in favour of Caesar's return; thus, although Cato had the *boni* element of the senate under his influence, the senate itself was afraid of the people.[38] Although Caesar had maintained that he would respect whatever decision the senate made, it is clear that there were many who feared Caesar, not just Cato. Cato had no compunction in continually proclaiming the danger that Caesar posed, which in the end, was justified. It was not only Cato who feared Caesar; others in the senate had proved that if they had to choose, they would choose Pompey.

While Curio had delayed the voting regarding the termination of Caesar's command, the senate had vacillated between Pompey and Caesar, with the end result in Pompey's favour. There should be no doubt that Cato's hand can be seen in the eventual capitulation of the senate and the *boni* towards Pompey in its refusal to deal with Caesar's requests. One of the men refused to go to his province, the other feared leaving his. Pompey perhaps had more reason to avoid leaving Rome as he would be beyond senatorial support if he left the city, but also, if war was to erupt (as it increasingly appeared), it was essential that Pompey be in Rome to deal with the threat of Caesar. Cato was ultimately justified in his appraisal of the situation, having had to deal with Caesar in 59 BCE, and knowing exactly what the man was capable of.

There are numerous problems regarding the trigger of the civil war, with Caesar arguing that he needed to defend his honour and *dignitas*, but it boils down to a disagreement between the senate, Pompey and Cato regarding Caesar's excessive demands and desires.

The *boni*, led by Cato, refused to compromise with Caesar, due to Caesar's continued demands that he be allowed to come into the city with his army nearby. Cato simply refused to believe that Caesar meant that he would disarm and come quietly into the city. This distrust coloured the discussions between the *boni*, the senate and Caesar. While there are many reasons, which have been discussed at length by other scholars regarding the civil war, perhaps one is also the personal and political hatred between these two men.

The senate was willing to consider all proposals. Even Cato finally saw reason – the senate asked that Caesar merely remain in his province, so that they could meet and discuss all the options available, but Caesar became less conciliatory. He wanted to meet with Pompey, but the latter refused, enraging Caesar. Pompey might talk about his commitment to the *res publica* but, apparently, Caesar saw an insult that Pompey might not have intended. Taking the moral high-ground, Caesar now argued that his personal *dignitas* had been threatened and blamed everyone but himself:

> Cato is goaded on by his old quarrels with Caesar and vexation at his defeat [for the consulship]. Lentulus is moved by the greatness of his debts, by the prospect of a military command and a province ... Scipio is stimulated by the same hope ... which he thinks that kinship will entitle him to share with Pompey ... Pompey, urged on by Caesar's enemies and by his desire that no one should be on the same level of authority with himself, had completely withdrawn himself from Caesar's friendship and become reconciled with their common enemies.[39]

Caesar had always felt a sense of superiority; his actions illustrate well his disregard for constitutional tradition, his recourse to illegal activities using the threat of violence and his refusal to follow the rules. They were for everybody else, not Caesar. It was this belief that was to draw Rome into civil war and provide Caesar with his moral justification for marching on Rome.

While there may be the idea that all eyes in Rome were focused on Caesar and his return, normal events, such as trials, elections and legislation continued during this period as well. It may have been a dominating issue, but Rome was not paralysed into non-action, nor did everyone fall into a panic regarding Caesar. The main disruption of this period was the death of Clodius in 52, and following Pompey's dictatorship regular elections ensued. Cato may not have been elected consul, but he still had formidable power in Rome. One way in which this was demonstrated was in drawing Pompey closer to the senate, so that the end contest became not just Pompey versus Caesar, but Pompey, Cato and the senate united against a common enemy.

8

Civil War and Caesar's Dictatorship

On 1 January 49 BCE, Pompey began to pressure the senate to make a decision about Caesar. Caesar meanwhile had sent a letter to the consul, C. Claudius Marcellus, who was persuaded by two tribunes to read it aloud. Caesar again reminded the people of all of his services to the *res publica* and referred to the fact that the people had granted him the right to stand for the consulship *in absentia*. Furthermore, he was prepared to lay down his command, but only if Pompey did the same.

Marcellus stated that he was willing to do whatever the senate decreed, and Pompey's father-in-law, Q. Metellus Scipio, rose and stated that he could assure the senate of Pompey's assistance, but they would have to decide how to act now. Perhaps if the senate had approved these measures, civil war could have been averted, but there was still one aspect unresolved (and it was unlikely that Caesar would compromise on this), he still demanded that he be allowed to stand for the consulship *in absentia*, and would not agree to any other proposition in this matter.

Caesar's unwillingness to stand for the consulship in person is in sharp contrast to his actions in 59, when he abandoned his triumph in order to stand for election. Caesar's reasons not to disband at this time may be due not just to the possible threat of prosecution, but also to Pompey's refusal to dismiss his own army. Caesar argued that he was fighting this time because of the insult to his *dignitas*, but this was not an issue *per se* back in 59. In 49, Caesar had reason to fear his enemies and knew that Cato, at the very least, would immediately mount a prosecution against him as well as the possibility of facing Pompey's soldiers without his own army, if he were to disband them. For all of his rhetoric arguing for a senatorial compromise, Caesar was unwilling to return to Rome as a private citizen, while the senate would not consider any alternative.

Cato suggested that the senate put all matters in the hands of Pompey and the *senatus consultum ultimum* was passed on 7 January 49. Under the cloud of martial law, Caesar had been stripped of his provincial command – L. Domitius Ahenobarbus was appointed as his successor. Tying to intercede their tribunician veto, Antony and Cassius were ignored and they fled the city, taking refuge with Caesar. Caesar argued that he had not left his province for any evil purposes, but merely to protect himself:

> [He sought to] defend himself from the insults of his foes, to restore to their position the tribunes of the people who at that conjuncture had been expelled from the state, to assert the freedom of himself and the Roman people who had been oppressed by a small faction.[1]

The scholar Christian Meier has stated that it was 'the determined opponents around Cato, [who] insisted that he must pursue his candidacy as a private citizen, and it was on this that all attempts at mediation failed. Cato declared that one should rather seek death than allow a citizen to dictate conditions to the Republic'.[2] Cato also spoke with Pompey, persuading him and others not to plunder cities subject to Rome and to not put any Roman citizens to death, except as a result of battle. Thus, according to Plutarch, Pompey's group received an excellent reputation for reasonableness and mildness.[3]

Informed that the senate would not allow him to stand for the consulship *in absentia*, Caesar concluded that war was the only answer and crossed the river Rubicon.[4] One thing that is clear is that neither side trusted the other. Diplomacy and negotiation had failed. The civil war had begun.

THE CIVIL WAR

On 10 January 49, Julius Caesar crossed the Rubicon with one of his legions. By crossing the river, which was the boundary between the Roman province of Cisalpine Gaul to the north and Italy to the south, Caesar was openly declaring civil war. He was leaving his province, with his army, and preparing to march on Rome. It is believed that Caesar commented '*Alea iacta est*' (The die is cast) as he crossed the river.[5] Individuals in Rome began to choose their sides.

Not knowing that Caesar only had one legion with him, the senate turned to Pompey to deal with the approaching threat. Although Cato had demanded that Pompey be made commander in chief at the beginning, this was rejected until the end of 49. There was no doubt some resistance from other military consulars, particularly Metellus Scipio and L. Calpurnius Bibulus, who would have resented Pompey's overall control at this stage of the conflict.

In early February, Pompey decided not to stay in Rome, but took many members of the senate, the reigning consuls and others to Capua. With a rear guard at Capua, with many of the *boni*, including Metellus Scipio and Cato, Pompey then went to Brundisium, where he was planning to go to the Eastern provinces to rally his extensive supporters there in the fight against Caesar. Although it might seem strange that Pompey left Rome, there are in fact several good reasons. In the first instance, Pompey had numerous supporters throughout the provinces and, perhaps looking to the example of Sulla a generation earlier, it was believed that Caesar too would eventually march on Rome. Another reason may have been the belief that once the provinces had been secured, the only matter left would be the city of Rome; furthermore, Pompey needed time to prepare his soldiers. Finally, also with the actions of Sulla overshadowing them, perhaps Pompey simply did not want any bloodshed in Rome itself. He would come as its saviour in victory, not as a renegade general threatening to overthrow the *res publica*, which was what Caesar was to do.

With Pompey building up his armies, Caesar turned his attention to Spain, with its leaderless army. On the way there in April, Caesar ran into his proconsular replacement L. Domitius Ahenobarbus, who had established his camp in central Italy, near Corfinium. Unfortunately, Domitius refused to engage with Caesar's army, but Caesar had no qualms – he marched up to Domitius' camp, fought his soldiers and defeated them easily. Domitius was routed, captured and his monies seized, but he was later released by Caesar. Caesar continued to strike with his usual speed along the passes to Etruria and overran Picenum. It was not an auspicious beginning for the Pompeian camp.

Arriving in June, Caesar was able to seize the Pyreenees passes against Pompey's forces and by the beginning of August, the Pompeian armies were defeated in Ilerda. In early September, the pro-Caesarian Decimus Brutus was able to defeat the Pompeian naval forces near Massilia and the besieged city then surrendered to Caesar. In October, Caesar came to Rome itself. He was then declared dictator of Rome, appointing Mark Antony as his *magister equitum* (literally 'master of the horse', in effect second in command) leaving him in charge of the city as he went to meet the Pompeian forces.

There had been some successes for Pompey in 49. Those opposed to Caesar had hurried to secure their own appointments and resources. The former praetor Varus seized Africa and was able to resist Curio's attempts to capture the area for Caesar. In late August, Curio was defeated and he committed suicide.

Other Pompeian appointments included Metellus Scipio, who was proconsul in Syria, Ap. Claudius Pulcher (brother of Clodius) was placed in command of Greece, while F. Cornelius Sulla recruited troops for Pompey, joining him in Epirus. L. Calpurnius Bibulus was placed in general command of Pompey's troops, which illustrates that while Bibulus may not have had success dealing with Caesar as his co-consul back in 59, his military attributes and experience were acknowledged and respected by Pompey.

Cato received command of Sicily, but he refused to engage in bloodshed and yielded the province to Pollio and Curio, who came to the island on Caesar's behalf. Cato left after telling the islanders to seek safety by joining the attackers so as to spare any destruction and deaths that might have ensued if

Brutus

Cato had joined in battle. In fact, 'Pompey trusted [Cato] enough to put him in charge of the garrison and naval squadron at Dyrrhachium'.[6] Yet there was something more to Cato: 'although of fighting age, [he] did not take part in the military engagements and perhaps he had told Pompey that he would not do so'.[7]

Cato was extremely reluctant to shed blood. While the senate might have the moral high-ground in relation to Caesar, it appears that Cato simply would not put ordinary men into combat in a battle that he perhaps thought of as a personal fight between himself and Caesar. In April 48, at the battle of Dyrrhachium, Caesar barely avoided a major defeat and retreated to Thessaly, but the turning point was a later battle, that of Pharsalus.

THE BATTLE OF PHARSALUS – 9 AUGUST 48 BCE

It is not clear whether Pompey was pushed into fighting against Caesar by his senatorial colleagues, but with a far superior numerical advantage of some 70,000–75,000 troops versus Caesar's 35,000, it was possible that following Dyrrhachium, a quick victory may have been possible for the Pompeians. One problem that Caesar faced was incomplete numbers within his legions, but his troops were much more experienced than Pompey's. Furthermore, Pompey had to contend with other commanders on his side, while Caesar himself oversaw his entire force.

Held by the river Enipeus on Caesar's left, the major action took place on the right side of Caesar's forces. Pompey hoped to use his superior cavalry in a two-front attack, with his slingers and archers as relief, while Caesar put his infantry in a fourth battle line in reserve. Pompey's objective was to tire out Caesar's forces, but Caesar's more experienced troops realized this and stopped their charge. Pompey, unable to communicate with his own soldiers, watched the stalemate.

Meanwhile, Labienus (on the furthest reach on Caesar's right) pushed the cavalry forward, but were met with Caesar's fourth battle line, which then swept around the back of Pompey's troops. Faced then with fresh Caesarian forces (the third line), the Pompeians began to panic and, in the confusion, Pompey fled. Moving in with his soldiers, Caesar is reported to have said at Pharsalus, 'he would have it so, after my great achievement, I, Gaius Caesar, should have been condemned by my enemies if I had not appealed to my army'.[8]

Fleeing from the battle, Pompey went to the island of Mytilene where he met with his wife Cornelia and son, Sextus Pompeius. Wondering where to go next, he eschewed the eastern provinces and sought refuge in Egypt. Waiting off the coast, the Egyptian government considered their response. Fearing that Caesar was on his way, the counsellors of young Ptolemy XIII advised that it would be better to kill Pompey in order to show their allegiance to Caesar, in hopes that no adverse attack would be forthcoming in what they considered a Roman war.

On 29 September 48 (believed to be Pompey's birthday), Pompey was lured towards a supposed audience on shore. Travelling in a small boat, he recognized some of his former comrades, but as he was preparing his speech for the king, two men entered the boat and stabbed him several times. They then decapitated the corpse, leaving the body unattended and naked, taking the head to the king. One of Pompey's freemen organized a simple funerary pyre and cremated the remains on the timbers of the small boat.

Pursuing the Pompeian army to Alexandria, Caesar's forces camped and became involved in the Egyptian civil war between Ptolemy and his sister, Cleopatra. The siege of Alexandra began shortly afterwards. Caesar later was to receive a small gift from Ptolemy; he was not pleased to be presented with Pompey's head in a box, and on receiving his signet ring, Caesar burst into tears. He was later to give Pompey's ashes and signet ring to Pompey's widow, Cornelia. It is believed that it was this action by Ptolemy that decided Caesar in favour of Cleopatra.

By December 48, Caesarian forces combined with Cleopatra's had won a decisive victory against Ptolemy in Alexandria. In the end, Caesar was able to depose Ptolemy, execute his regent and then install Cleopatra as ruler. During the battle, part of the great library of Alexandria caught fire and was burned down.

During the early part of 47, Caesar, along with Cleopatra, was able to finally route the Ptolemaic forces at the battle of the Nile, where Ptolemy was killed. At this point, Caesar finally relieved his troops in Alexandria. In May, Caesar redressed the defeat of the previous October, when he defeated Pharnaces at the battle of Zela. This is the infamous battle where Caesar reported his victory to the senate with *veni, vidi, vici* (I came, I saw, I conquered). Caesar then returned to Rome to quell a mutiny of his veterans.

In October 47, Caesar began his invasion of Africa.

NORTHERN AFRICA

Having heard of Pompey's death, Cato took control of the Pompeian forces and went along the coast to Cyrene, where Plutarch notes that the people received him kindly. It is believed that Cato controlled some ten thousand soldiers and after wintering, he led his army across to Utica. At the same time, there was a quarrel between Metellus Scipio and Varus as both tried to secure the favour of Juba, the ruler of Numidia.

Plutarch notes that as Juba was about to have an interview with Cato, he placed his own seat between those of Scipio and Cato, but Cato moved his seat to allow Scipio the middle position. Cato was then able to reconcile Scipio and Varus, but refused the overall command, noting that Scipio, as an ex-consul, had eminence over himself.

Scipio then tried to 'gratify' Juba by proclaiming that he would destroy the city of Utica as it had proclaimed its allegiance to Caesar, but Cato refused to allow this. Organizing the men of Utica, Cato established military quarters and built formidable trenches and palisades in front of the city. Scipio is reported to have called Cato a coward for sitting behind the fortifications, but Cato remarked that he would therefore take his troops back to Italy and face Caesar head-on, which seems more an insult against Scipio than evidence of Cato's cowardice.

THE BATTLE AT THAPSUS (FEBRUARY 46)[9]

Gathering their forces, the *boni* prepared to meet Caesar in batttle. Their army included some 10,000 men, an extremely powerful cavalry, the forces of local kings such as Juba, and some 60 war elephants. There were some small skirmishes, during which two legions deserted to Caesar. In the beginning of February, expecting reinforcements from Sicily, Caesar arrived in Thapsus and began to besiege the city.

At this point, Metellus Scipio and other commanders were forced to engage in battle. Scipio's army circled Thapsus but, anticipating Caesar's approach, this army remained in battle order flanked by elephants. Caesar utilized his usual approach, commanding the right side with the cavalry and archers flanked. Once the trumpeters had sounded the call to battle, the two sides began.

The elephants were surprised by the archers and began to withdraw, flattening the anti-Caesarian forces. After the loss of the elephants, Scipio began to lose ground and all hell broke lose. Caesar's cavalry destroyed the fortified camp and the opposition began to retreat. Juba's forces also abandoned the site and the battle was decided.

Although over 10,000 soldiers wanted to surrender to Caesar, they were instead slaughtered by his army, something that was extremely unusual for Caesar, who usually actively sought to recruit among the fallen Roman troops and proclaimed clemency for his enemies. It is not clear why Caesar (or his leaders) sanctioned such a move, but it may have been for the simple reason that, like Pharsalus, he intended Thapsus to be the ultimate victory, bringing an end to any anti-Caesarian revolt in North Africa. The war was now pretty much over, except for a few remnants of Caesarian opposition. For Cato, it was the end.

CATO'S DEATH – APRIL 46 BCE

When word came of Caesar's victory at Thapsus, Cato realized that the Republican resistance against Caesar had failed. Caesar was now the acknowledged ruler of Rome. Instead of seeking Caesar's pardon, although he urged his son and follow-ers to so do, Cato decided to end his own life in Utica, believing that there was no place for him under a Caesarian government. One could question whether it was the right decision, as Cato could have continued his protests against Caesar, perhaps even to joining Pompey's son, Sextus Pompeius or even, by force of personality, have driven Caesar out of Rome with his own troops.

Cato was aware that only a few remnants of anti-Caesarian resistance remained, and to Cato, Rome was a lost cause. It is doubtful that Cato would have eventually succeeded against Caesar and the bloodshed that would have resulted in enormous casualties was anathema to Cato's beliefs. Furthermore, *libertas*, a concept that Cato espoused, had been destroyed. With Caesar as ruler, there was no place for Cato.

Cato's death was the only recourse as he had lost all hope of escaping total destruction. '[His] alternative was having to appeal to the mercy of the hated victor Caesar', which was something that Cato would never have tolerated or even considered.[10]

Even if Caesar himself never used the word *clementia*, it was 'the situation, not the word, that men like Marcus Marcellus and Cato resented, the situation in which Caesar had acquired power over his equals by civil war and clearly intended to keep that power for some time afterwards'.[11] Indeed, Cato characterized conditions as '*arrogantiae, superbiae dominatusque unius mandatus*' (presumption, pride and the rule of one)[12] and sought death. Finally, as the historian Miriam Griffin points out, 'Cato, Caesar's most consistent enemy, who, after leading the resistance in Africa, declared that he was unwilling to be pardoned by Caesar because that would imply legal recognition of Caesar's position as tyrant through which he had acquired the power to save'.[13] Caesar was extremely angry with Cato, which was reflected in the vindictive nature of his later polemic, *Anticato*, which illustrated to others about what Caesar's infamous clemency really consisted of. Caesar never forgave Cato.

Plutarch records at great length the last hours of Cato's life in his *Life of Cato Minor* (67–70). After taking a bath, Cato sat dining with his friends and the magistrates of Utica. Over wine, literary topics and other pleasantries were discussed by those present, with a debate about the paradoxes of Stoicism. The Stoic concept of good and evil was mentioned, with a discourse about how the good man alone is free, while the bad are all slaves to their whims and ambitions. Cato broke into the discussion and maintained his argument with such vehemence that the others started to fear that Cato was planning to kill himself, thereby ending his current difficulties. Seeing their reaction, Cato returned to a more general conversation about those who had left, expressing his anxiety about their safe passage over the seas back to Rome.

When supper concluded, Cato took his customary walk with friends, but again, aroused their suspicions by embracing his son and friends with more than his usual kindness and concern. Cato then retired to his bedchamber and began to read Plato's *Phaedo*. Blaming a servant for misplacing his sword, he spoke harshly both to his son and companions, arguing that if he wanted to kill himself, he did not need his sword as there were numerous other methods he could use.

Cato began to contemplate his options, but returned to his book, reading through it twice and taking a short nap. Waking up around midnight, Cato asked his freeman to check on whether the sailing had been successful. After reporting that most of the ships had left, the servant told Cato that there was a heavy storm and a high wind which was delaying the final ships from embarking. Cato sent the servant back to offer any assistance and then slept for a few more hours.

As dawn approached, the servant told Cato that the harbours were quiet and went away from the bedchamber. Cato then took his sword and stabbed himself below the breast, but his motion was weak. In his death struggle, he fell from the couch. The noise alerted the household with servants, friends and Cato's son all rushing in, but he was still alive. Once Cato had recovered his senses, he pushed the physician away and tore at his bowels, finally dying.

Within hours, word had spread of Cato's demise and the townspeople were at the door, bemoaning his death and glorifying him as their saviour and benefactor. Even when rumours of Caesar's approach were heard, the people still refused to leave the house. Cato was buried near the sea with a statue of him with his sword in his hand erected later. Caesar, upon hearing of his death, is said to have responded, 'O Cato, I begrudge your death as much as you would begrudge me your life'.[14]

Cato's daughter, Porcia, would later marry her cousin, the future tyrannicide Brutus, while Cato's son joined in the later conspiracy against Caesar. Both of the main assassins, along with Cato's son, were to die at Philippi, with Porcia dying by her own hand. It would appear that a M. Porcius Cato served as a *delator* and suffect consul in 36 CE, but it is not certain that he belonged to this branch of the family.[15] Cato's death really was the end of the Porcii as well as Cato's beloved *res publica*. Yet his legacy would live on for generations.

THE END OF THE WAR: THE SECOND SPANISH COMMAND

Both of Pompey's sons from his third marriage remained a threat to Caesar. Gnaeus Pompeius and Sextus Pompeius, along with Titus Labienus, had escaped to Hispania. Two original Pompeian legions, which had enrolled in Caesar's army, now declared their allegiance to Gnaeus Pompeius and drove out the Caesarian proconsul. Able to raise another legion, the three men now had three strong, experienced legions to confront Caesar as he made his way towards the capital of the province, Cordoba.

Caesar travelled the 1,500 miles in less than a month and was immediately able to relieve the besieged town of Ulipia in early December 46, but could not secure Cordoba. Deciding against an open battle, Gnaeus Pompeius determined to wait Caesar out and the latter was forced to prepare for a winter campaign. Over January and February 45, Caesar slowly reduced his opposition, in particular, by taking the city of Ategua, which undermined morale and confidence on the Pompeian side. In early March 45, the two sides finally met on the plains of Munda in southern Hispania.

17 MARCH 45 BCE – THE BATTLE OF MUNDA

It is believed that Caesar was outnumbered by some 40,000 to 70,000 men (including cavalry and auxiliaries), and in the earliest stages, it was unclear how the course of the battle was progressing. The Pompeian army began the battle on a gentle hill less than a mile from the town of Munda, but after an unsuccessful attempt to draw Pompeius' army down the hill, Caesar led a charge.

The battle continued on for some time without any clear progress; the generals on each side then joined the ranks. The fighting was extremely fierce as many of those under Pompeius correctly believed that they would be shown no clemency by Caesar, having changed sides back to the Pompeian forces in late 46. In the end, Caesar's favourite legion began to push back the threatened left wing, but seeking a weakness in the Pompeian right wing, Caesar's cavalry launched a decisive thrust that turned the battle into a success.

With Caesar's army attacking the rear of Pompeius' army, Titus Labienus moved to intercept them, but miscommunication resulted in a belief that Labienus was actually retreating. At that point, the Pompeian army broke ranks and fled in the disorder. All of the Pompeian standards were captured, some 30,000 Pompeian soldiers were killed and Titus Labienus, once one of Caesar's most favoured generals, died. He was allowed a proper burial by Caesar, while both Sextus and Gnaeus Pompeius escaped.

Caesar then left his legate to besiege Munda and moved throughout the province to consolidate support. Both Cordoba and Munda, the latter after holding out for some time, were quickly retaken and Gnaeus Pompeius was found and executed. Sextus Pompeius, however, escaped to Sicily and would continue to pose a minor problem to Caesar, not being ultimately defeated until 35 BCE.

The atmosphere in Rome when Caesar returned was fraught with uneasy anticipation and fear. Caesar's well-known policy of clemency on the battlefield, excepting the massacre of the Pompeian forces at Thapsus and at Munda, was still untested in Rome itself. Caesar had a number of ideas and proposals as he returned to Rome, but there was still fear, as the scholar Christian Meier has noted 'for the time being, Caesar could do anything. Rome had to wait and see what he wanted. It was advisable to stay behind cover.'[16] Everything depended on Caesar.

Meanwhile, however, a literary war of sorts was occupying Rome during this uncertain time. Caesar's long-time enemy Cato, although dead in April 46 BCE, continued to colour senatorial sentiment. Ironically, Cato, in death, would perhaps be even more powerful than in life. At this stage, Cato's death became a viable political weapon against Caesar, which perhaps best shows that behind his policy of clemency, Caesar was anything but.

THE CONTINUED INFLUENCE OF CATO THE YOUNGER (AND CAESAR'S RESPONSE)

Within a few months of Cato's death in April 46, polemics, including both laudatory *Catos* and vindictive *Anticatos*, began to appear. Unfortunately, none of these have survived, but as later authors have remarked on them it is not difficult to surmise the content and sentiment in these accounts. On the positive side, both Cicero and Brutus composed eulogizing *Catos*, while Hirtius (cos. 43) and Caesar responded with vehement attacks. The latter backfired on Caesar and was at odds with his alleged clemency following his victory. This will be discussed in a moment.

THE PRO *CATOS*

The first eulogy for Cato that appeared was that of Cicero's, but he had problems in composing his *Cato*, fearing repercussions from the pro-Caesarian camp, as he notes 'If I steer clear of his utterances in the (senate) and of his entire political outlook and content myself with simply praising his unwavering constancy, even that would be odious for them'.[17] Nevertheless, Cicero persevered. His account began to be circulated around summer 46, just a few months after Cato's death. It appears to have dealt with Cato's childhood, but other details cannot be definitively determined. Although Cicero later said that he regretted writing his *Cato*, this may have been due not to any particular repercussions aimed towards Cicero himself, but rather reflected Cicero's withdrawal from political events following his daughter's death. He may not have wanted to be drawn into debate and discussion as he sank deeper into depression and introspection.[18]

The next positive account that appeared in 45 was Brutus', Cato's nephew and posthumous son-in-law (he had married Bibulus' widow and Cato's daughter, Porcia sometime in 46 or 45). How Brutus dealt with Cato can only be surmised. It would be reasonable to suggest that Cato's political career and importance was part of this account as Cicero took affront at its contents. At length, Cicero was to complain to Atticus that Brutus had overstated Cato's role in the decision-making process during the Catilinarian debates back in 63 BCE. He felt that Brutus had presented the debate as simply a debate (with Cato taking the honours) and not as the decisive moment of Cicero's consulship and indeed, his entire political career. Furious that Brutus' *Cato* had undermined his own consular glory, Cicero urged Atticus to persuade Brutus to modify his pamphlet in order to more accurately (according to Cicero) reflect the debate on the 5th December 63. This is most interesting, not that it reflects badly on Brutus and Cato *per se*, but clearly illustrates to the modern reader just how insecure Cicero really was about his contribution to the *res publica*. Whether Brutus paid any heed to Cicero's pleas is unknown, although the latter *Bellum Catilinae* by Sallust (written by 40 BCE) was to place Cato and Caesar in primary focus in the senatorial debates.

Other accounts also appeared, among them that of Fadius Gallus, who wrote a laudatory panegyric of Cato in mid 45. However, the most intimate and detailed of all of the Cato pseudo-economia was that of Munatius Rufus, a close friend and advisor to Cato himself. Although also lost, it is possible to reconstruct this account by looking at a much later account, that of Plutarch's *Life of Cato Minor*, which is an invaluable source and indeed, offers much of the evidence to illustrate the animosity between Caesar and Cato.

THE *ANTICATOS*

The *Anticato*s, however, appear almost to have been uniform in their tactics and vehemence. Shortly after Cicero's *Cato*, both the consul Hirtius and Caesar himself wrote vindictive accounts. On the 15 May 45, Cicero wrote to Atticus that there should be a great circulation of Hirtius' pamphlet and thus 'from their abuse (of Cato), his reputation may be greatly enhanced'.[19] What Hirtius specifically wrote is not clear, but its overall tone and approach seems to have attacked and ridiculed Cato to such an extent that, whatever its truth, the anti-Caesarian camp itself was amused at Hirtius' and not Cato's expense.

The same can be said for Caesar's *Anticato*. It is surmised that his pamphlet attacked Cato on the grounds of avarice, drunkenness and unworthiness of holding political office, rather than as the adversary that he really was. In Caesar's commentary on the civil war, he gives some insight into his pettiness, stressing that Cato's anger towards him was due to his longstanding hatred and Cato's own frustration at his defeat for the consulship.[20] Even the officer writing in the pseudo-Caesarian *Bellum Africum* acknowledged Cato's integrity.[21] Perhaps Caesar felt that it was better to ignore his enemy rather than try to deal with the numerous charges that Cato had levelled against him, almost from the beginning of his political career.

Whatever was written within Caesar's *Anticato*, it definitely backfired on the author. It was cruel, vindictive and self-destructive. The *Anticato* appears to have been written in two separate parts and, according to the historian Lily Ross Taylor, was 'presented, as Roman political pamphlets often were, as a speech for the prosecution ... thus, Caesar, whom the living Cato had vowed to bring to trial, was himself accusing his dead enemy'.[22]

While we do not know the specific charge, perhaps it was the same accusation that Cato may have threatened Caesar with – that of *maiestas* or treason against the state. There was anger and frustration in Caesar's attack. He simply could not understand his contemporary. Caesar had underestimated his colleague without ever quite realizing the political influence of his enemy. In many things that

Caesar had done or attempted to do, Cato had been there, trying to stop him, or at the very least, curb his excesses. In the end, Caesar simply could not stand Cato and in his *Anticato*, he mocked him with abandon. This work is perhaps one of the most vindictive pamphlets written during this post civil war period.[23]

Furthermore, the work itself undermined Caesar's platform of clemency. While there had been some trepidation when Caesar returned to Rome, this well-publicised clemency had done a great deal in calming both the city as well as the senatorial figures who were fearful of Caesar's aims and how he intended to secure his own power base. The *Anticato* caused a significant breach between Caesar and his colleagues, and what he had failed to again realize was that many of the survivors of the war had also supported Cato, not just within Roman politics but also during the war itself. Cato had, of course, led the anti-Caesarian forces in North Africa following Pompey's death in 48 until his own in April 46. This work, therefore, 'probably did [Caesar's] reputation no good, since many ... of the Caesarians had been under the impression of Cato's personality'.[24] It called into question just how forgiving Caesar really was.

CAESAR'S ACTIONS

It was not until September 45 that Caesar finally returned to Rome. Unlike Sulla, some forty years prior, Caesar's enemies had not been vanquished and feeling against him was running high. Nevertheless, a weakened senate had voted him triumphs as well as a number of extraordinary powers and honours, such as being named *praefectus morum* (overseer of morals, much like the censorship) and *dictator perpetuus* (dictator for life). Whether Caesar actually wanted these honours or rather that the senate felt it advisable to heap such rewards on him is not known, but 'even if the senators were not acting on his express wishes, they realised that he expected no less'.[25]

Whereas Pompey had set down his dictatorship/sole consulship in 52 after six months, the only precedent in living memory of another dictator was that of Sulla, who had retreated to private life after some two years. The senate may have felt that, as opposed to openly sanctifying any monarchical aspirations, offering the dictatorship may have reminded Caesar of the traditional role that the senate enjoyed within the Republican framework. The question remains whether Caesar felt any need for the senate or Republican necessities as he returned to Rome.

While his primacy had been assured, Caesar then had to deal with the destruction that the civil war had wrought and in particular, within the city of Rome itself. The provinces lay in disarray, ordinary political life had been rendered meaningless and the economic situation was in dire straits. Many of those who had helped in the running of the city, its government and provinces had perished in the war and it was not just an uncertain time for those colleagues remaining, but the city as a whole.

Meanwhile, however, Caesar's triumphs excited the people as they proceeded through the city, taking up to a whole day each with great spectacles. There were gladiatorial games, theatrical performances and massive feasts to entertain the people of Rome. Such a multitude had gathered that people were forced to sleep in tents or in the outdoors, and the festival went on for days. After this, Caesar distributed his booty. Some was given to urban populace, but most of the money went to his veterans. When one or two soldiers protested that the soliders should have received all of his booty, Caesar appears to have executed one of them, while having two other ritually sacrificed.[26] Overall, however, these triumphs allowed Caesar to consolidate his popular base; the senate was less pleased, with many grumbling about the expenses incurred as a result of the almost month-long celebrations.

One of Caesar's first moves was a general amnesty for all who had fought against him during the civil wars, thereby illustrating his break with earlier tradition; both Marius and Sulla's dictatorships had embarked upon violent and bloody attacks on their enemies, the repercussions of the latter's well-known to Caesar's contemporaries. In this, at least, Caesar was determined not to emulate Sulla, which in most likelihood did calm some of the fears of the senatorial and aristocratic classes (those who remained).

Caesar then began to plan a comprehensive social programme. The first measure was a reassessment of these eligible for free grain – although he cut the numbers significantly, Caesar proposed that large landowners be forced to hire one third of their labour from the urban poor as opposed to utilizing slave labour *en masse*. Caesar also proposed creating numerous resettlement colonies throughout the provinces as a way to relieve some urban congestion as well.

Turning to the social composition of the city, he allowed Greek teachers and doctors to acquire Roman citizenship as a means to promote education and stability, with the emphasis on the immigration of suitable non-citizens to Rome itself. Furthermore, he banned all *collegia*, which Clodius had re-introduced, as a means to control the urban gangs which had caused great unrest and violence during the 50s. He also proposed a general cancellation of a quarter of all debt owed, which helped not only to relieve some suffering, but also, continued to raise his popularity among the masses.

Caesar also focused on provincial management, limiting the terms of provincial governors and propraetors, to one year for propraetors and two years for proconsuls, which perhaps can be interpreted as an attempt not to allow any single individual an opportunity as Caesar himself had enjoyed in Gaul where he had had control of the province for some ten years. He also reformed tax policies by removing the dreaded tax collectors (such as evidenced by the Asian tax problems of the late 60s) by putting taxation back into the hands of the provincials themselves.

Perhaps his greatest accomplishment for the modern world was the reworking of the calendar. His complete overhauling of the solar year, as opposed to the lunar year, resulted in the year now lasting 365¼ days (with a leap day every four years), finally bringing the calendar year into synch with the seasons of the year – it is surmised that before this, one year had 444 days in it.[27] Caesar also proposed an extensive rebuilding programme for Rome, including a new rostra and a public library, while the senate building (which had been just been completed) was to be abandoned for a new marble project to be called the *curia Julia*. These plans would reach final fruition under his successor, Octavian (Augustus).

Caesar then began the lengthy process of re-establishing the governmental structure that the civil war had destroyed. The senate itself had been greatly depleted and Caesar raised its numbers to 900. For the new senatorial class, Caesar sought to reward various Italian provincials who had supported him and in effect, this had an added bonus of further unifying Italy – the process having begun back after the Social War of the early 90s, and perhaps, in this, Caesar succeeded in consolidating the Italian peninsula within the Roman structure. As for the magistracies, Caesar did two things: the first increasing the number of magistrates, while second resulted in controlling election results for the foreseeable future.

In this first measure, Caesar raised the number of praetors from 8 to 16, aediles from 4 to 6, with the quaestorship increasing from 20 to 40, but the functions of their offices remained the same.[28] Although Caesar was offered the chance to select magistrates, he chose instead to oversee the elections. It should be noted, however, that no elections actually took place in 47 or until the end of 45, while 46 saw Caesar appointing eight prefects who assisted Lepidus as *magister equitum*, while Caesar was away in Spain. In 45, it was not until October that Caesar gave up his fourth consulship in favour of Quintus Fabius Maximus and Gaius Trebonius as suffect consuls – Caesar, of course, still remained dictator. Indeed, for 44, one again sees Caesar controlling the magistracies and he placed individuals favourable to himself in positions of power.

CAESAR AS KING?

Continued honours were heaped on Caesar throughout 45 and into 44 BCE. Having been declared dictator for life and *pater patriae* (father of the country) by the senate, Caesar was indeed in control of the government. Although the urban masses had shown their support, particularly during the celebrations of 45 and with approval of some of his reformist schemes, it was nevertheless a precarious time for Caesar. Some of his actions during the last few months of his life served to illustrate Caesar's belief in his own superiority, which would serve to antagonize numerous senatorial colleagues, in particular, those he had so graciously pardoned.

For the first time, a Roman citizen, namely Caesar himself, was portrayed on coinage, contrary to customary practice. In this, Caesar clearly showed his belief that he was above the state and tradition. Furthermore, a new statue of Caesar was unveiled in the temple of Quirinus alongside those of the seven kings of pre-Republican Rome. A note of irony can perhaps be seen that the only other man aside from the kings who had a statue there was Lucius Junius Brutus, famed for his role in the revolt that led to the execution and expulsion of those kings.

Caesar also began to show signs of impatience with ceremonial responsibilities. When a senatorial delegation went to consult him at the new Temple of Venus (built by Caesar to celebrate his connection and thanksgiving to his patron deity), he refused to stand in deference. While he appears to have regretted his action, later baring his neck to his friends saying he was ready to offer it to anyone, it was not one of Caesar's better moves.

In the streets, a few individuals were calling him *rex*, or king but, in annoyance, Caesar initially refused to accept such a title. At a festival in February 44, Caesar was offered a crown by Mark Antony. Seeing the lacklustre support from the people, Caesar refused the honour. A second attempt saw Caesar stand to refuse, noting that 'Jupiter alone is king of the Romans' and 'I am Caesar, not king'.[29] As the people wildly applauded this gesture, Caesar appears to have retained his popular support as well as, perhaps, realizing the limit that the people would allow him. Rome was not ready for a king.

THE PLOT TO ASSASSINATE CAESAR

There have been numerous theories regarding the motivation behind the conspiracy to assassinate Caesar. Some are as mundane as simple hatred, whereas others are as outlandish as Caesar being equated to a Greek-style king, much like Alexander the Great, nullifying his Roman qualities and turning him into a tyrant of the old style, ripe for removal. Others have considered the fulfilment of Brutus' destiny as a descendant of the original slayer of Roman kings; revenge for Pompey or Cato's death (as Brutus was his nephew and posthumous son-in-law); or even that it was a logical philosophical response to tyranny.

There was indeed a loss of personal *dignitas*, with Caesar now controlling elections, selecting individuals for positions and appointing favoured people to take other administrative roles, often very lucrative. By assuming the dictatorship in perpetuity, Caesar had deprived many of participation in traditional Roman politics; the political offices had lost their importance as they were now given, not earned. There was an increasing frustration that, under Caesar, the rewards were nothing more than gifts from a benevolent ruler, hoping to distract his subjects from his own desires. It was a loss of freedom that many could not really reconcile themselves to and, in the end, this seething resentment would find fruition in a concerted effort to remove Caesar from power.

One interesting idea is that the senate was perhaps playing with Caesar, awarding him extensive honours not just to pander to his vanity, but to subtly remind people that Caesar was not an ordinary Roman anymore – the idea being that with each increased honour, more and more individuals would became resentful and that the urban masses would increase their own hatred towards him. This idea actually has some merit. Caesar had not won an overall resounding victory in the civil war and those that he had 'pardoned' subjected themselves to such a move for personal safety, but their own beliefs would not be subjugated within the parody of what passed for Republican politics under Caesar.

There were those who were generally pleased at their rewards, but many others resented Caesar's high-handedness and break with the traditional ways. In the end, it is possible that the many honours were a combination of genuine honour as well as an attempt to remove Caesar from the loop of accepted Roman practice.

It was Brutus, however, who provided the legitimacy that the conspirators needed to follow through on their plan, and he was, for a number of reasons, willing to comply. The refusal of Cato to accept Caesar's clemency was something that permeated throughout Roman society. Although he had urged his son, friends and followers to appeal to Caesar, it was an uneasy decision for many. Brutus had to reconcile the internal struggle. It was not just a question of the perceived insult to his family, such as his frustration over his mother's lengthy affair with Caesar, but also more recent events, such as Cato's death as well as how Caesar was treating the *res publica*.

As Cato's nephew, Brutus also grew to embrace philosophy and, in particular, appeared to embrace the best of Greek ideals, but this was also intermixed with his role in the Republic, family tradition and personal idealism. Brutus married Cato's daughter, Porcia (Bibulus' widow) and fought hard for Cato's recognition, particularly envisaging him as a role model contrasting severely with Caesar. Where Caesar indulged in clemency, Cato began increasingly to represent the fallen Roman world.

Another consideration was Brutus' awareness of being descended from the infamous Lucius Junius Brutus, who had assassinated the last king of Rome – Tarquinius Superbus – in 509 BCE. There were daily reminders that Brutus himself, by allowing Caesar to prosper, was ignoring the role that he was destined to play.

THE IDES OF MARCH (15 MARCH 44 BCE)

It is rumoured that in the days before Caesar's appearance in the senate on the Ides of March that there were balls of fire seen in the skies and that it rained blood – auspicious omens that foretold death and destruction. On the morning in question, one of Caesar's closest friends, Decimus, came to collect him and they walked through the streets to the Theatre of Pompey, where the senate was meeting, as the old *curia* had burnt down in the conflagration surrounding Clodius' death nearly a decade before and was not yet completely rebuilt.

It was the custom that Caesar would enter the assembly alone and unescorted. As he did so, the signal for the conspirators to gather was given and collectively, they attacked Caesar. A few minutes after 11 am, Julius Caesar lay dead, ironically near Pompey's statue. There had been some 23 stab wounds with the second strike being the mortal blow. Whether Caesar actually made the now infamous comment, '*Et tu, Brute?*', with all of its heavy significance, as he lay dying is not necessarily true, but it is true that it was not just the enemies of Caesar who surrounded him that day, but also his friends.

Did Caesar know of the plot? Although Shakespeare conveniently has the soothsayer prophesy to 'beware the Ides of March' to all who would listen, Caesar may have heard the rumours of a plot, but not believed how serious it was. Perhaps he believed his own propaganda and thought he was generally loved, respected and admired. It is difficult to ascertain just how Julius Caesar felt; much as during his political career he had demonstrated his reluctance to follow the rules, now there were no rules except what Caesar wanted. As Cicero said, 'the sun only rose because Caesar said so', this type of sycophantic behaviour may have had an extremely negative impact on him.[30] In the end, Caesar may have thought he was invincible and therefore, simply could not believe that anyone hated him, or the idea of him, so much as to plot his downfall. Caesar was dead, but perhaps not yet the Republic.

THE REPERCUSSIONS

While it is common to assume that Caesar's assassination meant that the republic died then and there, this is not necessarily the case. In the aftermath, the conspirators were free in Rome while the people waited to see what would happen. As consul, Mark Antony appeared to be following the line of stability and calming political tensions, but this was to change on the day of Caesar's funeral.

Antony gave a dramatic eulogy, capitalizing on the grief of the crowd, and when he began to read Caesar's will, the people were astonished and delighted to see that he had left his vast gardens as a public park and a sum of money to every male citizen. As the list of honours was read out, Antony seemed consumed by grief, stripping the bloodstained cloak off the corpse and raising it aloof on the tip of a spear. As the historian Josiah Osgood continues:

> The people, no longer merely the audience of this drama, joined Antony in his lamentation 'like a chorus'. It was monstrous: many of the murderers had been supporters of Pompey, but Caesar had spared them and given them posts in his government and his armies. As dirges were sung, some mimic blessed with a deadly accuracy called out a line from an old Roman tragedy: 'to think that I saved those men so they could destroy me'. The crowd was near to violence when somebody else suspended over the bier a wax effigy of Caesar – it would have been too difficult to lift the body – and twirled it around by a mechanical device so that all the twenty-three stab wounds could be seen.[31]

It was then that the crowd erupted, setting the senate *curia* on fire (again) and running through the streets, seeking the assassins, who had fled the Forum. On the 17th, Antony convened the senate and persuaded them to agree to an amnesty for the assassins, with Cicero urging him on. By agreeing not to declare Caesar a tyrant, it meant that new elections would not need to take place, and ordinary business could continue. One proviso was that the assassins had to leave the city, which Brutus gratefully did, but they were not declared public enemies.

Both Brutus and Cassius went to their provinces as legally recognized praetors. Brutus remained in Crete from 44–2 BCE. As things became calmer and more controlled, in June, the senate allocated the province of Cyrene to Cassius in his role as a praetor.

Antony continued to be consul, but soon Caesar's heir, his great-nephew Octavian, was to arrive in Italy. After a warm welcome from Caesar's troops in Brundisium, who had been readied in relation to Caesar's proposed war against the Parthians in the east, Octavian demanded some of the funds that Caesar had put aside for the Parthian campaign. He was to later seize the tribute sent by the eastern provinces, and started to amass his own army. Coming to Rome in May 44 BCE, he reached an uneasy truce with Mark Antony, who was to leave Rome shortly. It was not until 43 that the assassins were declared public enemies, and in a final battle at Philippi on 23 October 42 BCE, did the last vestiges and hopes for the republic finally fall. As Brutus died, it is recorded that his last words were:

> O wretched virtue, you were but a name, and yet I worshipped you as real indeed, but now, it seems, you were but fortune's slave.[32]

Conclusion

It was not inevitable that the Roman Republic would fall. One could argue that aristocratic competition and the levels to which individuals were willing to go to achieve power had irreparably destroyed the very foundations of Roman society, but this is too simple an answer. Due to changes in the army under Marius in the late first century BCE, soldiers increasingly looked to their successful generals to provide rewards, such as monies and land. Those generals, could, therefore, turn to their troops when they felt their own personal ambitions were being curtailed by other aristocratic figures, or even to overturn a senatorial decision or mandate. The civil wars of the 80s had an ominous tone to them, and Sulla's actions would overshadow much of the last decades of the Republic, but there are other factors to take into consideration.

The civil wars of the 80s had given a blueprint to any other aspiring dictator, but throughout the 70s, 60s and 50s, such threats as Lepidus or Sertorius in the 70s, Catiline in the 60s or even Clodius and Milo in the 50s were dealt with and the ordinary business of state continued, such as elections, trials and the proposal of legislation. It was not even the death of Caesar that caused the Republic to falter. Following his death, the assassins were persuaded not to challenge Caesar's legislation; the two main individuals involved – Brutus and Cassius – were sent as legally approved praetors to nearby provinces. It was not until 43 that the men were declared public enemies, and this was by Caesar's heir – Octavian. Furthermore, it was not until after the battle of Philippi that the *res publica* seemed doomed, but Pompey's son would continue to harass the second 'triumvirate' of Lepidus, Antony and Octavian until the mid-30s. Antony and Octavian, much like Pompey and Caesar, would fight another civil war, culminating in the defeat of Antony and Cleopatra at Actium in 31 BCE. It was then that Octavian, newly named Augustus, took over complete control of the Roman state, and the Republic was truly dead, although his carefully orchestrated programme of reconciliation with Republican traditions and the stability he offered clouded the issue of monarchy.

In the end, it was not Caesar or his death that meant the end of the republic. The state had survived Sulla and even Pompey as dictator in 52 BCE, but both had stepped down in the end and allowed the *res publica* to resume its path. In the end, the constant fighting would signal its end, but not for another 20 years after Caesar had crossed the Rubicon.

It may be convenient to blame Cato and the senate for not compromising with Caesar, but the reality is that when they were ready to do so, Caesar was not. He had been 'insulted' too much and would march to Rome to proclaim his superiority, his *dignitas* and his birthright. Yet nobody knows what might have happened if he had lived. He was prepared and ready to go to the east to deal with the Parthian threat, and perhaps with Caesar out of Rome for a few years, normal business and fewer Caesarian-influenced policies and elections could have resumed.

It is also too narrow to blame the assassins of Caesar. As consul Mark Antony did perhaps incite the people against the conspirators and while many fled Rome a month or so after Caesar's murder, Brutus and Cassius were nevertheless officially recognized in their roles as praetors. The senate acted accordingly, confirming their appointments and strongly advising that they leave Rome so that public order could be restored. Although Octavian came to Rome in May 44, he did not have the support and strength yet to try and fulfil Caesar's real legacy – that of domination of the *res publica*. It would take until the beginning of 43 until Octavian – with Antony absent – demanded that the conspirators be declared public enemies. It was almost two years later that the battle of Philippi destroyed one threat, not to the republic, but to Octavian; not even the eventual defeat of Pompey's son could consolidate Octavian's power. The end of the republic came with the deaths of Antony and Cleopatra, with Augustus now sole ruler.

While there are many good and reasonable ideas as to why the Republic fell, it is noteworthy that neither with Caesar as dictator, nor following his death, did anyone actually believe that the *res publica* was doomed. Caesar was ruthless in his pursuit of power, and his explanations cannot justify his actions. Rome had seen dictators, but with Caesar out of Rome for almost ten years, his path was unreasonable, destructive and, ultimately, destroyed a generation. He may have shown the way, but with his death, it was not apparent that the Republic was gone.

The assassins may have been naïve, but to blame them for not having the foresight to know what Caesar's heir intended is not helpful. As far as anybody in Rome in 44 BCE was aware, Caesar was dead, the masses were unhappy and Antony stepped in as consul to calm matters. Rome in 44–3 may have been in a precarious situation, but ordinary business continued. There was no revolution, there was no widespread destruction of Italy and, finally, there were hopes that the current system of government would recover. The republic was not yet dead.

In the line of formidable rulers, Rome had survived Marius' seven consulships, Sulla's dictatorship and other threats. Caesar may have commented that Sulla was a fool to have stepped down as dictator, but Caesar's own death did not ultimately cause Rome's destruction. This is of fundamental importance. The idea that it was one crisis after another until a war-weary world finally accepted Augustus is far too easy. One can easily blame Caesar, and indeed, his assassins might not have truly realized the repercussions of their act in the long-term, but it was Augustus who ended the republican system of government, by gradually eroding its traditions.

Pompey had stepped down from dictatorship, but Caesar would not. One *should* look at the increasing demands of public office, the need for evermore extravagant and excessive displays of wealth and the rivalry between aristocratic competitors that created conditions ripe for bribery and corruption. The issues surrounding land and the urban masses also played a major part. In the end, however, it was individuals and their actions that ultimately doomed Rome.

Sulla had marched on Rome. So did Caesar. Sulla had declared himself dictator. So did Caesar. Sulla had stepped down. Perhaps Caesar would have in time. This is a tantalizing 'what-if?' that historians delight in. What if Pompey had remained in Rome and met Caesar in one decisive battle? Would the end result be very different from what actually happened? While Caesar's future plans are only thoughts and desires, the reality was something quite different.

Caesar does deserve some of the blame, so do his assassins; this latter claim could also be laid at the senate's door and in the inaction of Mark Antony when Octavian came to claim his rights. It was a cumulative process, one that only really ended years later on the battlegrounds of Actium. It was never preordained, it was never thought possible and everybody believed that the republic would survive. After a generation had died in Caesar's civil war and Octavian's attacks against Brutus and Cassius at Philippi, another generation, unused to Republican practices, elections and normal senatorial business, were grateful to Augustus for finally bringing stability. It is that generation and their acquiescence in Augustus' rise to power that dealt the final blow. The ideas of the republic, its ideals of *libertas, virtus* and *iustitia*, would survive in literature, and for men who would never taste such freedom the *res publica* of Pompey, Caesar and Cato continued.

Notes

Notes to Chapter 1: What it Was to be Roman

1 Earl (1967), p. 33.
2 Lucilius 1196–1208.
3 Livy, 39:40.
4 Cic. *Att.* II.1
5 Sall. *BJ.* IV.7.
6 Millar (2004), p. 209.
7 Dupont (1989) p. 143.
8 Sall. *Cat.* 14.
9 Virgil, *Aeneid*, VI. 390.
10 Flower (1997), p. 23.
11 Bryant, *Handbook of Death and Dying* (2003), Sage: London, p. 311.
12 Bryant, *ibid.*
13 Nicolet (1980), p. 212.
14 Dunn (2005), p. 49.
15 Ibid, p. 54.

Notes to Chapter 2: A Blueprint for Civil War? Sulla and the 80s BCE

1 Plut. *Ti. Grac.* 19.5–6.
2 Plut. *G. Grac.* 4.1–3.
3 *ibid*, 14.4–5.
4 Taylor (1966), pp. 34–5.
5 Sall. *BJ.* 97.
6 It is difficult to convert Roman currency into modern equivalents.
7 Marching under the yoke is a particularly humiliating punishment. It has its origins from a Roman loss against the Samnites in 321 BCE, when the vanquished Romans were stripped of their weapons and forced to march one by one past the enemy. An even older tradition was for the conquered to bow and literally pass under a yoke used by oxen. In this case, however, the Roman swords were used.
8 Plut. *Marius.* 21.1–2.

9   Claridge (1998). Note that the existing senate house was moved from its original Republican location slightly.
10   Meier (1982, 1996), pp.159–60.
11   Cic. *Rab.* 7.20, 8.22.
12   Meier (1982, 1996), p.159.
13   App. *CW.* 135; Livy. *Per.* 71.
14   Diodorus Siculus 37.11.
15   Keaveney (1998), p. 22.
16   Vell. Pat. II. 14.
17   App. 1.38.
18   Livy. 75.7.
19   Vell. Pat. II. 17.1
20   App. *CW.* 1.49.
21   App. *CW.* 12.
22   App. *MW.* 21.88.
23   Plut. *Marius.* 34.3.
24   Plut. *Sulla.* 9.2.
25   Plut. *Sulla.* 9.5–7.
26   App. *CW.* 59.
27   App. *CW.* 60.
28   App. *CW.* I.67.
29   Plut. *Pomp.* 1.
30   Plut. *Marius* 45.1–2.
31   App. *MW.* 59.
32   App. *CW.* I.77.
33   Plut. *Pomp.* 8.
34   Plut. *Sulla.* 29.3.
35   Plut. *Sulla* 30.4.
36   Plut. *Sulla* 35.1.
37   App. *CW.* 96.
38   Dio 109.13.
39   Dio 109.20.
40   Vell. Pat. 28.4
41   Scholars are divided as to whether Caesar was born in 102 or 100. It is more likely that he was born in 100 as he was elected consul in 60 (at the age of 40). The normal age or 'his year' was 42, but as a patrician, Caesar could rely on an exemption to run two years earlier.
42   Plut. *Cat. Min.* 3.3
43   Vell. Pat. 28.2.
44   App. *CW.* I.100.
45   App. *CW.* I.106.

Notes to Chapter 3: The Up and Coming Generations: Rome in the 70s BCE

1   App. *CW.* I. 105.
2   Plut. *Suet.* 26.4–6.
3   Plut. *Caes.* 2.
4   App. *RH.* 71.
5   App. *RH.* 73–4.
6   Plut. *Lucullus* 16.1–7.
7   App. *RH.* 81.
8   App. *RH.* 82.
9   App. *CW.* I. 116.
10 Plut. *Cras.* 6–7.
11 J. Carcopino, *Daily Life in Ancient Rome* (New Haven: Yale), 1940, pp. 19–32.
12 Cic. *Verr.* 5.139.
13 App. *CW.* I. 121.38.
14 Plut. *Cras.* 12.
15 The *tribuni aerarii* were those not as wealthy as the *equites*, but, nevertheless, still from the higher classes. Caesar was to later remove their right to sit on juries in 46–5 BCE.
16 It appears that the agrarian bill might not have passed.
17 Plut. *Pomp.* 22.5–6.
18 Cic. *Verres.* I. 15. 45.
19 *CAH* 9, p. 227.
20 Cic. *Verres.* I. 2.4.
21 *Ibid*, I. 3.9.
22 *Ibid*, I. 32.82.
23 Plut. *Crass.* 12.3–4. The previous incident of their reconciliation, from Appian, appears similar to this telling. It is in the location of each account – Appian records that this was before they were consuls and both had armies on the outskirts of Rome, while Plutarch notes it was at the end of their consulship – that a difference can be seen.

Notes to Chapter 4: Hopes for the Future: Rome in the 60s BCE

1   Griffin (1993), p. 196.
2   Plut. *Pomp.* 26.3.
3   Plut. *Pomp.* 26.3–4; Dio 36.37.
4   App. *RH.* 98.
5   Dio 36.17.3.
6   Cic. *De har. resp.* 42.
7   Dio 36.38.1.
8   Dio 36. 38.3.
9   Plut. *Cic.*13.
10 Seager (1979; 2002), pp. 44–7.
11 Cic. *Man.* 10.27.

12   Cic. *Man.* 15.43.
13   Dio 36. 49.5–8.
14   Octavius also founded a city of Nicopolis in Epirus (Greece) following victory over Antony and Cleopatra at Actium in 31 CE.
15   Plutarch says it was extortion, but Asconius argues that it was for violent disorder during Cornelius' trial.
16   Wiseman (1994a), p. 342.
17   See Sall. *BC.* 18.5; Ascon. 92C, and Dio 36.44.3.
18   Suet. *DJ.* 9.
19   Salmon (1935), pp. 305–6. For alternative views, see Epstein (1987), p. 66 and Seager (1979, 2002), pp. 66–7.
20   Seager (1979, 2002), pp. 66–7.
21   Wiseman (1994a), p. 343.
22   Cic. *Murena* 38.37.
23   Cic. *Att.* I. 2.
24   Suet. *DJ.* 10.
25   It seems more probable that Cato would have brought prosecutions during his quaestorship and as the trials were conducted in 64, not 65, this is one definite sign of his holding the office in 64. Furthermore, Cato was born in 95 and would not have been eligible for election to quaestorship until after his 30th birthday; the election taking place in 65.
26   Dio 37.9.5.
27   Cic. *Cat.* 3.8.19.
28   Plut. *Cato min.* 16.5.
29   Gruen (1974), p. 277.
30   Dio 37.10.3–4.
31   Plut. *Cic.* 11.
32   Cic. *Q.F.* 64.
33   Stockton (1971) p. 72.

Notes to Chapter 5: Rome in Crisis? The Catilinarian Conspiracy of 63 BCE

1   Dio 37.25.2.
2   Cic. *Leg Agr.* 1.1–3.
3   Roscius had passed legislation in 67 that reserved the first 14 rows of the theatre for the equestrian order; the knights may have appreciated the gesture, the people evidently did not.
4   Plut. *Caes.* 7.2–5.
5   Dio 37. 37. 3.
6   Sall. *BC.* 26.
7   Dio 37.29.2–5.
8   Plut. *Cat. Min.* 20–1.
9   Seager (1979; 2002), p. 52.
10   Plut. *Cic.* 14.2.

11   See Cic. *Att.* 12.21 (SB 256).
12   Yavetz (1963), p. 498.
13   Suet. *Div Iul.*17.
14   Cic. *Fam.* V. 2.
15   App. *RH.* 111.63.
16   Dio 37.14.1–2.
17   Wiseman (1971), p. 359.
18   *Ibid*, p. 360.
19   Rickman (1980), p. 171.
20   Seager (1979; 2002), p. 49; see de Sousa (1999), pp. 179–182, which deals specifically with
     the situation in 62 BCE.
21   Cic. *Att.* I.17.
22   Cic. *Att.* I.18.
23   Tatum (1999), p. 64.
24   Cic. *Att.* I.14.
25   The *lex Aelia et Fufia* was designed to stop any additional senatorial measures during the
     period from election notices to election day.
26   Of the 22 possible consular slots from 90 to 80, only 13 men had held the position (Cinna
     × 4, Carbo × 3 and Sulla × 2); there were 8 deaths in office. See Gruen (1966): pp. 385–9.

Notes to Chapter 6: A First Triumvirate? Rome in the Early 50s BCE

1   Suet. *Div.Iul* 20.
2   However, a later (April or May) *lex agraria* regarding the Campanian lands was proposed
    and passed. This law was much more restrictive than the previous bill.
3   It is most likely that it was not the *lex agraria* that was the innovation, but the fact that
    a consul, rather than a tribune, proposed it. Plutarch notes that: 'for whatever political
    schemes the boldest and most arrogant tribunes were wont to practise to win the favour
    of the multitude, these Caesar used with the support of the consular power, in disgraceful
    and humiliating attempts to ingratiate himself with the people' (*Cato Min.* 32.1).
4   Plut. *Cat.Min.* 32.1.
5   Wiseman (1985), p. 369.
6   Taylor (1949), p. 133.
7   Wiseman (1985), p. 371.
8   See Cicero's letters *Att.* II.13 (April); *Att.* II. 16 (May); *Att.* II.19 (July); *Att.* II.21 (summer);
    and, *Att.* II.22 (October).
9   Cic. *Att.* II. 24.
10 Seager (1979; 2002), p. 106.
11 For clarification Cicero's letter *Att.* II.24 is the best (and most contemporary) source
    regarding suspicions about Caesar's involvement. Cicero's hatred (and fear) of Clodius
    is evident in other letters from this year, so the omission of Clodius from this particular
    event is particularly noteworthy.
12 See Cic. *Att.* II.19.

13 Cic. *Att.* II. 21.

14 Wirszubski (1950), p. 76. See also Cicero, *QF.* 1.2.15.

15 Cic. *Att.* II. 17 (May).

16 Cic. *Att.* II.20 (July).

17 Cic. *Att.* II. 21 (late summer).

18 Cic. *Att.* II. 23 (September/October).

19 Gruen (1974), p.99.

20 Scullard (1959; 1982), p. 116.

21 Tatum (1999), Oost (1955), pp. 98–112; Balsdon (1962), pp. 166–182.

22 Dio 38.12.3.

23 See Mouritsen (2001), pp. 44–5.

24 Tatum (1999), p. 132.

25 Tatum (1999), p. 114–49 offers an detailed analysis of Clodius' tribunate and legislation.

26 Gruen (1974), p. 292.

27 Tatum (1999), p. 140.

28 Cic. *De domo sua.* 22.

29 There was some debate that Clodius' mother may have a Servilii, but Wiseman has rejected this argument. Regardless, the two men were separated by only three years – Cato being born in 95, Clodius in 92, so it is entirely possible that this 'younger generation' had a connection of familiarity, if not actual relations. I am indebted to Professor Wiseman for clarifying the position.

30 See Chapter 7. Two specific speeches of Cicero's, the *de domo sua* and the *pro Sestio* imply a united front of Cicero/Cato versus Clodius, but there is no evidence to support Cicero's contention.

31 Lintott (1968), p. 197.

32 Cic. *QF.* 2.4.

33 Mitchell (1969), p. 293; Meier (1982; 1996) suggests that it took place in March, p. 273.

34 Steele (2001), p. 204.

35 Plut. *Cat.Min.* 39.1–3.

36 Tatum *The Patrician Tribune*, p. 221.

37 Plut. *Cat.Min.*, 41.4–5.

38 Seager (1979; 2002), p. 123.

39 Plut. *Cato Min.*, 43.1–5.

40 Catullus, no. 93.

41 Meier (1982; 1996), p. 289.

Notes to Chapter 7: Violence in Republican Rome: The Truth of the Late 50s BCE

1 Gruen (1974), p. 316.

2 Dio 39.61–2.

3 Gruen (1974), p. 322.

4 Dio 40.17.

5 Dio 40.46.

 6 Plut. *Crassus* 21.5–7.
 7 Cic. *Philippics.* 2.21.
 8 Cic. *Pro. Milo.* 28.
 9 Seager, p. 133–4; Tatum (1999), pp. 239–41, Sumi (1997) 81–5.
10 Dio 40.49.2–4.
11 Ruebel (1979), p. 236.
12 Asc. 35–35C; for Caesar, see Dio 40.50.3.
13 Plut. 48.3.
14 Plut. 47.3.
15 Seager (1979; 2002), pp. 134–5.
16 Plut. 48.1–3.
17 Plut. 48.2.
18 Suet. 27.1.
19 Dio 40.54.3.
20 Either by a stone thrown or he was executed.
21 Plut. *Pomp.* 55.4.
22 Dio 40.56.1–2; Cic. *Att.* 8.3.
23 Syme (1939), p. 40.
24 Taylor (1949), p. 150: 'Cato had vowed that he would accuse Caesar, and Cato could be depended on to keep his vows.' See Meier (1982; 1992), pp. 323–7 regarding the ambush by Gallic tribes against Caesar.
25 Plut. *Cat. Min.* 46.2–3; there is some debate about the chronology of Plutarch's account.
26 Taylor (1949), pp. 151–2.
27 Gruen (1974), p. 459.
28 Taylor (1949), pp. 150–1.
29 Shotter (1994), p. 76.
30 Dio 40.59.1.
31 Cic. *Att.* 5.11.
32 Caes. *BG.* 8.52.3.
33 Cic. *Att.* 6.
34 Cic. *Att.* 7.2.7.
35 Meier (1982; 1996), p. 334–5.
36 App. *CW.* II. 31.
37 Plut. *Cat. Min.* 51.5.
38 *ibid*, 51.5.
39 Caes. *BC.* I. 4.

Notes to Chapter 8: Civil War and Caesar's Dictatorship

 1 Caes. *BC.* 1.22.
 2 Meier (1982; 1996), pp. 345–6; Plut. *Cat. Min.* 64.2.
 3 Plut. *Cat. Min.* 53.4.
 4 Vell. 2.49.4; App. *BC.* 2.34.134–40.

5   Another alternative, attributed to the poet Menander, was 'Let the die fly high!'
6   Fantham (2003), p. 104.
7   *ibid.*
8   Suet. *Div. Iul.* 304.
9   Some scholars date this to April.
10 Van Hooff (1990), p. 173.
11 Griffin (2003), p. 160, who contradicts Yavetz (1983), p. 174. Also, Fantham (2003), p. 105.
12 *Anticato* fr. 5, Klotz; see Yavetz (1983), p. 175.
13 Griffin (1986b), p. 194.
14 Plut. *Cat. Min.* 72.2.
15 Syme (1939), p. 492, fn. 1.
16 Meier (1982; 1996), p. 431.
17 Cic. *Att.* XII.4 (SB 240).
18 Cic. *Att.* XII.4 (SB 240).
19 Cic. *Att.* XII.44 (SB 285).
20 Caes. *BC.* I.4.
21 [Caes]. *BA.* see 23 where Cato is referred to as a '*homo gravissimus*' and related the affection felt by the people of Utica in 87–8. This work, long attributed to Caesar, has been shown not to be his.
22 Taylor (1949), p. 171.
23 Obviously, Cicero's *Philippics* are another example, but belong to the post-Caesarian period.
24 Rawson (1975), p. 213.
25 Meier (1982; 1996), p. 433.
26 Meier (1982; 1996), p. 446.
27 Additional days were inserted back into the year 46, with days added to the end of different months, see Bickerman, E.J., *Chronology of the Ancient World.* London (Thames and Hudson) 1980, p. 47.
28 Scullard (1959; 1982), p. 147.
29 Suet. *Div. Iul.* 79.
30 This is from a television programme, cited by Gilchrist, J. 'Caesar: Left Winger?', *The Scotsman.* 16 December 2002, p. 4.
31 Osgood (2006), p. 12–13.
32 Plut. *Brutus.* 52.4–5.

Bibliography

PRIMARY SOURCES

(all in translation)

Asconius, *Commentaries on Speeches of Cicero*. (trans. R. G. Lewis), Oxford: 2006.

Appian, *Roman History*, vols. I–IV, (trans. Horace White) Loeb: 1912–1913.

Catullus, *The Complete Poems*, (trans. Guy Lee) Penguin: 1990.

Caesar, *Civil Wars*, (trans. A. G. Peskett), Loeb: 1914.

Cicero, *The Three Speeches on the Agrarian Law Against Rullus*, vol. 6 (trans. J. H. Freese) Loeb: 1930.

—*The Verrine Orations*, vols 7–8, (trans. L. H. G. Greenwood), Loeb: 1928; 1935.

—*Pro Lege Manilia, Pro Caecina, Pro Cluentio, Pro Rabirio Perduellionis Reo*, vol. 9, (trans. H. Grose Hodge), Loeb: 1927.

—*In Catilinam I–IV, Pro Flacco, Pro Murena, Pro Sulla*, vol. 10 (trans. C. Macdonald) Loeb: 1977.

—*Pro Archia, Post Reditium in Senatu, Post Reditum ad Quirites, De Somo Sua, De Haruspicum Responsis*, vol. 11, (trans. N. H. Watts), Loeb: 1923.

—*Pro Milone*, vol. 14, (trans. N. H. Watts), Loeb: 1931.

—*Philippics*, vol. 15, (trans. Walter C. A. Ker), Loeb: 1926.

—*Letters to Atticus*, vols. 22–4, (trans. D. R. Shackleton Bailey), Loeb: 1990; 1999.

—*Letters to Friends*, vols. 25–7, (trans. D. R. Shackleton Bailey), Loeb: 2001.

—*Letters to Quintus and Brutus*, vol. 29, (trans. D. R. Shackleton Bailey), Loeb: 2002.

Dio, *Roman History*, vols. 1–9, (trans. Earnest Cary). Loeb: 1914–1927.

Diodorus Siculus, *Library of History*, vol. 12, (trans. Francis R. Walton), Loeb: 1967.

Livy, *History of Rome*, (trans. A. C. Schlesinger), Loeb, 1959.

Lucilius, *Remains of Old Latin*, vol. 14, (trans. E. H. Warmington), Loeb: 1938.

Sallust, *Catiline's War, The Jugurthine War and Histories*, (trans. A. J. Woodman), Penguin: 2007.

Suetonius, *The Twelve Caesars*, (trans. Robert Graves), Penguin 1957; 1979.

Plutarch, *Fall of the Roman Republic*, (trans. Rex Warner, notes Robin Seager), Penguin: 2006.

Makers of Rome, (trans. Ian Scott-Kilvert), Penguin, 1975.

Velleius Paterculus, *Compendium of Roman History*, (trans. Frederick Shipley) Loeb: 1924.

Virgil, *The Aeneid*, (trans. David West) Penguin: 1990.

SECONDARY SOURCES

Baldson, J. P. V. D. (1962) 'Roman History 65–50: Five Problems', *JRS* 52: 134–41.

Brunt, P. (1971) *Social Conflicts in the Roman Republic*, (London: Norton).

—(1988) *The Fall of the Roman Republic and Related Essays*, (Oxford: OUP).

Claridge, A. (1998) *Oxford Archaeological Guides – Rome*, (Oxford: OUP).

Drummond, A. (1995) *Law, Politics and Power*, (Stuttgart: Historia).

Dunn, J. (2005) *Setting the People Free: The Story of Democracy*, (London: Atlantic).

DuPont, F. (1989) *Daily Life in Ancient Rome*, (Oxford: Blackwell).

Earl, D. C. (1961) *The Political Thought of Sallust*, (Cambridge: CUP).

—(1967) *The Moral and Political Tradition of Rome*, (Ithaca, NY: Thames and Hudson).

Edwards, C. (1996) *Writing Rome*, (Cambridge: CUP).

Epstein, D. F. (1987) *Personal Enmity in Roman Politics 218–43 BC*, (London: Croom Helm).

Fantham, E. (2003), 'Three Wise Men and the End of the Roman Republic', *Caesar Against Liberty?* (eds F. Cairns and E. Fantham) Arca (43): 96–117.

Finley, M. I. (1983) *Politics in the Ancient World*, (Cambridge: CUP).

Flower, H. (1997). *Ancestor Masks and Aristocratic Power in Roman Culture*, (Oxford: OUP).

Frank, T. (1933) *Economic Survey of Ancient Rome*, (Baltimore: Johns Hopkins).

Garnsey, P. (1988) *Famine and Food Supply in the Graceo-Roman World*, (Cambridge: OUP).

Gelzer, M. (1968) *Caesar: Politician and Statesman*, trans. P. Needham (Oxford: OUP).

—(1969) *The Roman Nobility*, trans. R. Seager (Oxford: OUP).

Goar, R. (1987) *The Legend of Cato Uticensis from the First Century BC to the Fifth Century AD*, (Bruxelles: Latomus).

Goldsworthy, A. (2000) *Roman Warfare*, (London: Cassell).

Griffin, M. (1973), 'The Tribune C. Cornelius', *JRS* 63: 196–213.

—(1986a), 'Philosophy, Cato and Roman Suicide: I', *Greece & Rome* 32.1: 64–77.

—(1986b), 'Philosophy, Cato and Roman Suicide: II', *Greece & Rome* 32.2: 192–202.

—(2003), 'Clementia After Caesar: from Politics to Philosophy', *Caesar Against Liberty?* (ed. F. Cairns and E. Fantham) Arca (43): 157–182.

Gruen, E. (1968) *Roman Politics and the Criminal Courts: 149–78 BC*, (Cambridge, Mass: Harvard University Press).

—(1974) *The Last Generation of the Roman Republic*, (Berkeley: University of California Press).

Harris, W. V. (1985) *War & Imperialism in Republican Rome*, (Oxford: OUP).

Keaveney A. (1998) *Rome and the Unification of Italy*, (London: Routledge).

Kunkel, W. (1966) *An Introduction to Roman Legal and Constitutional History*, trans. J. M. Kelly (Oxford: OUP).

Lintott, A. (1968) *Violence in Republican Rome*, (Oxford: OUP).

—(1999) *The Constitution of the Roman Republic*, (Oxford: OUP).

Meier, C. (1982; 1996) *Caesar*, (London: Fontana Press).

Millar, F. (1998) *The Crowd in Rome in the Late Republic*, (Ann Arbor: University of Michigan).

—(2004) *Rome, The Greek World, and the East*, (Chapel Hill: UNC).

Mitchell, T. N. (1986) *Cicero: the Ascending Years*, (New Haven: Yale University Press).

—(1991) *Cicero: the Senior Statesman*, (New Haven: Yale University Press).

Mouritsen, H. (2001) *Plebs and Politics in the Late Roman Republic*, (Cambridge: CUP).

Nicolet, C. (1980) *The World of the Citizen in Republican Rome*, trans. P. S. Falla (Berkeley: University of California Press).

Nippel, W. (1995) *Public Order in Ancient Rome*, (Cambridge: CUP).

Oost, S. I.(1955), 'Cato Uticensis and the Annexation of Cyprus', *CP* 50: 98–112.

—(1956),'The Date of the *Lex Iulia de repetundis*', *AJP* 77: 19–28.

Osgood, J. (2006) *Caesar's Legacy*, (Cambridge: CUP).

Patterson, J. R. (2000) *Political Life in the City of Rome*, (Bristol: Bristol Classical Press).

Rawson, E.(1975) *Cicero: A Portrait*, (London: Allen Lane).

—(1978) *The Politics of Friendship: Pompey and Cicero*, (Sydney: Sydney University Press).

—(1985) *Intellectual Life in the late Roman Republic*, (London: Duckworth).

Rickman, G. (1980) *The Corn Supply of Ancient Rome*, (Oxford: OUP).

Ruebel, J. (1979) 'The Trial of Milo in 52 BC: A Chronological Study', *TAPA* 109: 231–49.

Salmon, E. T.(1935), 'Catiline, Crassus and Caesar', *AJP* 56: 302–16.

—(1939), 'Caesar and the Consulship for 49 BC', *CJ* 34: 388–95.

—(1969) *Roman Colonisation Under the Republic*, (London: Thames and Hudson).

Scullard, H. H. (1959; 1982) *From the Gracchi to Nero*, (London: Routledge).

Seager, R. (1979, 2002) *Pompey the Great*, (Oxford: Blackwell).

Sherwin-White, A. N. (1973) *The Roman Citizenship*, (Oxford: OUP).

Shotter, D. (1994) *Fall of the Roman Republic*, (London: Routledge).

de Souza, P. (1999) *Piracy in the Graeco-Roman World*, (Cambridge: CUP).

Stockton, D. (1971) *Cicero*, (Oxford: OUP).

Steele, C. (2001) *Cicero, Rhetoric and Empire*, (Oxford: OUP).

Sumi, G. (1997) 'Power and Ritual: The Crowd at Clodius' Funeral', *Historia*: 80–102.

Syme, R. (1939) *The Roman Revolution*, (Oxford: OUP).

—(1964) *Sallust*, (Berkeley: University of California Press).

—(1979), 'A Roman Post-Mortem', *Roman Papers I*, (Oxford: OUP), 205–17.

Tatum, W. J. (1999) *The Patrician Tribune – Publius Clodius Pulcher*, (Chapel Hill: UNC).

Taylor, L. R.(1949) *Party Politics in the Age of Caesar*, (Berkeley: University of California).

—(1960) *The Voting Districts of the Roman Republic*, (Rome: American Academy in Rome).

—(1966) *Roman Voting Assemblies*, (Ann Arbor: University of Michigan).

Vanderbroeck, P. J. J. (1987) *Popular Leadership and Collective Behaviour in the Late Roman Republic*, (Amsterdam: Gieben).

Van Hooff, A. (1990). *From Autothanasia to Suicide: Self-Killing in Classical Antiquity*, (London: Routledge).

Ward, A. M. (1977) *Marcus Crassus and the late Roman Republic*, (Columbia and London: University of Missouri).

Wiedemann, T. (1994) *Cicero and the End of the Roman Republic*, (Bristol: Bristol Classical Press).

Wiseman, T. P.(1971a) *New Men in the Roman senate 139 BC to AD 14*, (Oxford: OUP).

—(1971b), 'Celer and Nepos', *CQ* 21: 180–2.

—(1985) (ed) *Roman Political Life 90 BC–AD 69*, (Exeter: University of Exeter Press).

—(1994a), 'The senate and the *Populares*: 69–60 BCE', *CAH* 9 (1994): 327–67.

—(1994b), 'Caesar, Pompey and Rome: 59 to 50 BC', *CAH* 9 (1994): 368–81.

Wirszubski, C. (1950) *Libertas as a Political Ideal at Rome*, (Cambridge: CUP).

Yavetz, Z.(1958),'The Living Conditions of the Urban Plebs in Republican Rome', *Latomus* 17: 500–17.

—(1963), 'The Failure of Catiline's Conspiracy', *Historia* 12: 485–99.

—(1969) *Plebs and Princeps*, (Oxford: OUP).

—(1983) *Julius Caesar and his Public Image*, (London: Thames and Hudson).

—(1984), 'The *Res Gestae* and Augustus' Public Image', in *Caesar Augustus: Seven Aspects*: (Oxford: OUP).

Index